THE STATE OF AFRO-AMERICAN HISTORY

The State of
Afro-American History

PAST, PRESENT, AND FUTURE

Edited by Darlene Clark Hine
With an Introduction by Thomas C. Holt

LOUISIANA STATE UNIVERSITY PRESS

BATON ROUGE AND LONDON

Designer: Joanna V. Hill
Typeface: Sabon
Typesetter: G & S Typesetters
Printer: Thomson-Shore
Binder: John Dekker & Sons

LIBRARY OF CONGRESS CATALOGING IN PUBLICATION DATA

The State of Afro-American history.

Essays presented at the American Historical Association conference held in Oct. 1983 at Purdue University.

Includes index.

1. Afro-Americans—History—Congresses. 2. Afro-Americans—Historiography—Congresses. I. Hine, Darlene Clark. II. American Historical Association.
E184.5.S83   1986   973'.0496   85-24138
ISBN 0-8071-1254-2

10 9 8 7 6 5 4 3 2

To Afro-American historians
past, present, and future

CONTENTS

Today Afro-American history is a respected and legitimate field of American history. During the past three decades, and especially since the civil rights struggles of the 1960s, interest in Afro-American history has flourished. This was not always the case. There was a time when black historians endured the humiliation of discrimination within professional societies, were prohibited from researching in southern archives on a free and open basis, and had their work dismissed or undervalued by their white professional colleagues. In spite of limited opportunities and professional ostracism, many black historians nevertheless researched and wrote exemplary works on the Afro-American historical experience. Scholars such as Carter G. Woodson, Benjamin Quarles, John Hope Franklin, W. E. B. Du Bois, Lorenzo Greene, Charles Wesley, A. A. Taylor, and Helen Edmonds persevered in the face of adversity to make the world see black Americans as actors and creators of history instead of so many hapless victims of forces beyond their control.

The student protests of the 1960s did much to force professional historians to take seriously the study and teaching of Afro-American history. To be sure, their loud and insistent demands for the inclusion of black history courses into secondary and college curricula occasioned many cheap debates and much resistance. Controversies raged over who would or could teach such courses and about the uses and abuses of history. In an effort to respond to the burgeoning interest, schools, colleges, and universities added the black experience to their curricula, and some textbook publishers included blacks in their histories. However, it soon became apparent that the mere inclusion of blacks into the historical record in a contributionist or token fashion was inadequate. What was needed was a fundamental reconceptualization of all of American history with the experience of black Americans at center stage.

By the mid 1970s a significant body of fresh and revealing literature about black America was pouring from the presses. This new history was characterized by bold interpretations and diverse methodologies based on the use of heretofore unexamined sources and documents. Historians of the new slavery studies have, for example, imaginatively extracted fragments of the black experience from deeds, wills, estate papers, court records, tax books, census lists, medical records, slave narratives, black autobiographies, folklore, newspaper advertisements, diaries and personal letters of white planters and their wives, and even tombstones in country cemeteries, as well as from linguistics and material artifacts. New monographs challenged traditional interpretations of slavery, emancipation, and urbanization and expanded our understanding of the institutional structures and factors that have shaped the experiences of blacks in America. We now know that emancipation provoked the most fundamental questions of economy, society, identity, and polity. The new status of former slaves transformed the nature of social interaction and conflict in the South. With this expanded understanding we were for the first time able to comprehend and appreciate the complexities of black responses to enslavement, freedom, and ghettoization. As a consequence of the proliferation of scholarship, teachers of black history confront an embarrassment of riches. So many books are of such high quality as to make course assignment selection difficult.

As we approach the twenty-first century, the time has come to assess and evaluate the historical outpouring of the last few decades. But beyond assessment and evaluation is the challenge of charting new directions, raising new issues and concerns about the future of the context and nature of black history. Those questions and demands posed by the students of the 1960s are still germane, still urgent, and still in need of considered response. We in this field remain concerned about the teaching of Afro-American history in secondary and post-secondary schools and the continuing need to revise textbooks. To be sure, blatant and overt racism and

stereotypes no longer pollute the pages of most American history textbooks. Yet, the expectation of a fundamental reconceptualization of American history as reflected in textbooks remains a distant dream. Much of the
new scholarship, the fresh interpretations and insights, have not been incorporated into the textbooks used in schools around the country. Thus, it
would appear that we have only just begun our work.

The American Historical Association is to be commended for its willingness to sponsor the state-of-the-art conference on the study and teaching of Afro-American history held in October, 1983, at Purdue University.
The Lilly Endowment is to be equally applauded for providing the requi-
site financial support, as are the National Endowment for the Humanities
and Purdue University.

This volume culminates the efforts and thoughts that were invested in
planning and financing the conference. It is a collection of sharply focused
essays designed to capture the interest of scholars, teachers, and students
and to demonstrate disciplined analysis of a vital field in American history.
No attempt was made to present a unified point of view or to create point-
less dispute. The authors invited to prepare the conference papers included here were asked simply to help point the way to a meaningful perception of the Afro-American experience during slavery, emancipation,
and urbanization and to offer some suggestions as to how we may collec-
tively probe more deeply and ask new questions of our sources.

All but one of the papers included in this volume were presented at the
conference. The advisory committee decided after the conference that the
volume would be incomplete without a synthesis of recent scholarship on
black women's history. We all hope that this essay will underscore, in part,
the need for more scholarly attention to this important topic, as it is the
intention behind both the conference and this volume to call for historians
and teachers to be as concerned with the actual researching and study of
Afro-American history as with the politics of its dissemination.

ACKNOWLEDGMENTS

Thanking the dozens of people who helped to make possible the American Historical Association Conference on the Study and Teaching of Afro-American History held in October, 1983, at Purdue University and this volume of essays is a long-awaited pleasure. My gratitude to these fine people for their assistance at every stage in the four-year development of this project continues to increase.

Respecting the demands on their time and energies, I initially approached with trepidation my friends and colleagues Robert L. Harris, Jr., of Cornell University, Thomas C. Holt at the University of Michigan, Alton Hornsby, Jr., of Morehouse College, Armstead Robinson at the University of Virginia, and Rosalyn Terborg-Penn at Morgan State University. To my delight, each one readily agreed to help with writing and reviewing numerous drafts of the conference proposal and selecting the speakers and commentators. They likewise agreed to chair sessions at the conference and to critique the essays included in this volume. I owe special thanks to my colleague Harold Woodman of Purdue University, for it was he who first suggested that a major conference on black history be organized and it was upon his initiative that David Van Tassel, then vice-president of the AHA's Teaching Division, was persuaded that the AHA should sponsor the event. I would also like to acknowledge the participation of Mikaso Hane of Knox College, who served as a liaison between the AHA Teaching Division and the conference advisory committee.

Throughout the development and execution of this project, the staff of the American Historical Association labored with consummate skill, dedication, and professionalism. I am deeply indebted to Samuel Gammon, executive director of the AHA; to Noralee Frankel, special assistant for women and minorities; and to Jamil Zainaldin, deputy executive director, for their enthusiastic support. A grant from the National Endowment for the Humanities to the AHA enabled faculty members from historically black colleges and universities to attend the conference.

I would like to offer a special bouquet of heartfelt thanks to Laura Bornholdt, who as vice-president of the Lilly Endowment, provided the substantial financial resources necessary to transform a dream into reality. Those of us who study and teach black history applaud her vision and relentless commitment to the advancement of scholarship in this field.

It gives me great pleasure to thank all of the program participants, including those who chaired sessions and in general made the conference a success. Specifically this includes my Purdue University colleagues, Donald Berthrong, Thelma L. Snuggs, Geneva Gay, and Monroe Little (of Indiana University and Purdue University at Indianapolis), and Robert Ringel, dean of the School of Humanities, Social Science, and Education, and Felix Haas, executive vice-president and provost. I thank the historians from around the country who agreed to participate in this first-of-its-kind conference. For many of them, taking part in the conference meant shifting priorities and delaying completion of their own research projects. Their contributions can now be appreciated by all of us interested in the field.

The editors of Louisiana State University Press were good and conscientious people with whom to work. To Beverly Jarrett, who early recognized the publishing potential of the project, I say simply, thank you for seeing this project through the final stage. Two other special people provided able assistance throughout the duration of this project—my associate Patrick K. Bidelman and my one-in-a-million secretary, Cynthia FitzSimons.

Finally, a refrain of thanks is owed to the over two hundred teachers, scholars, school administrators, and representatives of university presses who attended the conference. For my family, specifically my husband Johnny Brown and daughter Robbie Davine, mere words will not convey the depths of my gratitude for their love, understanding, and support.

THE STATE OF AFRO-AMERICAN HISTORY

INTRODUCTION

Whither Now and Why?

THOMAS C. HOLT

These papers are divided into two major areas of concern, reflecting the dual purpose of the conference for which they were prepared. The first area is the creation of histories, that is, research and writing; the second area is the dissemination of these histories, through classrooms, textbooks, museums, and popular media. Some of the papers are essentially intellectual and historiographical in focus; others, dealing with issues that are necessarily political and institution-oriented, might be considered to be of a different sort entirely. They might seem to be; but they are not, because intellectual and political considerations are pervasively connected and interactive, especially in Afro-American history.

Professor Franklin reminds us that Afro-American history itself has a history and that we are part of perhaps its most important and productive phase thus far. His description of the generational succession of Afro-American historians makes it clear that each generation was motivated by a mission, and that the mission was shaped by perceptions of the conditions and needs of black people at the time and by the general imperatives imposed by the larger society in its relations with blacks. Thus the research and writing of history is itself a reflection of history and politics, and the dissemination of new histories is political action with historical consequences.

Franklin's description of four generations of Afro-American scholarship emphasizes the intimate interaction between history as lived by a generation and the historical emphasis of that generation's scholars. The late-nineteenth-century Afro-American historians' concern with proving the compatibility of blacks with American life came in an age when colored peoples everywhere were assaulted by genocidal rhetoric and action. The "contributionists" of Carter G. Woodson's generation struggled against a racial climate that denigrated black achievements in American life and culture. The integrationist faith of the third generation drew sustenance from the efforts of blacks and their white allies to pull down the anachronistic edifices of Jim Crow and segregation.

Pushing Franklin's schematic further, one can assume that the nationalist orientation of so many fourth-generation scholars might involve a reaction to the negative implications of integration. They came of professional age during a period when both political and scholarly discourse were suffused with claims that the black community was racked by debilitating pathologies, and that these pathologies must be eradicated if integration were to be successful. The legacy of black history, it seemed, was only a crippled culture and a degraded community.[1] Consequently, the fourth generation has sought to make the invisible Negro not only visible, but real, human, and capable of action in the world. It is not accidental that many members of this generation are veterans of social movements that taught them that an oppressed people are not just victims, but are capable of heroic and effective action. Perhaps they may be forgiven the arrogance of sometimes thinking that they were the first to discover this.

For the most part, the papers included here represent assessments of the ongoing process of researching, writing, and disseminating Afro-American history as viewed by this post-sixties fourth generation of historians. The historiographical papers delineate three major periods of Afro-American history: slavery, emancipation, and urbanization. This periodization is itself a contribution to the development of the field. As Professor Franklin points out, there has been a dramatic expansion of topics, sub-fields, and specialization during the past decade. But it is also impor-

---

1. Two complementary works, one in history and the other in public policy, stimulated much of this response: Stanley M. Elkins, *Slavery: A Problem in American Institutional and Intellectual Life* (Chicago, 1959), and Daniel P. Moynihan, *The Negro Family in America: The Case for National Action* (Washington, D.C., 1965). Actually, novelist Ralph Ellison, reacting against a black "image drained of humanity" as found in American fiction, best expressed the impatience of his and subsequent generations with the "sociological Negro." See *Shadow and Act* (New York, 1953).

tant to sustain the coherence of Afro-American history as a study of our collective experience, and this depends on a clear perception of its major movements across time and space, and of the intersections and connections among its various themes.

Undeniably the central fact of the Afro-American experience before 1865 was slavery. The African background has relevance to the Americas largely in the context of how slavery dictated critical choices among new cultural possibilities. The African cultural inheritance strongly influenced, but could not determine, the choices made. The free black experience, abolitionism and protest, black participation in American wars, these cannot be considered as distinct from and uninfluenced by the fact that the overwhelming majority of blacks were slaves. Similarly, the central fact of the immediate postslavery experience is that for more than half a century the overwhelming majority of the black population was bound by the iron grip of southern sharecropping and tenancy. And, finally, the great urban migrations of the twentieth century not only reshaped the life chances and cultural choices of urban dwellers, but had a significant impact on the lives of those left behind. The roots of the Civil Rights Movement lay in northern, as well as southern, cities.

Furthermore, I would draw attention to an interpretation latent in this periodization: the central thread or definitive phenomenon in each period was how the social labor of blacks was mobilized and reproduced. Slave labor conditioned, if not dictated, one set of social relations and cultural forms; juridically free labor as sharecroppers and tenants shaped another; and incorporation into the mature capitalist labor relations of the urban North, still another. The best of the recent literature reflects how such matters as family life, cultural expression, the social and economic roles of women, the community itself, and political organization were all shaped and reshaped in each period by the social relations implied in the existing labor relations. As the papers and commentary here show, recognition of this fact and the detailed working out of its implications are clearer and more advanced in studies of slavery and emancipation than in those of the subsequent period. Perhaps this is because the issue is more difficult to evade when we are confronting the brutal coercion of slave and postslavery labor systems.

The idea that the social relations of labor constitute the starting point for any examination of the Afro-American experience is only implicit in the periodization framed by these papers. But other common themes are more explicit. All three historiographical papers argue that an Afrocentric perspective is essential to any attempt to reconstruct the Afro-American experience, but that simultaneously one must locate that experience within the context of larger American, and indeed global, developments. Thus Leslie Owens pushes us to align ourselves with the slave's perspective on slavery. We must understand that the African's central cultural focus was kinship, the family, the lineage group, or what he summarizes as "the generational matrix." Our understanding of emancipation, Armstead Robinson tells us, must begin with the perspective of the freedpeople themselves, their values, their world view. Freedom meant not only economic and geographical mobility, but "new horizons of autonomy." And if we are to finally escape Gilbert Osofsky's ahistorical, stultifying "enduring ghetto" model for black urban life, Kenneth Kusmer urges, we must examine the black community's responses, its cultural values, its institutional matrices, its view of the world.[2] Black urban residences were not just slums; they were living communities. All of this adds up to a unanimous rejection of the degradation/deficit models spawned during the riotous sixties. Degradation and deficit there were; but there were also adjustment, adaptation, and struggle. In short, the victims, be they slaves, sharecroppers, or slum dwellers, were also capable of remarkable acts of cultural creativity in response to oppression. There was pressure, but there was also grace under pressure.

But putting black people back at the center of their history is not the only prerequisite to creating a complete history of the black experience. Our attempt to view the Afro-American experience from the bottom up—to reclaim the perspective and lived experience of black people—must also include a sustained effort to account for and place that experience in the larger context of external forces. Clearly slavery and emancipation were part of a worldwide process of labor mobilization, capital formation, and, eventually, the political-military domination of much of the globe by European powers. As Owens reminds us, slavery and the slave trade are crucial links among the histories of Europe, the Americas, and Africa. And the abolition of slavery in the United States, Eric Foner points out, took place in the context of a dual revolution involving the transformation of social,

2. Gilbert Osofsky, "The Enduring Ghetto," *Journal of American History*, LV (1968).

political, and labor relations in the North as well as the South. The making of the black working class, Robinson adds, must be linked to the making of the white working class if we are to understand such apparently disparate phenomena as Populism and Booker T. Washington. Meanwhile, Kenneth Kusmer argues here that the examination of forces internal to the black community must be articulated along with the external forces that constrained and shaped that community's initiatives and choices. In his study of Cleveland he has demonstrated the crucial impact of technological and organizational changes in communications, transportation, and commerce on the evolution of the ghetto and in forming the template of twentieth-century race relations.[3]

The proposition that Afro-American history cannot be understood separate from broader national and even international developments is the corollary of another: an understanding of black history is central to the study of American history. Franklin suggests that Afro-American history should be recognized as "a centerpiece" of American history, that it provides "a very important context in which much if not the whole of the history of the United States can be taught and studied." Thus Afro-American history becomes a window onto the nation's history, a vantage point from which to reexamine and rewrite that larger history. This is true not simply because blacks should be included for a more accurate portrait, but more because their inclusion changes many of the basic questions posed, the methods and sources for answering those questions, and the conclusions reached.

Much of the work in this volume echoes Franklin's point and lends itself to the suggestion that, having established Afro-American history as a valid and legitimate endeavor within the profession, we look now to change that profession, to refocus its Eurocentric, male-dominant view of the world. Eric Foner argues, for example, that federal-state relations must be viewed differently if the black perspective is incorporated. Similarly, Armstead Robinson suggests that interracial politics and class relations in the late-nineteenth-century South appear in a different light if we take account of the internal dynamics *within* the black community.

Our task, then, is twofold: to put black people at the center of their history and to put the black experience at the center of American history, by

3. Kenneth Kusmer, *A Ghetto Takes Shape: Black Cleveland, 1870–1930* (Urbana, 1976).

reinterpreting that history in light of that experience. We can write no genuine history of the black experience without attempting to see our ancestors face to face, without straining to hear their thoughts and desires, without groping for the textures of their interior worlds. But having done that, we then must establish linkages between that interior world and the external developments and movements in the larger world; for only in that way can that history lay any claim to centrality in the national experience. Thus we are charged with a formidable task indeed. We must move between two levels of experience. We must occupy two vantage points simultaneously. We must do history inside out and back again.

Clearing this much ground lays bare the unspoken question central to these papers and to the conference that produced them, a question that was implicit in Franklin's chronology: Whither the fifth generation of Afro-American historical scholarship? The question is not simply a matter of what the various research agendas will look like, but what the unifying mission will be. Does our assessment of the work of the fourth generation suggest the next necessary steps before us? Obviously, the issue runs far beyond simply inserting blacks into American history, beyond simply moving out of the woodpile and into the parlor. We now must begin the work of redecorating the very mansion itself. For the more difficult questions that face us have to do with the way the craft is pursued. Much of our earlier attention has been focused on learning the craft and proving our ability to use it. But the larger implication of much recent work is that the practice of craft, the ways of knowing, are inseparable from the knowledge and understandings produced.[4]

---

4. And here I must acknowledge that the most important source for my thinking on this point and much of what follows was not the conference papers, but the provocative work on similar problems in anthropology by Christopher Davis-Roberts. Perhaps it is because the sources of knowledge in her discipline are also the objects of study that the problematic role of the scholar, as observer and interpreter, is most clearly exposed. (See "A Left-handed Ethnography," unpublished MS, 1984). Once we recognize this problematic, a host of others are thrown up in its wake: the "legitimacy" of populist sources of knowledge, the problem of alien claims on and interpretation of that knowledge, the possession of the products created from these sources. Much of the discussion of the black scholar and the community found in the conference papers might be more fruitfully reformulated in terms of this series of problematics, which have applicability to the profession as a whole. An interesting effort to confront, at least partially, some of these problems can be found in a work of history written by sociologist Elizabeth Raul Bethel.

For example, the biases that left slaves, as people, out of the history of slavery were not simply racial. They more often had to do with what could be considered legitimate and illegitimate sources. This in turn had to do with how knowledge, or fact itself, was defined. The scope of the problem is suggested by the striking similarities in the problem of sources confronted by students of women's history, working-class history, or that of cultures that left no written records. Shifting our focus from the question of representative content to the question of sources, therefore, raises the larger and interrelated issues of methodology and perspective. The extensive empirical work that has been done and which is assessed by the essays that follow should allow us now to rectify at the theoretical level the essence of complaints of our own and preceding generations of historians. The reason Afro-Americans were so long excluded is not because they had no history, an impossibility where life and experience exist; nor that that history was unimportant, a notion easily contradicted by reference to almost any political and economic development; nor that there were no sources from which to write that history—clearly there were and are. Most of the sources we rely on today were available at least since the 1930s and 1940s, and many earlier still.[5] Rather, it was that these sources remained unseen. What we see is a function of where we stand. And where we stand is a function of our political and social relations.

I mean "political" here in its broadest sense. Historians themselves are products of history, and therefore blacks who write history or whites who choose to write black history will tend—to varying degrees, of course—to assume an oppositionist stance in relation to the national history. Such a stance is implied by their experience in the first instance, and by their choice in the second. In any event, this is the gauntlet laid down, even if not taken up.

When Owens argues, therefore, that the slave's presence and passive

---

In *Promiseland: A Century of Life in a Negro Community* (Philadelphia, 1981), the people are to a large extent sources for the history, collaborators in its writing, and claimants to the product.

5. Two striking examples are the WPA slave narratives collected during the 1930s and the archival records of government department, such as the Freedmen's Bureau and War Department—used so effectively to re-create the emancipation experience from the freedpeople's point of view by Ira Berlin, Joseph Reidy, and Leslie Rowland, *Freedom: A Documentary History of Emancipation, 1861–1867* (Cambridge, England, 1982).

resistance exposed the contradictions in liberal-democratic thought and practice and thereby forced a maturing of the nation's guiding ideology, he is restating a venerable theme in Afro-American literature and thought. It is more than a rhetorical flourish.[6] Our task is to seize this counter-point, so obvious in black experience, and build out from it viable counter-interpretations to the received traditions such as "the growth of the American republic," and "the progress of democracy." All this takes us beyond merely inserting blacks into "white" history or establishing their contributions and role, however begrudging, in building Western civilization. The issues here are not just ones of political economy, but ways of understanding the world. And, conversely, not just how we think about the world, but how we make it.

Making the world is undeniably a political act. Writing histories that imply alternative ways in which the world might have been made are also political acts. In this light, the problem of disseminating such histories in classrooms and museums and through the public media takes on added significance and added difficulty. Both Bettye Gardner and Robert Hayden insist that since the sixties there have been retrenchment and retreat from the well-publicized efforts to achieve ethnic diversity in public school curricula and textbooks. And other conference participants report that attempts to do more than merely paste colored faces into existing texts are seldom welcomed by textbook publishers. Robert Brent Toplin informs us that films, too, are still likely to represent, at best, a "grossly exaggerated version" of recent historical scholarship. Clearly, material that attempts to push beyond the mere inclusion of the black experience and to challenge cherished values and national myths will experience even greater difficulty.[7]

None of the contributors offers easy solutions to these problems, only

6. I have argued elsewhere that the emancipation era was a moment of truth for many of the central tenets of liberal-democratic thought. Slaves in the Americas had a different view of the world than their emancipators, and acted on it. See J. Morgan Kousser and James M. McPherson (eds.), "'An Empire over the Mind': Emancipation, Race, and Ideology in the British West Indies and the American South," in *Region, Race, and Reconstruction: Essays in Honor of C. Vann Woodward* (New York, 1982), 283–313.

7. The counterattack often takes the form of arguments to restore the "majesty" of the American story, meaning a coherent narrative, and implying a homogenous national identity and a teleological purpose. For example, see Frances Fitzgerald, *America Revised: History Schoolbooks in the Twentieth Century* (New York, 1980), 97–105.

more struggle and work. Hayden suggests that professional historians must become more involved with the public schools. Toplin suggests that we be more integrally and conscientiously involved, from conception to production, in the film projects we lend our names to as consultants. Clearly, any attempt to influence public education must recognize that the content of textbooks and public school curricula are determined not simply by professional standards but by political values and actions as well.

On the other hand, the papers by Carole Merritt and John Fleming underscore the vital link between finding the sources essential to our work and the dissemination process. First, by educating the general black public that the common, everyday material artifacts around them are of value and can be historical texts, we might encourage them to preserve, collect, and donate such artifacts to museums and other repositories; and at the same time, we might stimulate the preservation of written documents as well. Secondly, Merritt makes the important point that the immediacy of material artifacts "is of particular benefit to a people who have felt alienated from history, who have been led to believe that they have little or no claim to a significant past." Thus the creation of a history-conscious public is crucially linked to the creation of histories.

And, of course, all this, too, is part of a longer tradition in Afro-American scholarship, part of the history of our history. As Franklin reminds us, Carter G. Woodson was the first to publish a historical periodical aimed at a popular audience, *The Negro History Bulletin*, and that the Association for the Study of Negro Life and History always included public school teachers among its membership and readers and sessions on teaching at its annual meetings. Moreover, the concern manifested in these papers with the black scholar's role in and responsibility to the black community, with that community's claims on the scholar, all resonate with the writings of Woodson, Du Bois, and others more than half a century earlier.[8]

History both transmits and creates culture; it follows then, as Nathan Huggins warns, that myth, symbolism, and the affirming-legitimizing function of history cannot be ignored. On the other hand, Nell Irvin Painter chastises those who hesitate "to investigate black life fully," follow-

8. W. E. B. Du Bois, *The Education of Black People: Ten Critiques, 1906–1960*, ed. Herbert Aptheker (New York, 1973); Carter G. Woodson, *The Mis-Education of the Negro* (Washington, D.C., 1933).

ing wherever the story leads, even into unflattering areas. Our history's ultimate power, Vincent Harding tells us, is in its "truth telling"; its ultimate aim, both Harding and Franklin agree, is to reshape the present and to create visions of a new future, not only for black Americans but for the whole society. Implied here is the notion that the future is somehow imprinted in the past, not because of any mystical determinism, but because minds are shaped for action by their understandings of the past.

In a 1960 essay reflecting on the imminent destruction of segregated education, Du Bois warned of "even more difficult problems of race and culture" implicated in the progress he foresaw: "Because what we must now ask ourselves is when we become equal American citizens what will be our aims and ideals and what will we have to do with selecting these aims and ideals. Are we to assume that we will simply adapt the ideals of Americans and become what they are or want to be and that we will have in this process no ideals of our own?"[9] "No!" is the answer these essayists would seem to return to Du Bois' query. The task of this generation and the next is to make good the implied promise in that reply: that the revitalization of Afro-American history be the basis for both a new American history and a new history in America.

9. Du Bois, "Whither Now and Why," *The Education of Black People*, 149.

I PROLOGUE

On the Evolution of Scholarship in Afro-American History

JOHN HOPE FRANKLIN

Every generation has the opportunity to write its own history, and indeed it is obliged to do so. Only in that way can it provide its contemporaries with the materials vital to understanding the present and to planning strategies for coping with the future. Only in that way can it fulfill its obligation to pass on to posterity the accumulated knowledge and wisdom of the past, which, after all, give substance and direction for the continuity of civilization.

According to my calculation, there have been four generations of scholarship—of unequal length—in Afro-American history. The first generation began auspiciously with the publication in 1882 of the two-volume *History of the Negro Race in America* by George Washington Williams and ended around 1909 with the publication of Booker T. Washington's *Story of the Negro*. Although it is difficult to characterize this first period of serious scholarship in the field, it is safe to say that the primary concern of the writers was to explain the process of adjustment Afro-Americans made to conditions in the United States. Whether it was the aggressive integrationism of George Washington Williams or the mild accommodationism of Booker T. Washington, the common objective of the writers of this period was to define and describe the role of Afro-Americans in the life of the nation. They by no means shared the same view of the past or the same way of writing history; they delineated the epic of Afro-American history in the manner that their talents and training permitted. They wrought as well as they could; and they wrought well.

There were no trained, professional historians among them, with the exception of W. E. B. Du Bois, who deserted the field shortly after he entered it. As he roamed across the fields of history, sociology, anthropology, political science, education, and literature, Du Bois became one of the few people ever who could be considered truly qualified in the broad field of Afro-American studies. Likewise, it is impossible to confine Du Bois to one generation. His life spanned three generations, and he made contributions to each of them. Others of the first generation were able, industrious, and well focused. They were historians more interested in espousing the causes of human beings than in adhering strictly to the canons of history. They provided panoramic, even pictorial views of Afro-Americans from the earliest times to the present. They wrote of "The Progress of the Race," "A New Negro for a New Century," and "The Remarkable Advancement of the American Negro." As one of them said, in commenting on post–Civil War Afro-Americans, "Starting in the most humble way, with limited intelligence and exceedingly circumscribed knowledge . . . they have gone on from year to year accumulating a little until the savings, as represented by their property, have built churches, erected schools, paid teachers and preachers, and greatly improved the home and home life." Obviously their concern was with adjustment, adaptation, and the compatibility of Afro-Americans with the white world in which they were compelled to live.

The second generation was marked by no special fanfare until the publication of Du Bois' *The Negro* in 1915, the founding of the Association for the Study of Negro Life and History also in 1915, the launching of the *Journal of Negro History* in 1916, and the publication in 1922 of Carter G. Woodson's *The Negro in Our History*. Woodson was the dominant figure of the period. He was not only the leading historian but also the principal founder of the association, editor of the *Journal*, and executive director of the Associated Publishers. He gathered around him a circle of highly trained younger historians whose research he directed and whose writings he published in the *Journal of Negro History* and under the imprint of the Associated Publishers. Monographs on labor, education, Reconstruction, art, music, and other aspects of Afro-American life appeared in steady succession, calling to the attention of the larger community the role of Afro-Americans, more specifically the contributions they had made to the development of the United States. The articles and monographs reflected prodigious research and zeal in pursuing the truth that had *not* been the hallmark of much of the so-called scientific historical writing produced in university seminars in this country some years earlier.

Woodson provided the intellectual and practical leadership of the second generation. With his strong sense of commitment, he offered the spirit and enthusiasm of a pioneer, a discoverer. He even provided the principal theme for the period when he said—in his writings and on numerous occasions—that it was the objective of him and his colleagues "to save and publish the records of the Negro, that the race may not become a negligible factor in the thought of the world." Nor should the record of Afro-Americans become a negligible factor in their own thought, Woodson contended. Thus he began doing everything possible to keep the history of Afro-Americans before them and before the larger community as well. Every annual meeting of the Association for the Study of Negro Life and History had several sessions devoted to the teaching of Afro-American history in the elementary and secondary schools. In 1926 Woodson began the annual observance of Negro History Week to raise the consciousness of Afro-Americans regarding their own worth and to draw the attention of others to what Afro-Americans had contributed to American civilization. Shortly thereafter he launched the *Negro History Bulletin*, a magazine for students, teachers, and the general public. Forty years before this country began to observe History Day, there was Negro History Week. Fifty years after the beginning of the *Negro History Bulletin*, the American Historical Association was still wrestling with the idea of a popular history magazine for students and the general public.

The second generation of Afro-American historical scholarship was coming to a close some years before Woodson's death in 1950. Perhaps a convenient place to mark the beginning of the third generation is with the appearance in 1935 of W. E. B. Du Bois' *Black Reconstruction*. Although Du Bois had gone to some length to disassociate himself from efforts toward racial integration when he left the NAACP the previous year, *Black Reconstruction* reflected little of the separatist sentiment that characterized some of his other writings in 1934 and 1935. In his book on Reconstruction, as the subtitle indicates, he was interested in "the part which black folk played in the attempt to reconstruct democracy in America." In this attempt Du Bois saw merit in blacks and whites working together, es-

pousing the same causes, voting together, and promoting the same candidates. If his book lacked the scholarship of *The Suppression of the African
Slave Trade*, which had appeared forty years earlier in 1896, it achieved a
level of original interpretation seldom if ever matched by the most profound students of history.

The third generation of Afro-American historical scholarship spanned,
roughly, a twenty-five-year period that ended with the close of the 1960s.
Most of the members of this generation were, like Du Bois, interested in
the role that Afro-Americans played in the nation's history. Their training
was similar to that of the second generation, but their interests were different. They looked less to Afro-American achievements and more to the interactions of blacks with whites, and more to the frequent antagonisms
than to the rare moments of genuine cooperation. They tended to see
Afro-American history in a larger context, insisting that any event that affected the status of Afro-Americans was a part of Afro-American history
even if no Afro-Americans were directly involved. Mississippi's Theodore
Bilbo, reading Rayford Logan's *What the Negro Wants* (1944) to his colleagues in the United States Senate and interpreting it for their benefit, was
as much a part of Afro-American history as was Heman Sweatt's seeking
admission to the University of Texas Law School.

The third generation experienced the fire and brimstone of World War
II. Its predicament was not one that Adolf Hitler created but one created
by the racial bigotry within their own government and in the American
community in general. While all Afro-Americans were exposed to this special brand of racial perversion in the form of eloquent, if shallow, pro-
nouncements against worldwide racism, Afro-American historians were
especially sensitive to the persistent hypocrisy of the United States from
the colonial years right down to World War II. Small wonder that they had
difficulty maintaining a semblance of balance in the face of studied racial
discrimination and humiliation. One of them declared that the United
States government was "guilty of catering to the ideals of white supremacy." Another called on the United States to "address herself to the
unfinished business of democracy," adding somewhat threateningly that
"time was of the essence." If anyone doubts the impatience and anger of
Afro-American historians during those years, he or she should examine
the proceedings of the annual meetings of the Association for the Study of

Negro Life and History or follow the activities of the historians themselves.

A salient feature of this generation was the increasing number of white historians working in the field. Some years earlier the second generation of historians had indicated that there were numerous areas in which work needed to be done. White historians entered the field to share in the work. One of them published the first extensive study of slavery in almost forty years and another wrote an elaborate work on the antislavery movement. Still another presented the first critical examination of Negro thought in the late nineteenth century. Interestingly enough, hostile white critics called these white historians "neo-abolitionists." Others worked on Afro-Americans in the antebellum North, Afro-American intellectual history, racial discrimination in education, and Afro-Americans in urban settings. Meanwhile, university professors began to assign dissertation topics in Afro-American history to white as well as Afro-American students. They also participated in the annual meetings of the Association for the Study of Negro Life and History and contributed to the *Journal of Negro History*. By the end of the 1960s Afro-American history was no longer the exclusive domain of Afro-Americans.

I believe that Carter G. Woodson would have been pleased with this involvement of white historians in the third generation of scholarship. When he founded the *Journal of Negro History* in 1916, he invited white scholars to sit on the editorial board and to contribute articles. He was, nevertheless, a man of shrewd insights, and I am not suggesting for a moment that he would have approved of or even tolerated whites of the third generation whose motives were more political than scholarly. Even so, he would have welcomed papers for publication in the *Journal of Negro History*, whether submitted by whites or blacks, so long as they were the product of rigorous scholarship and were not contaminated by the venom of racial bias. I knew him well and spent many hours with him each year between 1940 and 1950, when he died. He would have been appalled at the bickering that enveloped the association in the 1960s over the question of whether white historians should be permitted to participate in the work of the association. He had always insisted that men and women should be judged strictly on the basis of their work and not on the basis of their race or the color of their skin.

In the fourth generation, which began around 1970, there emerged the largest and perhaps the best-trained group of historians of Afro-America that had ever appeared. The Afro-Americans in the group were trained, as were the white historians, in graduate centers in every part of the country, in contrast to those of the third generation, who had been trained at three or four universities in the East and Midwest. No area of inquiry escaped their attention. They worked on the colonial period, the era of Reconstruction, and the twentieth century. They examined slavery, the Afro-American family, and antebellum free blacks. Their range was wide, and they brought educational, cultural, and military subjects, among many others, under their scrutiny.

These new approaches as well as the accelerated intensity in the study of Afro-American history were greatly stimulated by the drive for equality that had already begun in the third period. In their insistence that they be accorded equal treatment in every respect, Afro-Americans summoned the history of the United States to their side. They had been here from the beginning, they argued, and had done more than their share in making the country rich and great. Since history validated their claims, it was important that the entire nation should become familiar with the facts of Afro-American history. Consequently, it should be studied more intensely, written about more extensively, and taught more vigorously. Institutions of higher education came under pressure to add courses in Afro-American history and related fields and to employ specialists in the field. Responses were varied. One dean at a leading predominantly white university said that he had no objection to a course in Afro-American history, but it would be difficult in view of the fact that there was not sufficient subject matter to occupy the teachers and students for a *whole* semester. Another rushed out and persuaded one of the leaders in the black community, who happened to be a Baptist minister, to teach a course in Afro-American history. Despite the intellectual, educational, and political considerations affecting their decisions, many colleges and universities incorporated courses in Afro-American history into their curricula.

It was the frenetic quality of the concerns of university administrators that cast doubts on their interest in maintaining high academic standards in the area of Afro-American studies. As students intensified their demands for courses in this area, university officials seemed more interested in mollifying students than in enriching the curriculum with courses taught by well-trained professors who maintained high standards. The results were that some courses were staffed by persons whose familiarity with what they taught was minimal and whose approach tended to confirm the views of the dean who thought there was not sufficient subject matter in Afro-American history to span an entire semester.

It is nothing short of marvelous that under the circumstances scholarship in Afro-American history moved to a new high level of achievement. Some claimed that those who taught were not doing the researching and writing and, thus, were not adding to the body of knowledge that was needed in order to satisfy our doubting dean. That was true, to some extent, but it was no less true in, say, diplomatic, cultural, intellectual, or economic history. There have always been more purveyors than creators of knowledge in all fields, and there is nothing fundamentally wrong with this, I suppose. We who teach *and* do research and write tend to think that the dual activity is more healthy intellectually, but that is a matter of opinion. What is remarkable in the field of Afro-American history is not that there were so many teachers who did not write but that there were so many who did.

Perhaps it was because scholars in the field of Afro-American history saw so many opportunities to reinterpret their field that such a large number of them were engaged in researching and writing. There was zeal, even passion, in much that they wrote, for they were anxious to correct all the errors and misinterpretations of which earlier historians had been guilty. Thus, they undertook to revise not only the racist historians of an earlier day but the Afro-American historians of an earlier generation as well. There was not always the grace and charity and certainly not the gratitude that one might expect of persons whose work almost invariably rested on the work of their intellectual godfathers. That, however, was relatively unimportant, especially if the work they produced was of the highest quality and made a solid contribution to the scholarship of Afro-American history. This was true often enough that one could blush more often in pride than in sorrow.

Some writing, nevertheless, was stimulated by publishers who were anxious to take advantage of a growing market. Under pressure from their agents and editors, some scholars produced works that had the sole merit of having been written with more than deliberate speed. When the speed was not great enough to produce "instant" books, publishers prevailed on some scholars to anthologize the writings of others. Some of the products were of great merit, bringing together as they did the best writings of some of the leaders in the field. Some of the products, however, were excellent illustrations of how scholars and scholarship can be corrupted by the prospect of monetary gain. Many anthologies were literally thrown together, without any thought being given to arrangement or organization and without any introduction, interpretation, or connective tissue. The only thing that one can say of such works is that they were not alone in the nature and extent of their compromise with intellectual integrity. Lecturers could be just as bad or worse. One recalls how in the early 1970s one of the "authoritative" lecturers in Afro-American history broke an engagement at a leading western university and simply informed them by telegram that he had been offered more money to lecture at another institution. Perhaps more common were "instant" professors, black and white, who rushed into the field to make a quick reputation as well as a quick buck. Unhappily, college and university administrators did not display the same skill in detecting the charlatans in this field that they did in some other fields. Thus, the field often suffered from the presence of so-called authorities whose abilities were no higher than their motives.

At this point one must not dwell on defects of scholarship or even the character of the scholars. Time will take care of such matters, without even so much as a suggestion from us as to how we should like to settle them. Instead, we could better serve the present *and* the future by attempting, as historians, to take lessons from the last century and use them to make certain that this generation will make significant improvements over what preceding generations had to offer.

In his *History of the Negro Race in America* (1882), George Washington Williams was extremely critical of Frederick Douglass for various positions he took on slavery and freedom in the years before the Civil War. We could excoriate Williams, as did his contemporaries, but that would be unfair without at least first understanding Williams' impatience with a political party that had betrayed not only the freedmen but Frederick Douglass, their chosen spokesman, as well. Likewise, one could be extremely critical of Carter G. Woodson's preoccupation with the achievements of Afro-Americans, but one should remember that Woodson was hurling historical brickbats at those who had said that Afro-Americans had achieved nothing at all. One could likewise be extremely critical of the historians of the third generation for their preoccupation with what may be called "mainstream history." In the process, some claim, they neglected some cherished attributes of Afro-American life and history, such as race pride and cultural nationalism. Such claims overlook the important fact that the historians of the third generation were compelled by circumstances to fight for the integration of Afro-American history into the mainstream of the nation's history. Their fight to integrate Afro-American history into the mainstream was a part of the fight by Afro-American students to break into the graduate departments of history in every predominantly white university in the southern states and in very many such institutions outside the South. It was also a part of the fight of Afro-Americans to gain admission to the mainstream of American life—for the vote, for equal treatment, for equal opportunity, for their rights as Americans. They pursued that course in order to be able to refute those, including our favorite dean—our favorite whipping boy, incidentally—who argued that Afro-Americans had little or no history. They also did so in order to support their argument that Afro-American history should be recognized as a centerpiece—an adornment, if you will—of the history of the United States.

The excoriations and strictures heaped on one generation of Afro-American historians by succeeding generations could better be spent on more constructive pursuits. Better trained and with better means of communication, they could, for example, seek to tell us more than we already know about malingering and sabotage among slaves. They could devote more attention to writing vignettes if not full biographies of hundreds of important Afro-Americans, the remembrance and recognition of whom are endangered by neglect and the passage of time. They could devote some of their energies to helping us understand how it is, in a country committed to the dignity of man, that so much energy has been spent throughout its history to maintain the proposition that Afro-Americans have no dignity and, therefore, are not deserving of respect. Thomas Jefferson argued it when he likened Afro-Americans to the orangutan. Fourth generation historians of Afro-America have come close to arguing it by claiming that slaves, as a whole, were not only content but were imbued with the Protestant work ethic that gave them a sense of commitment to what they were doing. No area of intellectual endeavor needs such stumbling blocks to truth, whether it comes out of the eighteenth century or out of the last quarter of the twentieth century.

The implications of all of this for the teaching of Afro-American history are profound, to say the least. As a relatively new field, at least only recently recognized as a respectable field of intellectual endeavor, it is alive and vibrant. This is why it can easily attract and excite a large number of graduate and undergraduate students. It provides, moreover, a very important context in which much, if not the whole, of the history of the United States can be taught and studied. It also provides an important context in which much of the history of the United States can be reexamined and rewritten. In its unique position as one of the most recent areas of intellectual inquiry, it invites the attention of those who genuinely seek new avenues to solve some of the nation's most difficult historical problems. And, if it is a valid area of intellectual inquiry, it cannot be segregated by sex, religion, or race. Historians must be judged by what they do, not by how they look.

I like to think that it was more than opportunism that increased the offerings in Afro-American history in the colleges and universities across the land. I like to believe that it was more than the excitement of the late 1960s that provided new opportunities to teach and learn Afro-American history. I prefer to entertain the thought that in addition to those other considerations there was the valid interconnection between the history of a people and their drive for first-class citizenship. The quest for their history, lost and strayed, was a quest in which black and white alike could and did participate, as both teachers and writers of history. The drive for first-class citizenship was a drive whose immediate benefit could be enjoyed only by those who had been denied it or by those others who at least truly understood the loathsome nature that such denial represented.

Some members of the fourth generation, no doubt, will regard this sentiment as optimistic if not maudlin. I would be the first to say that there is some of both in it. I would only add that when one begins a poem, a hymn, a short story, or even a history, one must be optimistic about its completion and about what it seeks to teach. If one believes in the power of his own words and in the words of others, one must also hope and believe that the world will be a better place by our having spoken or written those words.

II SLAVERY STUDIES

The African in the Garden: Reflections About New World Slavery and Its Lifelines

LESLIE H. OWENS

Until very recently most thinking on the subject of American Negro slavery was still dominated by the influence of the subject's first interpreter, Ulrich Bonnell Phillips. This observation is meant to underscore that most of our revised approaches to the study of slavery and particularly slave personality have appeared during a span of years covering little more than the past decade. Scholars of the post–World War II period have increasingly grouped their investigations into psychological and economic categories, but even refined approaches in these areas have not moved us as far from the past as many now tell us we should be. Yet a characteristic that recent studies share—some for better, some for worse—that has added much to our insights into slavery and American consciousness is a desire to get inside the black man or woman's skin in an effort to see things from his or her perspective and thus to make coherent the impact of harsh historical circumstances on the black psyche.

A variety of concerns that have played central roles in shaping the discussion of slavery throughout the twentieth century have often clashed with private and public black sensibilities. The impact of slavery on millions of Africans shipped to the New World remains a troubling subject. The precise number of victims of the Trade continues to be an elusive area of investigation, but what is clear from the extremes in estimates ranging from Phillip Curtin's (*The Atlantic Slave Trade*, 1969) revised low of ten million to older projections of up to fifty million or more is that past generations have tampered with the evidence. Since much of the data is inappropriate to the needs of scholars, the impact on generations of Africans of the forced migration of millions of their ancestors over a period of nearly four centuries has generally escaped wider systematic explorations. However, what is increasingly apparent is that, whatever figures are used, historians and the general public tend to treat them literally, with lower estimates coming mostly from white scholars and higher ones from black scholars. That the matter remains open to heated debate is perhaps healthy, and its spin-off into the important areas of the mortality and birth rates of Africans in the Western Hemisphere has led to equally heated discussions about the treatment of Africans in different geographic areas and the survival characteristics shared by them and their children.

The issue of how many of the most vigorous African males and females were snatched from their homelands, or of their mortality and birth rates, will never be resolved. Yet, understanding the slave trade in the historical and comparative context of populating the New World and depopulating the African continent should prove helpful in grasping the larger and more revealing story of the impact of the Trade on African family members on both sides of the Atlantic. The taking of Africa's most important resource —human beings—played a devastating role in the lives of slave-era Africans both at home and abroad and greatly facilitated the conquest of Africa by Europeans in the nineteenth century. While Europe and the New World advanced, Africa unavoidably declined, although their relative positions in the world order on the eve of the slave trade were as near equals. The slave trade made possible Europe's leap into the industrial age. Could not an equal influx of manpower and capital formation harnessed by Africans have done something similar for their lands?

In the context of much of the suggestive scholarship of our day, the need to investigate parallel economic, political, and social happenings in Africa and the New World during and immediately after the slave trade— perhaps within the covers of a single study—seems a long overdue undertaking. Even though the mathematics of the Trade continues to elude us, its generational and chronological advance can be brought into clearer focus.

Just as individuals of the international slaveholding powers fashioned uneven views of their relationships to a section, a nation, and the world, so too the African forged conceptions of his place in a world that depended so much on his labor and energies for its building. The clarification of such world views and their social, political, and economic implications are of paramount importance for the future directions of slave studies. Africans, after all, had been spirited from their continent for great deeds. As was their custom, many assessed the controlled existence others had arranged for them, compared it to their own keen awareness of a structured past and place in history, and became central figures at leading the New World into a conscious era of freedom.

The slave trade shattered family units and societies central to understanding African historical developments and the shaping of African attitudes about Europeans and vice versa, but the Trade also hardened Africans to the corrupted value systems of their captors. Shackled in the bellies of ships and in the Caribbean islands, Africans experienced the brunt of what modern slavery's psychoeconomics would mean for their lives and heritage. Here the predominance of an African majority in most areas continued the pattern of African blood ties and alertness to history that distinguished their immediate past. Africans were saturated with historical family ties based on blood relations and perhaps more prone to think of family and history in expanded terms as a reference point for much of the strength of their identities. They were not a nuclear (conjugal) oriented people as Europeans were and thus found it only natural to reach out to their oppressed brothers and sisters. The reach became more difficult with time, but such blood ties should be labeled more than simply lingering "Africanisms." They unlock an institutionally structured way of ordering the world and provide a practical link to a past that could not be erased. Yet, conclusions persist in the literature that the black past can hardly be found.

I would like to suggest a need for closer attention to generational evidence within the slave community. Such evidence is not as limited as widely supposed; both the narratives and plantation records are useful, offering the possibility of more precise descriptions of the internal forces and traditions holding communities of slaves together amidst the disruption of high mortality and the evolving domestic trade. Generational methodology seems particularly important for the period before the cutoff of the international slave trade, a period covering the major part of modern slavery.

In a similar framework our approaches to comparative history need to be in part recast. There is much to be learned from comparative efforts encompassing more limited regional differences, island differences, and differences and similarities between parts of the same century. Such approaches have rarely been attempted but promise to provide us with a far more comprehensive feel for the impact of slavery on the African and of the African on slavery.

In slavery, whites as well as blacks faced many assaults—cultural and physical—on their sense of being; whites, for instance, suffered a series of memorable defeats in the Haitian and Latin American revolutions. The island communities of the Caribbean and the countries of Latin America never developed into—nor were they intended to—the promised land that mainland North America talked about. The Old South intended Africans to learn that they were a part of something larger, that, although their numbers were great from plantation to plantation, they lived in an expanding region peopled by more whites than any other place in the hemisphere. And the Africans were to be the tools of this expansion along new frontiers. Slaves' visions thus grew with the world around them as they continued to build on the knowledge of how others expected their lives to be played out.

The appearance of Robert Fogel and Stanley Engerman's *Time on the Cross* moved the economics of slavery to center stage alongside psychological considerations of the institution. To critique the limitations of this study is not my present purpose, but Fogel and Engerman's *Cross* is one of the few economic studies that adds the variable of human blood to its design in a manner predated by such scholars as Eric Williams and C. L. R. James. The economics of blood, as slavery must also be referred to, has too often escaped cliometricians and other economic investigators. Yet, there are few precedents in world history for so many people directly or indirectly benefiting from the blood, sweat, and tears of others; so enormous an advance toward ironic notions of free enterprise and democratic institutions appeared to grow from so enormous a suppression of the rights of one's fellow man.

The idea of earned wealth used by most economists and historians had profound impact on the African mind. In contrast to almost all other Americans, African-Americans came to understand why the fruits of their labor did not convert to financial or material gains for themselves, their families, or communities. They therefore gained an insight into the workings of the nascent free enterprise system not shared by most of its architects and potential benefactors. Understanding what they learned has not occupied much economic history, but our considered looks at the economic notion of profit maximization as a key characterization of plantation owners' behavior in relationship to the management of their properties necessitate clearer delineations of profit's meaning in the eyes of slaves for their own upkeep and treatment.

In this regard, the kinds of profit to be made at the local level via interplantational trade and bartering cannot be calculated into our economic models. This is due partly to the nature of the evidence that remains and partly to the resistance of many researchers to searching available plantation records for what they imply about economic and human behavior modeling. Slaveholders had frequent connections, often through their slaves, with other slaveholding and nonslaveholding farmers throughout the South as the region increased its economic and psychological dependency on slave labor. The conclusion that the economic picture of slavery throughout an entire century—particularly the nineteenth—is fundamental to understanding the dynamics of the institution's profits in a world-market climate makes a great deal of sense for understanding the dynamics of black-white dependency as well. By accepting the reasonable notion that the choice of producing cash crops of scale (cotton, tobacco, rice, etc.) is a vital factor distinguishing slaveholders in the South from nonslaveholders in the North and elsewhere, we learn not only a great deal about the ideology of production and class structure but how the individual and collective presence of the African intruded into every area of regional, national, and international life and how well many Africans understood this.

In terms of the larger connection between slave labor and freedom, slaves' associations with New World land arrangements fired their desires for landholding just after emancipation in all parts of the hemisphere. Land meant the great opportunity to put many of their skills to work for themselves, and, combined with education, it engaged their spirits like almost no other topic. To say that the skilled working of land by slaves contributed to the prosperity of the slave regime in ways that simply prolonged their own bondage is to miss the point that I am trying to establish here, for in this scenario the slave is simply the true captive—body and soul—of the master class. Instead, many bondsmen utilized their worth to the economic markets to help modify those markets and the systems of race relations that existed. The pursuit of this kind of mutuality or symbiosis may bring us nearer to understanding the roles of slaves in the economics of slavery and the enthusiasm with which they approached life following the Civil War and even in earlier times when often the feeling that freedom was imminent ran high.

The wealth of the planter and the so-called pride that some slaves took in it were perhaps savored because slaves could see beyond their agony and could sense that the sweat of their labors had creative force capable of taming the earth's resources. This may strike many as a strange connection between the good intentions of the enslaved and the evil manipulations of masters, but for slaves and many others in the working class it possessed the character of relations between labor and management even when managers did little more than hold the whip. Slaves understood the earthly failings and limitations of their masters in managing both human and real property. The stereotypes nurtured by slave medicine and later by scholars such as U. B. Phillips bespeak the doubts of men confronted with the black capabilities that produced the life-styles whites enjoyed. Africans under primitive conditions were after all able to do something in the Western Hemisphere that Europeans were not. They were able to harness Paradise. That Paradise and blacks have been inseparable in the annals of the ancient past and in present-day scholarship has played no small part in the development of scholarly considerations of the origins of civilization and the creative energies that such origins imply.

One of the more neglected and important areas for slavery investigations to pursue embraces the field of women's studies. Our grasp of the diversification and nuances between sexual roles of women and men in bondage is seriously deficient and requires further readings of the narratives, plantation records, and other available sources. The Caribbean islands and Latin America suffered a shortage of African women for many years, as did sections of the Old South down to the census of 1830. One consequence of this shortage is that the work and sex roles of women and men continue to be blurred, thus hampering researchers in their ability to provide accurate portrayals and syntheses of the varieties and significance of the roles played by African women and the impact of these roles on womanhood, family life, and male-female relations. At times the devastating disparity of numbers between men and women on Caribbean and Latin American plantations brutally reshaped homelife traditions, sexual life-styles, and the meaning of agricultural production for Africans, who had long ago evolved institutions far more sensitive to these requirements than those of their European counterparts. Slavery as it was known in Africa sought generally to leave victims within the reach of the family, and the use of women as prostitutes and concubines seems rare.

Still, the place of women in African cultures and their sporadic existence in many sections of the New World constitute a prime example of worlds in collision. And there was no way for slave traders to blunt such a wrong—when they saw it as that—without compounding the dimensions of the wrong on both sides of the Atlantic. The African was the first to seize this point in the tug-of-war that body and emotions were placed in. Yet, inasmuch as slavery was inevitably changed by the increased incorporation of women under its yoke, the nature of this evolving bondage needs more balanced and detailed analysis. For males in regions where there were few or no women, the physical and spiritual divide separating their lives as slaves from memories or traditions of the continent added greatly to their understanding of the exact nature and intent of their captors. Their captors had cut a central thread of African life and made the identification of slaveholders with the forces of evil indelible.

In the Old South the researcher sometimes comes across manuscript references to plantations largely peopled by female slaves. What we might learn about the treatment of women as differentiated from men is not always clear, but we need to gain insight into how and why such situations arose. Evidence that relates to sterility rates among female slaves needs both systematic gathering and interpretation in the search to broaden our perceptions of the pressures on the family unit. Better insights into the complementary nature of the slave household's division of labors between wife and husband are important doorways to understanding family life. Domestic abuse in the quarters has been overstated, as has the plantation evidence said to support it. Wives understood, as did their husbands and growing children, that slavery was the great compromiser. The affections of wives and husbands are areas that interpreters have seldom appreciated or explored, and husbands were not generally emasculated—viewed as boys—by the mythical domination by wives in the quarters. Both men and women realized that their capacities for loving could bring an intimacy even to bondage marital ties that those who oppressed them might never know themselves.

Comparative statements about the associations of slave women with slave mistresses have been few. Their connections in both the workplace and in their respective social systems might give us better balanced interpretations of matriarchal and patriarchal assertions that dot the literature. Mary Boykin Chesnut's well-known observation that mistresses felt akin to slaves in their servitude within the southern system has many antecedents in the plantation journals and diaries kept before the war. But the real-life link between such feelings and the plantation scene serves us best as we look further at male-female relations, woman-child relations, and the roles of relatives within the master-slave setting. It was the slave who, despite separation from loved ones, frequently had more people surrounding him or her who were referred to in familial terms, and this is an important realm of the African woman's influence. Ultimately, it is perhaps an irony of circumstance that often more references to the comfort provided by kinship ties occur in the confines of the quarters than in the Big House.

Our depictions of the quality of life in the quarters could also bring us closer to unlocking the reach of the quarters into the African past and memories of family associations. The physical resemblance of many quarters to residential compounds that appear on the coast of West Africa is unmistakable. And, as these compounds were synonymous with family life, other similarities may spring from the actual physical configuration of the quarters housing. By gaining a closer idea of housing arrangements— who lived next to whom and how often, if at all, the family living space mirrored uneven slave status and family formations—we may find ourselves more capable of penetrating the quarters' silences. On large estates the cabin grouping of skilled slaves and field slaves sometimes alerts us to status differences as well as family ties and friendships. And on occasion, recently purchased slaves occupied selected cabins or space in a family seasoned in helping recent arrivals in the adjustment process. Did childless women live in family units? Some did, some did not. As a rule, we don't know. Did a driver, handpicked by a slaveholder, rule over the quarters and establish his particular style? Probably not in ways previously suggested, despite his authority. Differences in life-styles based on religious or worldly inclination among slaves also shaped the family and quarters space and affected the roles of older bondsmen in influencing the patterns of life among younger adults and children.

In the 1920s southern congressmen nearly succeeded in having a federal statue to the black mammy erected in the District of Columbia. Their efforts met with considerable resistance within the black community, but their actions betrayed more than just racial bigotry. The mammy frequently played a crucial role in whites' upbringing and sometimes their public lives. Such roles may not have been ones that altered the face of slavery and later race relations, but the references by southern leaders and other members of the ruling class to their motherly mammies should be treated as more than simple affection for a tragic figure whose emotions were misdirected under the weight of slavery. The evidence may be particularly important where it bears upon reaction to blacks as a whole in some important moments in local and national history. Even as some mistresses tried to fathom and match the sexual allure they believed potent slave women somehow possessed even in the condition of servitude, many were driven to questioning the dimensions of their own personalities and humanity as they observed slave women in restricted bloom about them.

Focusing on slaves as women and men of course means that we acquire increased knowledge about their children, with considerable stress on the many children who were parted from their families by sale. The general status of the slave child has received little serious scholarly attention. Yet, slave children received a great deal of attention from a plantation system bent on turning a margin of profit. Children are often so closely connected with the behavior of adults and parents that the historical record needs considerable maturing. Fuller discussions about matters such as the proportion of children to adults on average size plantations as well as the numbers of children who found themselves part of the international and domestic slave trades can lead us to more informed debates about slave family structure and the economic orientation and priorities of the Peculiar Institution.

Some writers at times have written about slave children as if their bondage was somehow divorced from the conditions of slavery their parents endured. Evidence to support such views is occasionally cited from the slave narratives, but consider how remarkably such a childhood contrasted to harsh adult slave life. And in the end this view is more a commentary about parents than children. One almost must believe that "happy-go-lucky" adults conveyed little of their own sufferings to their children. This would indeed have been a slavery of the master's making. But it is doubtful that any slave parent or quarters resident could have allowed offspring to be so ill-prepared—as the logic of this position would have it—for the rigors of bondage. Instead, most children were well schooled in the lessons of slavery early on in their lives. This schooling does not mean that they did not enjoy times of fun and games and parental affection that allowed their minds and hearts to develop in ways beneficial to life among their peers, but they were well versed in the realities and carefully garnered joys that were the lot of a plantation bondsman.

One area relating to childhood should be stressed. A clearer view of how slave children were reared is of major importance for understanding the configuration of slave breeding. If the breeding of slaves in selected regions as opposed to others moves us closer to the variations in treatment of slaves from spot to spot, it may also help us to understand plantation to plantation variations within the local neighborhood. Present evidence is often suggestive of situations on the local level where one plantation or more served as the human reproductive center for neighbors, much in the fashion of the interplantation trade in other goods. This dimension of the domestic slave trade has remained hidden, yet its pursuit and further confirmation may give us some knowledge about the extent of slave intermarriages on local plantations and a wider grasp of why such arrangements were made with more regularity than we have perhaps realized.

The reluctance with which many scholars have explored and discussed slave breeding is itself stimulus for controversy. Some have looked for specific plantation breeding sites though often without looking in plantation records. Others have alleged that the search would add little to our awareness of the institution unless researchers were able to establish a one-on-one relationship between breeding slaves and a plantation's overall margin of profit. This suggestion, however, ignores much direct and corroborative evidence available in plantation manuscripts. But what it may ignore most is the expressed intent of many slaveholders to make a profit no matter how that had to be accomplished or defined. The Parker-Gallman slave farms sample, as Richard Sutch has elaborated on, demonstrates that "selling states had higher fertility ratios than did the buying states." Yet it seems unnecessarily tentative merely to suppose that slaveholders in many areas of the Old South (especially in older eastern slave states) tampered with the sexual habits of some of the slaves under their charge. The record speaks often of such tampering for real or imagined profit, and the use of sources beyond the manuscript census would illuminate some of these findings more fully. With the high rates of sterility and infant mortality in the quarters, attention to sexual situations of slaves and slaveholders assumed much the form of crude family planning. It could be a brutal and insensitive method that tossed slaves' emotions aside, but even within the quarters some viewed an occasional arrangement as essential to the perpetuation of the line.

The Africans' resistance to their bondage, especially in the United States, is perhaps the most sensitive and controversial area of slave investigation. Often the question is raised: Why didn't Africans in the United States resist their bondage more? The question is used almost as an epitaph about the suggested past behavior of a people and perhaps about their future course of development. But the question is misleading—perhaps deliberately so—and is one that slaveholders probably never would have posed. Initially what it promotes is arguments between blacks and whites. Still, this is indicative of a fundamental misunderstanding about resistance from the outset. First, the perceptions of black and white Americans about resistance have always been divergent. Indeed, the idea that one can count the number of resistance incidents in slavery has done much to damage real consideration of resistance patterns. Resistance among slaves even in the plantation records seems to accord little with what has been written about it by a great many researchers.

For most blacks, resistance to American society's oppressive features has been an almost automatic part of their personality and identity in historical touch with the earliest days of the overseas trade. Whereas Western scholarship has frequently confused resistance with bloodshed as a fundamental ingredient, Africans have often perceived it as an inner stance coiled to preserve identity. The striking material differences in Western and African cultural modes which linger in our day have tended to make blacks reliant on what has come to be called soul. This development is by no means accidental but in great measure is in line with most important African traditions. It is of course intended by association to designate whites as soulless. Africans (blacks) have continued to think of themselves as the people of soul and humanity, which is in fact the most forceful resistance they could offer to a hostile environment deceived by its own democratic impulses.

Yet obviously soul is not enough or an end in itself. Many in the slave setting were thrown off guard by white America's profession of an extension of soul in the notion of equality for all. Blacks—slaves and free—continued to believe in this notion as they fought for freedom in the Revolutionary War, the War of 1812, the Civil War, and other lesser-known struggles. In these wars for freedom the black presence was a continued statement of resistance and rebellion against the practices of abuse and discrimination so characteristic of the New World. For example, the thousands of Africans who escaped to "freedom" during the Revolutionary War have never been sufficiently recorded or interpreted. Their resistance at the start of the American Republic was a massive indictment of a system gone bad. Those who fought for American freedom did just that; that is, they fought for an honest definition of freedom in line with their conceptions of the justice due the soul. And there is no little irony in this.

If the historian's search for Nat Turners in the Old South is little satisfied, the impact of Nat Turner lies all around the landscape. Blacks gained their freedom in the blood struggles in Haiti and other parts of Latin America. They set up maroon communities in the mountains of Jamaica and launched the Republic of Palmares (America's first) in the Brazilian jungles. But perhaps only in the United States did their resistance and presence have the lasting impact on conceptions of democracy so fundamental to any understanding of the evolving Western world's institutional structures and dreams. American blacks early on set the standards for what freedom was and was not. The price of their resistance was/is a painful and destructive relationship with white America. But their economic prowess in captivity and their dashed expectations that Americans were people of their word fueled the American dream of equality like few other developments in the Western Hemisphere.

Their resistance, then, was to the notion that men were not created equal and entitled to equal rights. Nonblacks on the American scene could little understand this conception without its accompanying racial biases, but it receives no better expression than in the lives of plantation slaves. Slaves not only made the economics of the New World possible but also made the New World's dream of democracy a reality at the price of their lives. In each instance they were closest to the effort that would make the political economy of the New World a reality, though it would never be the reality they sought and knew to be possible. This does not of course disparage the resistance attainments that were the deeds of African relatives throughout the hemisphere. My effort is to express a needed balance between the successes of physical violence in the context of New World developments and the expanded dimensions of thinking about freedom that the presence of blacks in the United States pushed.

COMMENT

EUGENE D. GENOVESE

Leslie Owens, having decided to range so widely in a short paper, should not be surprised to hear that he has risked unleashing frustrations, the more so since he has peppered the paper with some exciting if occasionally obscure challenges. What, for example are we to make of his reference to those Africans in the garden who alone "were able to harness Paradise"? He appears to mean that the slaves, not their masters, did the psychologically liberating labor in the garden of southern myth that lay at the heart of the plantation pastoral. If so, Owens is calling for a deeper understanding of the ramifications for blacks as a complement to the brilliant analysis that Lewis P. Simpson has offered for whites.[1] Owens also insists, in the tradition of W. E. B. Du Bois, that, in consequence, the slaves and their descendants, not the masters and theirs, embodied the finest aspirations of southern culture. Still, his claim that only Africans, nowhere Europeans, harnessed Paradise clearly refers to the cultural development of the United States and the rest of the Western Hemisphere. If so, the northern farmers, not to mention the southern yeomen, are getting short shrift. If, however, as Owens hints in his curious reference to antiquity, his invocation of Paradise does not refer to the myth of the garden—to the New

---

1. Lewis P. Simpson, *The Dispossessed Garden: Pastoral and History in Southern Literature* (Athens, Ga., 1976); also, Simpson's contributions to the symposium *Southern Literary Study: Problems and Possibilities*, eds. Louis D. Rubin, Jr., and C. Hugh Holman (Chapel Hill, 1975).

World pastoral to which he alludes with an edge of contempt—then he needs to speak a good deal more clearly or invite a multiplicity of mutually exclusive readings.

I suspect that Owens can clarify his meaning and defend his thesis and I ask only that he do so. But he may have a much more difficult time in defending the suggestion, which he advances cautiously, that the slave trade ruined Africa's chance to industrialize before Europe. I confess to being surprised to find a unilinear interpretation of history ensconced in Owens' work and am by no means sure that it does the Africans and other non-European peoples justice. England, in any case, not "Europe" effected the industrial revolution that transformed the world, and England had become a capitalist country several centuries earlier. The European continent, as well as Africa, had maintained various forms of precapitalist social relations, and it is doubtful that the African forms would have evolved into bourgeois forms without outside intervention. To the contrary, they appear to have been a good deal more stable than those of Western Europe—a judgment that implies not the slightest cultural, social, or moral inferiority. For these reasons, among others, Eric Hobsbawm's demonstration that the industrial revolution probably could only have occurred in a single country provides a salutary check against the tendency to romanticize, and thereby inadvertently denigrate, the historical experience of the Third World.[2]

So much for the caveats and expressions of frustration that Owens well knew he would provoke. He has, nonetheless, tossed out many fruitful suggestions and, even more impressively, has offered a rich context within which they may be explored. That context is political economy, which provides the bedrock for his projected reexamination of familiar themes. Consider his subtle, excruciatingly courteous discussion of the historical literature on "the slave personality." Avoiding unnecessary polemics and cheap shots, he begins by observing that an initial postwar fascination with the debilitating effects of slavery on the slave passed inexorably into the opposite—a concern with the slaves' active response to enslavement and with their struggle against it. Thus he wisely rejects the rigid separation of frontal opposition and the almost imperceptible daily struggles at every level of experience. As he says, the slaves' ability to defeat the fero-

2. See esp. E. J. Hobsbawm, "The Crisis of the Seventeenth Century," in Trevor Aston (ed.), *Crisis in Europe, 1550–1660* (Garden City, N.Y., 1967).

cious attempts to infantilize and emasculate them proved multidimensional and often silent. Since the slaves' struggle for "soul" itself constituted a massive and historically decisive form of resistance, he properly calls for further and more specific work, although I am sure that he intends no slight to the work of Blassingame, Gutman, Levine, Litwack, Raboteau, Sobel, Starling, and others.

Owens especially calls for an extension and deepening of Herbert Gutman's pioneering work on the black family and the role of kinship networks and child rearing. I would caution only on one point. He writes, "Generational methodology seems particularly important in the period before the cutoff of the international slave trade—covering a major part of modern slavery." But for the United States, unlike the rest of the hemisphere, the great period of slavery expansion, including and especially the demographic explosion, followed the cutoff, with incalculable effects on the black population, the overwhelming majority of which, approaching totality by 1860, was born American and enslaved. Hence the cultural link between Africa and Afro-America remains an especially formidable problem.

In any case, Owens poses these questions in a way that makes two contributions of capital importance, and for good measure he forcefully insists upon their interrelation. First, he draws attention to the history of black women, whom he places at the center, not merely of family and social life, but of the economic and spiritual life as well. He cannot be faulted for saying that slave women have not been studied adequately, although it should be noted that a beginning is being made by a growing number of scholars. What especially remains to be done, as he suggests, is a careful analysis of the grounding of the female experience in the labor process, for so long as the discussion of women's roles is restricted to consideration of family life, slave socialization, and interracial relations—as important as these subjects continue to be—the full significance of slave women to the formation of the black community in and beyond slavery must remain obscure.

Thus Owens' first big contribution passes into his second—his restoration of political economy, and with it the labor process, to center stage. If I read him correctly, he is aiming a hard blow not only at certain debilitating tendencies in the historiography of slavery, but also at the more widespread tendency among American historians to pretend that culture can be studied in a manner abstracted from political economy, understood in its original and vital meaning of the politics and economics of class relations. Indeed, his paper deserves the closest attention for its tentative projection of the link between political economy and the most vexing and elusive effects of slavery on the individual and collective minds of both masters and slaves.

Enslavement, he argues, gave blacks a unique vantage point from which to evaluate and demystify "free enterprise and democratic institutions." He means, I believe, much more than that slaves found themselves in a position to expose the hypocrisy of their masters and of the national political culture. He implies something deeper, well beyond questions of hypocrisy and bad faith: that black people, first as slaves and then as a beleaguered minority, have been able to grasp more readily than others the organic connection between republican, liberal, and democratic aspirations, honestly held and often intrinsically admirable, and the class exploitation that has remained their social foundation.

Owens is pointing us in the right direction and is challenging us to bring to the surface the political implications of our social history. He is also gently chiding us to recognize that only by such an effort can we transform our fascination with the psychology of master and slave into a historically meaningful project and thereby avoid the pit of voyeurism that constantly opens before those who enter upon such terrain.

I have one criticism. He argues that blacks learned early and well the blood meaning of profit maximization, and, accordingly, he stresses the importance of the market in shaping the mentality of all classes and both races. These are valuable insights that invite no quarrel. Yet they are curiously one-sided, as Mr. Owens himself proceeds to show. For no sooner does he call for a deeper study of both white and black psychology in the light of profit maximization economics, than he reminds us that that very economics was bound up with "the dynamics of black-white dependency." And even more suggestively, he notes that the slaves used their economic roles "to help modify those markets and the systems of race relations that existed." To these excellent observations I can only add that profit maximizing in markets, including a market in the bodies of laborers, must suffer more than mere qualification in the absence of a market in labor-power. In short, I agree with Owens on the nature of the slaveholding stick but fear that he has grasped the wrong end of it. Specifically, I believe that the entire problem could more fruitfully be studied with reference to the plantation experience as household, albeit as household embedded in a world market that generated practices and attitudes which contradicted its ideal essence.[3]

Be that as it may, he has returned the discussion of slavery as a social system, and of its psychological ravages and ramifications, to the terrain of political economy, where it belongs. Let us hope that his message is received with the attention and respect it deserves.

3. For an elaboration of the possibilities inherent in this framework, see Elizabeth Fox-Genovese, "Antebellum Southern Households: A New Perspective on a Familiar Question," *Review*, VII (Fall, 1983), 215–53.

COMMENT

JACQUELINE JONES

Leslie Owens' evocative paper "The African in the Garden: Reflections About New World Slavery and Its Lifelines" presents us with a wealth of images and ideas. Obviously it will not be possible for me to comment fully on each of the issues he has raised concerning the dynamics of race relations in plantation society and the political, social, and demographic implications of slavery. Therefore, I would like to confine my remarks to two particular themes that appear especially worthy of further study. The first deals with the inherently political nature of Afro-American culture—how the slaves' consciousness of their own bondage affected power relationships between blacks and whites not only during the slave era but long afterwards as well. The second theme focuses on the fate of Afro-American women under slavery—the distinctiveness of their experiences compared with those of their husbands, sons, and African foremothers as well as with those of white women. I would like to suggest that closer examination of these two themes will illuminate not only the peculiar human relationships forged by the white supremacist imperative in the antebellum South, but also the basic institutional and ideological underpinnings of American society in general.

Owens suggests at several points in his paper that slave culture produced among black men and women a unique political sensibility akin to radical class consciousness: "In contrast to almost all other Americans, African-Americans came to understand why the fruits of their labor did not convert to financial gains or material gains for themselves, their families, or communities." As a result, they "gained an insight into the workings of the nascent free enterprise system." Here he seems to suggest that oppression "freed" blacks from illusions about the American political and economic system, illusions that would continue to affect whites, rich and poor, North and South, throughout American history. Hence we may surmise that this Afro-American consciousness amounted to a kind of collective spiritual (not material) liberation in some paradoxical way. Further, because black people appreciated their own "creative energies" and their ability to "harness Paradise," they found in this appreciation a release from the mythic, egalitarian America cherished by so many whites regardless of ethnic or class background. For example, especially after the early nineteenth century, white men came to associate material well-being with the ability of individuals to exploit the labor of others, whether slaves, factory hands, or domestic servants. But blacks as a group persisted in their quest for family autonomy and, once emancipated, economic self-sufficiency.

Owens also encourages us to refine our notions about blacks' "resistance to American society's oppressive features" by suggesting that such resistance "has been an almost automatic part of their personality and identity." Certainly, if we consider the various forms that resistance may assume, then we need not measure a group's struggle for freedom and equality exclusively on the basis of violent revolt or even daily instances of work slowdowns and carelessness. Resistance is as much a state of mind as it is a physical action. Owens' treatment of this issue indicates that the time is ripe for a fresh look at W. E. B. Du Bois' argument contrasting the cooperative ethos in Afro-American culture with the strident individualism characteristic of white middle-class males.[1] If it is true that the values espoused by blacks present the most dramatic and enduring challenge to American material self-seeking, then this challenge must be considered in light of what we know about the attempts of other subgroups to resist a work ethic defined in such personalistic terms.

My second point stresses the observation made by Owens that "our grasp of the diversification and nuances between sexual roles of women and men in bondage is seriously deficient." Unfortunately, he seems a bit

1. W. E. B. Du Bois, *The Souls of Black Folk: Essays and Sketches* (Chicago, 1904).

too tentative in his own speculations when he says, "What we might learn about the treatment of women as differentiated from men is not always clear, but we need to gain insight into how and why such situations arose." Owens' own book, *This Species of Property: Slave Life and Culture in the Old South* (1976) raises intriguing questions related to the sexual division of labor in the quarters, including the suggestion that slave men actually scorned women's work like cleaning, clothes washing, cooking, sewing, and intimate forms of child rearing.[2] This division of labor, which differed from the plantation owner's more opportunistic approach to task assignments, reminds us that the slaves' respect for traditional sex roles could serve to reinforce the integrity of their own families in opposition to the whites' emphasis on political hegemony and profit making.[3] In this connection, I find most interesting Owens' observation that slave women, surrounded by friends and kin, rarely had to face the intense isolation endured by white women on plantations. In contrast, I strongly disagree that, as he has claimed, the sexual exploitation of slave women by white men indicated that these women were in "restricted bloom" and thus somehow less constrained than their tight-laced Victorian mistresses.[4] The physical abuse of black women by their masters only intensified their victimization and heightened their vulnerability to wrathful white wives.

As recently as a couple of years ago, Darlene Clark Hine wrote in a perceptive article, "To Be Gifted, Female, and Black," that "a deep, pervasive, and centuries-long conspiracy of silence surrounds the creative expressions, strivings, and struggles of the African American woman."[5] After a promising start by Angela Davis in 1971, the literature on slave women has grown only fitfully and slowly in contrast to the burgeoning of interest in Afro-American culture, family, labor, and white women's history. This historiographical trend is aptly expressed in the title of a recent anthology of articles in black women's studies—*All the Women Are White, All the Blacks Are Men, But Some of Us Are Brave* (1982).[6]

2. Leslie Owens, *This Species of Property: Slave Life and Culture in the Old South* (New York, 1976), 195.

3. Jacqueline Jones, "'My Mother Was Much of a Woman': Black Women, Work, and the Family Under Slavery," *Feminist Studies*, VIII (Summer, 1982), 235–70.

4. Cf. Catherine Clifton, *The Plantation Mistress: Women's World in the Old South* (New York, 1982).

5. Darlene Clark Hine, *Southwest Review* (Autumn, 1982), 357.

6. Angela Davis, "Reflections on the Black Woman's Roles in the Community of

Nowadays, however, we find an abundance of evidence to indicate that this imbalance in the historical record will be redressed in the near future, perhaps even dramatically so.[7] Black feminists—those whom Alice Walker has called womanists—have inspired recent explorations of black women's unique experiences from a variety of disciplinary perspectives. These writers reject the contention of radical white feminists that sex is the primary organizing principle for all societies and that class and racial factors are incidental to it.[8]

Research on sex roles within the contemporary black community needs to be extended to include their historical antecedents, especially during slavery and the immediate postbellum period. Particularly useful for this is the concept of a dual system of power and authority within Afro-American culture—one part formal and dominated by men, the other informal and dominated by women. It alerts us to the shortcomings inherent in the terms *matriarchy* and *patriarchy* as applied to either community life or household structure. Similarly, preoccupation with the dichotomy between the public (male) sphere and the private (female) sphere obscures the ways in which black women's domestic obligations have blended into community welfare work over the generations.

If, as James Oakes has argued in *The Ruling Race: A History of Ameri-*

Slaves," *Black Scholar*, IV (December, 1971), 3–15. Gerda Lerner (ed.), *Black Women in White America: A Documentary History* (New York, 1972), contains primary documents on slave women. See also Mary Ellen Obitko, "'Custodians of a House of Resistance': Black Women Respond to Slavery," in Dana V. Hiller and Robin Ann Sheets (eds.), *Women and Men: The Consequences of Power* (Cincinnati, 1977). Gloria T. Hull, Patricia Bell Scott, and Barbara Smith (eds.), *All the Women Are White, All the Blacks Are Men, But Some of Us Are Brave* (Old Westbury, N.Y., 1982).

7. For recently published works, see Darlene Clark Hine and Kate Wittenstein, "Female Slave Resistance: The Economics of Sex," in Filomina C. Steady (ed.), *The Black Woman Cross-Culturally* (Cambridge, Mass., 1981); Bell Hooks, *Ain't I a Woman? Black Women and Feminism* (Boston, 1981); Dorothy Sterling, *We Are Your Sisters: Black Women in the Nineteenth Century* (New York, 1984). Other works include Deborah White, *Arn't I a Woman? Female Slaves, Sex Roles, and Status in the Antebellum Plantation South* (New York, 1985), and Jacqueline Jones, *A History of Black Women, Work, and the Family from Slavery to the Present* (New York, 1985).

8. For collections of essays by black feminists, see Toni Cade (ed.), *The Black Woman: An Anthology* (New York, 1970); Cherrie Moraga and Gloria Anzaldua, *This Bridge Called My Back: Writing by Radical Women of Color* (Watertown, Mass., 1981); Hull, Scott, and Smith (eds.), *But Some of Us Are Brave*; Alice Walker, *In Search of Our Mothers' Gardens: Womanist Prose* (San Diego, 1983); Barbara Smith (ed.), *Home Girls: A Black Feminist Anthology* (Watertown, Mass., 1983).

can Slaveholders (1982), slavery was a significant form of aggressive capitalist enterprise, then the plantation was a microcosm of American society, and the status of slave women tells a larger story about the mutually reinforcing power systems of capitalism, white supremacy, and patriarchy.[9] Female slaves were exploited in various ways, depending upon whether a slaveholder chose to define them as blacks, which meant working in the fields with the men, or as women, which meant performing domestic tasks at the Big House. Similarly, depending on the needs of a growing, industrializing economy, different groups of white women have been alternately drawn into the traditional "male" realm of the paid labor force or restricted to the "female" realm of the household. On one level, then, the nexus between slave women's productive and reproductive functions and the slaveholder's profit motive bespoke a more general relationship between women's work and capitalism.

However, the exploitation of slave women was not necessarily an extreme form of the oppression endured by all American women, including whites. Persistent assaults on the stability of black family life, represented most dramatically by the violent abuse of black women by white men, revealed that black people as a group would continue to define their own interests as fundamentally different from those of other aggrieved groups. Owens alludes to the political significance of black family life, a point that Herbert G. Gutman and Eugene D. Genovese have developed for the slave era and one that might be extended to the present day as New Right budget-cutting measures continue to fall disproportionately on poor black mothers, fathers, and their children.[10]

An analysis of slave women's roles—especially in relation to those of their menfolk—is problematic for several reasons. First, we must reject the stereotype of the disorganized or nonexistent slave family and at the same time recognize that oppression played a part in shaping black women's and men's expectations of one another and that, given the constraints imposed upon them by a racist society, marital partners were not always able to live up to these expectations. I am not entirely convinced,

9. James Oakes, *The Ruling Race: A History of American Slaveholders* (New York, 1982).

10. Herbert Gutman, *The Black Family in Slavery and Freedom, 1750–1925* (New York, 1976); Eugene D. Genovese, *Roll, Jordan, Roll: The World the Slaves Made* (New York, 1974); Coalition on Women and the Budget, *Inequality of Sacrifice: The Impact of the Reagan Budget on Women* (Washington, D.C., 1983).

for example, that slaves accepted each other's limitations with the equanimity implicit in Owens' comment that "wives understood, as did their husbands and growing children, that slavery was the great compromiser." It is not at all clear that slave husbands always absolved their wives of all responsibility in instances of rape or sexual harassment initiated by white men.

Second, we must comprehend the strength, resilience, and resourcefulness of black women—articulated so eloquently by Sojourner Truth in her defiant pronouncement, "Ain't I a Woman?"—without either romanticizing the conditions that these women endured or assuming that all women triumphed over them. The contrast between the black female fieldhand and the genteel Victorian white lady is indeed a striking one, but we should not assume that the slave's objective condition was in any way better than that of her mistress. Again, some recent interpretations of male-female sex roles and family life under slavery go too far in portraying these relationships as conflict-free and as somehow more open and honest than those between women and men in the "free" social order.[11]

Owens might disagree with this point, reminding us of his argument that the slaves' consciousness of their oppression gave them a sort of psychic advantage over other Americans in general and over their tormentors in particular. Perhaps it is best to end with the image conveyed by his title, "The African in the Garden." Whatever its promise or potential, the biblical paradise of Eden was doomed from the start (though of course we would all agree that Eve should not be held exclusively responsible for the subsequent shortcomings of all humankind). Perhaps in their superior understanding of—or confrontation with—original sin American-style, Afro-Americans gained "insights" of a particular kind. But over the years, as the whites around them came to enjoy more fully the blessings of material prosperity and democratic citizenship, these insights brought blacks cold comfort indeed. Whatever the spiritual benefits or "soul" blacks may have gained came at the expense of justice; simply put, their "liberation" from a slavish devotion to capitalism and its attendant myths exacted a price that was just too high for any people ever to have to pay.

11. For example, Deborah White suggests that emancipation resulted in a "loss" of black women's "equality" with black men; freedom amounted to "a decline in the status of black women." "Ain't I a Woman? Female Slaves in the Antebellum South" (Ph.D. dissertation, University of Illinois–Chicago Circle, 1979), 51.

III EMANCIPATION STUDIES

The Difference Freedom Made: The Emancipation of Afro-Americans

ARMSTEAD L. ROBINSON

Emancipation studies already stands at the cutting edge of scholarly explorations into Afro-American life and history. This preeminence will continue at least through the remainder of this decade and reflects the critical role that the death of slavery played in the overall history of Afro-Americans. In fact, the experience with emancipation, spanning the two generations from 1860 to 1920, occupied the critical moment of transition between the dominant modes of black life in American society: the slavery period and twentieth-century urbanization. During the sixty-year interval that links slavery to urbanization, American society attempted to cope with the consequences of black freedom. Only by being free laborers could blacks have participated so readily in the twentieth-century population movements that dramatically transformed the geographic locus and the economic focus of Afro-American life. Thus, the tasks of describing and analyzing the social forces that contributed to these revolutionary transformations constitute the *raison d'être* for the study of emancipation.

At the heart of the challenge posed by the death of slavery lay the necessity of incorporating four million former chattel slaves into American society and economy. Prior to the Civil War, the Peculiar Institution established the boundaries of blacks' participation in American life. The laws governing chattel slavery accomplished this by involuntarily appropriating the fruits of black labor at the same time that they restrained black freedom of movement. So successfully did this system work that, for a quarter of a millennium, the Peculiar Institution served as the bedrock upon which the entire structure of antebellum southern society and economy rested.[1] Not only did slavery define the broad outlines of social class relationships within southern society, but this system of production also played a critical role in fashioning the pattern of interdependent regional economic specialization that undergirded antebellum American economic development, a pattern that also linked this developing economy to the expansion of international capitalism.[2] Precisely because emancipation precipitously destroyed a status quo that predated the American republic, this social revolution brought with it the urgent necessity of developing mechanisms for incorporating the newly freed into the national economy.

Under almost any conceivable set of circumstances, the adjustment to emancipation would have imposed a major crisis upon post–Civil War American political economy,[3] even without the disruptive impact of the industrial revolution. However, the onset of full-scale industrialization served to further complicate what could not have been other than a most trying ordeal. Economists now date the "take-off" of the American industrial revolution to the years between 1860 and 1914, precisely the same era during which the results of the Civil War compelled this society to undertake a new accommodation with Afro-Americans.[4] The simultaneous advent of emancipation and industrialization made it virtually inevitable that southern society would experience a powerful combination of internal and external pressures. Indeed, this combination would prove sufficiently powerful to stimulate revolutionary changes both in the patterns of relationships within that region's social structure and in the relationships between the southern economy and the rapidly changing economy of the nation as a whole.

Within the South, this confluence of forces compelled all of the region's

1. Eugene D. Genovese, *The Political Economy of Slavery: Studies in the Economy and Society of the Slave South* (New York, 1965), 13–39.

2. Douglas C. North, *The Economic Growth of the United States, 1790–1860* (New York, 1966); Elizabeth Fox-Genovese and Eugene D. Genovese, *Fruits of Merchant Capital: Slavery and Bourgeois Property in the Rise and Expansion of Capitalism* (New York, 1983), 34–75.

3. Eric Foner, *Nothing But Freedom: Emancipation and Its Legacy* (Baton Rouge, 1983), 1.

4. Harold G. Vatter, *The Drive to Industrial Maturity: The U.S. Economy, 1860–1914* (Westport, Conn., 1976), 37–86.

social classes and racial groups to grapple for new moorings, a process that could have no other outcome than the complete destruction of the antebellum social order.[5] Former masters and former slaves could not avoid engaging in bitter struggle, since, in general, societies experiencing the demise of unfreedom have discovered that the former masters of the unfree attempt to retain as much of their former dominance as possible.[6] Furthermore, the peculiar pattern of antebellum southern agrarianism that saw slaves producing most of the exportable surplus while the non-slaveholding white majority remained on the periphery of the market economy could not survive the rapid postwar expansion of commercial farming, textiles, and extractive industries into the "backcountry" hinterland.[7] By the turn of the century, emancipation and industrialization would produce profound changes in the labor requirements of the southern economy. With white laborers inextricably entwined in the tentacles of the market economy, the South grew much less dependent upon black labor than it had been during antebellum times.[8] And, it was this tendency toward the emergence of a pool of underemployed southern black laborers that made for the World War I migrations.[9]

Being free did make a difference.[10] For former slaves, freedom opened new horizons of personal autonomy and facilitated hitherto unrealizable degrees of economic and geographic mobility. In fact, no other single

5. Harold D. Woodman, "Sequel to Slavery: The New History Views the Postbellum South," *Journal of Southern History*, XLIII (November, 1977), 523–24; Thavolia Glymph (ed.), *Essays on the Postbellum Southern Economy* (College Station, Texas, 1985).

6. Eric Hobsbawn, *The Age of Capital, 1848–1875* (London, 1975), Chap. 10; Eugene Genovese, *The World the Slaveholders Made: Two Essays in Interpretation* (New York, 1969), 22–23.

7. C. Vann Woodward, *Origins of the New South, 1877–1913* (Baton Rouge, 1951), 291–320; Steven Hahn, *The Roots of Southern Populism: Yeomen Farmers and the Transformation of Georgia's Upper Piedmont, 1850–1880* (New York, 1983); Pete Daniel, *Breaking the Land: The Transformation of Cotton, Tobacco, and Rice Cultures Since 1880* (Urbana, 1985).

8. Harvey Perloff (ed.), *Regions, Resources, and Economic Growth* (Baltimore, 1960), 175–80.

9. Florette Henri, *Black Migration, the Movement North, 1900–1920: The Road from Myth to Man* (Garden City, N.Y., 1976), 50–51.

10. Leon F. Litwack, *Been in the Storm So Long: The Aftermath of Slavery* (New York, 1979), 502–56; Herbert G. Gutman, *The Black Family in Slavery and Freedom, 1750–1925*, (New York, 1977), 461–75.

event exerted more pervasive influence over the lives of nineteenth-century Afro-Americans than did emancipation. On the eve of the Civil War, fully 90 percent of this nation's 4.2 million blacks lived as chattel slaves; the balance of the black population existed at the margins of unfreedom whether they lived north or south of the Mason-Dixon Line.[11] The three Reconstruction-era constitutional amendments that followed inevitably from wartime emancipation carried important advances in their wake.[12] These amendments eliminated chattel slavery as a racially exclusive legal category at the same time that they conferred citizenship and voting rights upon Afro-Americans whether "born" or "shot" free. Even though American society found it enormously difficult to accord to freedmen the same social and economic mobility that white Americans claimed as their birthright of freedom, it does seem clear that being free made a significant difference in the quality of life for most Afro-Americans.

As perhaps nothing else can, the reflections of former slaves reveal the dimensions of the task facing scholars studying the American experience with emancipation. According analytic importance to firsthand evidence from the freed people is of special relevance because one of the great pitfalls confronting those who would study emancipation is a marked tendency toward a brand of economism that reduces the process of postslavery social change to a mere reflex of economic forces.[13] Slavery scholars have already demonstrated the critical contribution that careful attention to the values and the ideology of the slaves makes to a comprehensive analysis of the culture of the Peculiar Institution.[14] So too must students of emancipation realize that what former slaves and their descen-

11. Ira Berlin, *Slaves Without Masters: The Free Negro in the Antebellum South* (New York, 1974), 217–49; Leon Litwack, *North of Slavery* (Chicago, 1961), 153–86.

12. Mary Frances Berry, *Military Necessity and Civil Rights Policy: Black Citizenship and the Constitution, 1861–1968* (Port Washington, N.Y., 1977), 100–107.

13. Robert Higgs, *Competition and Coercion: Blacks in the American Economy, 1865–1914* (Cambridge, 1977); Joseph D. Reid, "Sharecropping as an Understandable Market Response: The Postbellum South," *Journal of Economic History*, XXXIII (March, 1973), 106–30; Stephen J. DeCanio, *Agriculture in the Postbellum South: The Economics of Production and Supply* (Cambridge, 1974); Jay R. Mandle, *The Roots of Black Poverty: The Southern Plantation Economy After the Civil War* (Durham, N.C., 1978).

14. Eugene Genovese, *Roll, Jordan, Roll: The World the Slaves Made* (New York, 1974), 3–7; Lawrence Levine, *Black Culture and Black Consciousness: Afro-American Folk Thought from Slavery to Freedom* (New York, 1977).

dants thought and did made an enormous difference in the outcome of postslavery developments both inside and outside of the South. Precisely because the years immediately following the Civil War afforded Afro-Americans their first opportunity to realize dreams long deferred during the nightmare of slavery, it is imperative that emancipation studies strive for a balance between history viewed from the "top down" and history viewed from the "bottom up."

I propose to outline some of the more significant lines of investigation that await scholars interested in the study of emancipation. Although historiographic questions remain important, my purpose is not to critique the existing literature so much as it is to define the limits of current research. Three interrelated sets of questions seem likely to dominate the emancipation studies research agenda. The Civil War origins of the postwar labor system constitute the first line of inquiry that demands attention. Following this, it seems essential that scholars study the process of social differentiation among the recently freed during the initial decades after emancipation. Finally, significant attention must be focused on the origins and the outcomes of postslavery black migrations to areas both inside and outside of the South. These suggestions are intended to stimulate debate about the topics that demand attention, about the kinds of questions that ought to be posed, and about the types of sources that are available to help supply creative hypotheses concerning the numerous unresolved issues confronting the field of emancipation studies. Out of this dialogue should emerge the material from which scholars can finally construct the long-overdue synthesis about American emancipation.

I

Emancipation emerged as an official Civil War policy only after prolonged examination of practically every other alternative for saving the Union.[15] In fact, Lincoln's apprehensions about the peacetime aftershocks certain to emanate from the emancipation temblor prompted him to move very cautiously in the matter of declaring that the only path to defeating the

15. John Hope Franklin, *The Emancipation Proclamation* (Garden City, N.Y., 1963), 29–54.

Confederacy lay through laying waste the foundations of southern society.[16] Lincoln knew that his fellow northerners did not wish emancipation to provide a pretext for the massive resettlement of job-hungry former slaves in the "Free States."[17] Recognizing these political realities, the president promised that he would find some distant place beyond the foreseeable territorial boundaries of the United States to which he would transport the former slaves once the Civil War had run its course.[18] Obviously, Lincoln hoped that resettlement would resolve once and for all the questions posed by the troublesome presence of millions of freed persons of African descent.[19] Ultimately, the fortunes of war forced his hand. Lincoln moved to proclaim emancipation because of three major developments: the unexpected strength of the Confederacy, the danger that Great Britain and France might recognize the Confederacy, and the inability of his commanders in the field to cope with the black freedom struggle unintentionally ignited by the conflict between North and South.

Although neither the Confederacy nor the Union intended to foment a freedom struggle, nothing that either government could do seemed to avail against slaves' determination to exploit the North-South conflict to win their own freedom.[20] For example, the city of Nashville surrendered to the northern invaders in early February, 1862, almost a year before Lincoln promulgated the final Emancipation Proclamation. Yet in the immediate aftermath of the city's capitulation, slaves celebrated joyously throughout the Nashville region, supremely confident that the onrushing columns of blue-clad Yankees signified the final coming of the long-hoped-for "Day of Jubilo." An elderly slave captured the mood of the moment when he cried out:

16. LaWanda Cox, *Lincoln and Black Freedom: A Study in Presidential Leadership* (Columbia, S.C., 1981), 3–43.

17. V. Jacques Voegeli, *Free but Not Equal: The Midwest and the Negro During the Civil War* (Chicago, 1967), 1–29.

18. Abraham Lincoln, "Second Annual Message," in James D. Richardson (ed.), *A Compilation of the Messages and Papers of the Presidents* (Washington, D.C., 1896–1899), VII, 3340–42.

19. Charles H. Wesley, "Lincoln's Plan for Colonizing the Emancipated Negroes," *Journal of Negro History*, IV (January, 1919), 7–21; Warren A. Beck, "Lincoln and Negro Colonization in Central America," *Abraham Lincoln Quarterly*, VI (September, 1950), 162–63; Paul J. Schieps, "Lincoln and the Chiriqui Colonization Project," *Journal of Negro History*, XXXVIII (October, 1952), 418–53.

20. James Ford Rhodes, *History of the Civil War* (New York, 1919), 49–50.

> Oh Praise and Tanks
> De Lord He Come
> To Set de People Free
> An' Massa Tink it Day ob Gloom
> An' We ob Jubilee
> Oh Nebber You Fear
> If Nebber You Hear
> De Driver Blow His Horn.[21]

Long before "Massa" Lincoln decided to proclaim emancipation, millions of southern blacks concluded that defeat for their masters meant freedom for them.[22] Scholars still know far too little about this initial phase of the emancipation experience. In fact, analyzing the wartime origins of slavery's demise probably holds the key to understanding the variety of strategies that freedpeople employed during the immediate post–Civil War period.[23] Although no more than a quarter of the prewar slave population gained freedom as a result of the Emancipation Proclamation, it nonetheless remains clear that effective control over slaves disappeared from almost all of even the most remote plantations long before the surrender at Appomattox.[24] The pervasiveness of this loss of mastery reflected the impact of the revolution in attitudes unleashed by the onset of the war, a revolution of rising slave expectations that helped impel Lincoln toward proclaiming emancipation.[25]

Material for understanding the wartime demise of slavery is almost embarrassingly abundant. The published collection of WPA slave narratives speaks eloquently and at great length about the variety of ways that freedom came to wartime slaves.[26] In fact, these narratives probably reveal more about the emancipation experience than they do about the Peculiar

21. In Armstead L. Robinson, "Day of Jubilo: Civil War and the Demise of Slavery in the Mississippi Valley, 1861–1865" (Ph.D. dissertation, University of Rochester, 1977), 499.

22. Benjamin Quarles, *The Negro in the Civil War* (Boston, 1969), 42–56.

23. Louis D. Gerteis, *From Contraband to Freedman: Federal Policy Toward Southern Blacks, 1861–1865* (Westport, Conn., 1973), 193; C. Peter Ripley, *Slaves and Freedmen in Civil War Louisiana* (Baton Rouge, 1976).

24. Robinson, "Day of Jubilo."

25. James L. Roark, *Masters Without Slaves: Southern Planters in the Civil War and Reconstruction* (New York, 1977), 68–108.

26. George Rawick (ed.), *The American Slave: A Composite Autobiography*, (Westport, Conn., 1972 and 1978).

Institution. Another important source lies in the records relating to emancipation located in the National Archives. The recently inaugurated edition of these records offers a skillfully chosen sample of the voluminous materials bearing upon the demise of slavery that were compiled by the northern and southern armies as well as by various agencies of the federal government.[27] In addition, the diaries, journals, and home letters of northern soldiers and missionaries serving in the South contain invaluable accounts of the destruction and reconstruction of the southern labor system.[28]

Additional evidence about the demise of wartime slavery abounds in the records kept by embattled slaveholders, many of whom were women unfamiliar with the routines of slave management. The pleas these women dispatched to their relatives and also to local, state, and national officials vividly depict the rapid erosion of control over slaves made newly restive by reports about war pitting their masters in combat against northern "abolitionists." In turn, the inability to cope effectively with this erosion played a critical role in prompting the Confederate government to undertake draft and taxation policies that alienated the nonslaveholding majority from the southern cause, an alienation which took the forms of draft resistance, desertion, and tax evasion; most of this activity took place in the southern "backcountry."[29] Since these wartime conflicts had their roots in the political economy of the antebellum South and since much of southern political history in the immediate postwar years revolved around struggles between former slaveholders and "backcountry" yeomen, it would appear that careful analysis of wartime social developments may help explain hitherto inexplicable trends, such as the hotly contested postwar debt relief movement and the involvement, during the initial years of Congressional Reconstruction, of scores of thousands of southern yeomen in biracial Republican parties.[30]

27. Ira Berlin, Joseph P. Reidy, and Leslie S. Rowland, *Freedom: A Documentary History of Emancipation*, Series II of *The Black Military Experience* (New York, 1982).

28. For an exemplary demonstration of the contributions such sources can make, see Willie Lee Rose, *Rehearsal for Reconstruction: The Port Royal Experiment* (New York: 1964).

29. Albert B. Moore, *Conscription and Conflict in the Confederacy* (New York, 1924), 228–54; Robinson, "Day of Jubilo."

30. Armstead Robinson, "Beyond the Realm of Social Consensus: New Meanings of Reconstruction for American History," *Journal of American History*, LXVIII (September, 1981), 286–87.

Of even greater significance for emancipation studies, however, is the way that the assertion of blacks' claim to control over their persons and over the fruits of their labor power precipitated wartime struggles that prefigured postwar battles over the meaning of freedom. When the elderly slave near Nashville proclaimed his belief that freedom meant that blacks never again needed to fear the blowing of the driver's horn, he was articulating an ideological viewpoint widely held among the freedpeople, a cultural perspective that would confound practically every postwar attempt to reimpose slavelike forms of involuntary labor.[31] By examining carefully how these struggles resolved themselves during the Civil War, scholars can gain insight into the normative values that former slaves brought to their postslavery confrontations with the coming of free labor. The particular focus of these wartime struggles varied quite significantly, generally in keeping with the type of labor systems in which particular groups of slaves worked and the proximity of the slaves to the northern invaders. Thus, dimensions of time and place remain critically important for analysis of the wartime origins of the transition to a free labor economy.[32] By conceptualizing the war years as the stage upon which a spectrum of types of slavery gave way to a variety of types of free labor, students of emancipation will gain understanding of the social origins of labor readjustment in the various subregions that constituted the postwar southern economy.

II

Once the Civil War actually came to an end, southerners of all social classes and racial groups undertook the task of adjusting to the dawning of a new era. The three decades immediately following the war produced major changes in southern society, as defeat and emancipation forced a massive reshuffling of the balances of political and social power. In the same way that freedom from slavery raised the possibility of blacks' realizing dreams of economic independence, so too did the enfranchisement of former slaves and the disenfranchisement of many former slaveholders

31. Levine, *Black Culture and Black Consciousness*, 136–89.
32. Bell Irvin Wiley, *Southern Negroes, 1861–1865* (New Haven, 1938), 3–23; W. E. B. Du Bois, *Black Reconstruction in America, 1860–1880* (New York, 1935), 55–83.

open the door to a whole new style of southern politics that featured an alliance between poorer blacks and poorer whites. Unfortunately, this biracial lower-class politics could not long endure without the stable social foundation that very broadly based black land ownership might have provided; and further, the victorious national government revealed little of the iron-fisted determination called for by this situation. As a result, biracial lower-class politics failed during Reconstruction, only to experience a revival when the corrosive effects of New South-style economic development reignited fires of popular anger in the forms of the Farmers' Alliance and the Populist Movement. Ultimately, this second coming of biracial lower-class politics failed as well, victimized by divisions within and between various social classes and racial groups.[33] In its stead arose the grim specter of Jim Crow, that cradle-to-grave system of racial segregation that symbolized the abnegation of the optimistic dream about the meaning of freedom to which former slaves clung so fiercely during the initial enthusiasm for the "Day of Jubilo."[34]

Perhaps no group felt more immediate optimism about what emancipation could mean than did the freedpeople. So much of the story of war and emancipation conformed to the cherished biblical scenario of the Children of Israel's escape from bondage that most former slaves could not avoid believing themselves headed for the Promised Land.[35] Land was what the freedpeople craved more than anything else, for they understood that ownership of land constituted the essential prerequisite for independence from coercive external influences.[36] Indeed, if any single cultural theme summarized freedmen's visions of the world that would ensue from slavery's demise, it was this dream of a life in which an agrarian people could make their own decisions about how to organize their lives, decisions that would enable them to be "free" in the fullest sense of the term.

This dream would die aborning, betrayed in the first instance by the perfidy of Lincoln's successor, in the second by the reluctance of the Re-

33. Lawrence Goodwyn, *Democratic Promise: The Populist Moment in America* (New York, 1976), 493–514.

34. C. Vann Woodward, *The Strange Career of Jim Crow*, 2nd revised ed. (New York, 1966), 67–109.

35. Levine, *Black Culture and Black Consciousness*, 136–38.

36. Edward Magdol, *A Right to the Land: Essays on the Freedmen's Community* (Westport, Conn., 1977), 137–73.

publican party to countenance the politically motivated expropriation of private property, and in the final analysis by the spread of capitalist agriculture that, through a process of consolidation that rendered semisubsistence family farming an increasingly nonviable undertaking, used debt as the primary mechanism to force small farmers from the land. Instead of finding their Promised Land in the independent proprietorship that blacks thought would result from Yankee promises of land after war's end, the freedpeople struggled to make do as best they could, focusing on activities in the economic sphere, in voluntary social organizations, and in politics: the kinds of activities that allowed them to construct a community suited to their perceptions of their own needs.

Freedmen hungered for land. To a people long accustomed to working involuntarily on someone else's land, the ownership of even a modest plot of ground symbolized irreversible independence from external control. After the Civil War ended, keen disappointment awaited land-hungry freedmen. Although there never was enough land available for even a quarter of the freedmen who yearned for it, Congress did pass a bill in February, 1865, that created the Bureau of Refugees, Freedmen, and Abandoned Lands to supervise the redistribution of land abandoned by former Confederates. Unfortunately for even the small group of freedmen who might have obtained land through the Freedmen's Bureau, Lincoln's assassination gave his southern-born successor, Andrew Johnson, the opportunity to grant thousands of presidential pardons to southern landowners threatened with confiscation.[37] Congress subsequently refused to enact legislation that could have ordered massive confiscation of southern lands, in large measure because such seizures would establish the potentially dangerous precedent of sanctioning the violation of private property rights for the explicit purpose of giving working people ownership of the means of production.[38] With land redistribution eliminated from its functions,

37. William McFeely, *Yankee Stepfather: General Oliver Otis Howard and the Freedmen* (New Haven, 1968), 94–114; Donald G. Nieman, *To Set the Law in Motion: The Freedmen's Bureau and the Legal Rights of Blacks, 1865–1868* (Millwood, N.Y., 1979).

38. David Montgomery, *Beyond Equality: Labor and the Radical Republicans, 1862–1872*, 2nd ed. (Urbana, 1981), 335–86; Ronald Davis, " 'Good and Faithful Labor': A Study of the Development and Economics of Southern Sharecropping, 1860–1880" (Ph.D. dissertation, University of Missouri, 1974).

the Freedmen's Bureau turned its attention toward the task of making "good and faithful" laborers out of freedpeople determined to gain independence.

Freedmen refused to accept this betrayal passively. Of the many protests that dot the records of the Freedmen's Bureau, none speaks more eloquently of the world view of the vast majority of freedpeople than one that occurred early in 1866. Bayley Wyatt, a freedman from Yorktown, Virginia, addressed a meeting called to protest an order directing local freedpeople to return to prewar owners land that the blacks had been led to believe would soon be theirs. Wyatt spoke with fierce anger and with great conviction as he articulated the freedpeople's grievances against their emancipators:

> We now as a people desires to be elevated, and we desires to do all we can to be educated, and we hope our friends will aid us all dey can. . . .
>
> I may state to all our friends, and to all our enemies, that we has a right to the land where we are located. For why? I tell you. Our wives, our children, our husbands, has been sold over and over again to purchase the lands we now locate upon; for that reason we have a divine right to the land. . . .
>
> And den didn't we clear the lands and raise de crops ob corn, ob cotton, ob tobacco, ob rice, ob sugar, ob everything? And den didn't dem large cities in de North grow up on de cotton and de sugars and de rice dat we made? Yes! I appeal to de South and to de North if I hasn't spoken de words of truth.
>
> I say dey have grown rich and my people is poor.[39]

Neither the eloquence of Bayley Wyatt's oratory nor the accuracy of his social analysis availed much in the struggle over the forms in which freedpeople's labor power would be appropriated in the postwar South. It appears that initially most landowners preferred to continue as much of the antebellum pattern of centralized control as was possible; they did so by promising to pay wages at the end of the crop year while making few substantive alterations in the manner in which black labor was to be organized. However, these arrangements bore such a strong resemblance to slavery times that most freedmen resisted signing contracts that made a

---

39. Magdol, *A Right to the Land*, 172; Janet Sharpe Herman, *The Pursuit of a Dream* (New York, 1981).

mockery of their new freedom. This response was particularly marked among blacks who worked in capital- and labor-intensive crops such as sugar, tobacco, and rice, although the Cotton Kingdom experienced its share of conflict over the same set of issues.[40] As a result, a wide range of experiments with "free" labor arrangements took place, with varying combinations of wages, shares, and tenancy appearing throughout the South.[41]

The diversity of contractual arrangements did not obscure a startling unity of cultural purpose among the freedmen: their determination to assert their new status by removing black dependents from the labor force. Freedmen insisted upon shielding young children, pregnant women, and the sick and the elderly from the heavy field labor that had been their brutal lot during slavery. In the Cotton Kingdom, for example, by 1870 almost 40 percent fewer blacks were involved in field labor than had been the case in 1860, a result directly attributable to the withdrawal of dependent labor from the fields.[42] Although this minor reform could not prevent landowners from driving most landless freedmen into the status of agrarian proletarians, it nonetheless remains significant that the decentralized share-cropping system that came to dominate postwar southern agriculture afforded black families an approximation, however crude, of the independent family proprietorship that had been their initial goal.

Freedmen worked diligently to expand the realms of their lives in which they exercised autonomy. Some of the most intriguing research now under way concentrates on the processes through which freedpeople erected an infrastructure of religious, educational, and social institutions that the blacks themselves controlled.[43] Many of the invisible institutions of the slavery period materialized in quite concrete forms during the initial post-

40. Joseph P. Reidy, "Sugar and Freedom: Emancipation in Louisiana's Sugar Parishes," paper, American Historical Association annual meeting, 1980; Barbara J. Fields, *Slavery and Freedom on the Middle Ground: Maryland in the Nineteenth Century* (New Haven, 1985); Michael Wayne, *The Reshaping of Plantation Society: The Natchez District, 1860–1880* (Baton Rouge, 1983), 31–71.

41. Harold D. Woodman, "Post–Civil War Southern Agriculture and the Law," *Agricultural History*, LIII (January, 1979), 319–37.

42. Roger L. Ransom and Richard Sutch, *One Kind of Freedom: The Economic Consequences of Emancipation* (Cambridge, 1977), 44–46.

43. Armstead L. Robinson, "Plans Dat Comed from God: Institution Building and the Emergence of Black Leadership in Reconstruction Memphis," in Burton and McMath (eds.), *Toward a New South* (Westport, Conn., 1980), 71–102.

war years. Black churches sprouted throughout the South.[44] Although many of these structures owed their existence at least partially to the work of northern missionaries, the bulk of religious institution building occurred beneath the aegis of denominations that catered more or less exclusively to blacks. In the educational sphere, freedmen displayed what one missionary described as "a greedy fondness for books."[45] Nothing better illustrates the priorities that former slaves carried into freedom than the virtually universal acknowledgment that most freedmen spared nothing to educate first their children and then themselves.[46] This commitment to community uplift, a commitment brilliantly articulated by Bayley Wyatt, manifested itself through the emergence of a panoply of voluntary self-help organizations, groups such as benevolent and mutual aid societies, lodges, literary associations, etc.[47]

Scholars interested in analyzing the freedpeople's pursuit of autonomy can turn to a number of enormously rich sources. The archives of the Freedmen's Bureau remain the indispensable starting point for serious study of the immediate transition from slavery to freedom. Although there were never enough bureau agents to provide the help freedpeople required, these agents did leave a thick latticework of weekly, monthly, quarterly, semiannual, and annual reports about topics ranging across every aspect of the freedpeople's lives. Another important but still underutilized source appears in the records of the Freedmen's Savings and Trust Company, the so-called Freedmen's Bank. Before this institution went bankrupt in 1872, it opened savings accounts for tens of thousands of blacks across the South. The deposit ledgers kept by the branches of the Freedmen's Bank are a gold mine of information. Not only do many of these ledgers record information about the physical characteristics of depositors, who generally lacked birth certificates, but these bookkeepers also listed their

44. Carter G. Woodson, *The History of the Negro Church* (2nd ed.; Washington, D.C., 1945); E. Franklin Frazier, *The Negro Church in America* (New York, 1964); Clarence E. Walker, *A Rock in a Weary Land: The African Methodist Episcopal Church During the Civil War and Reconstruction* (Baton Rouge, 1982).

45. *Memphis Argus*, August 23, 1865.

46. William Preston Vaughn, *Schools for All: The Blacks and Public Education in the South, 1865–1877* (Lexington, Ky., 1974), 1–22.

47. For a sample of some of the growing literature on institution building among the freedpeople, see Peter Kolchin, *First Freedom: The Responses of Alabama Blacks to Emancipation and Reconstruction* (Westport, Conn., 1972); Robert Francis Engs, *Freedom's First Generation: Black Hampton, Virginia, 1861–1890* (Philadelphia, 1970).

depositors' best estimate of the location of family members. Armed with lists of names drawn from Freedmen's Bureau and Freedmen's Bank files, it is possible to collate information about specific individuals from sources as varied as the manuscript returns of the United States census, state tax and prison records, and county and municipal sources such as birth, death, and marriage records, property tax rolls and voter registration rosters, police arrest blotters, and the files of local relief agencies. This combination of types of records opens the exciting possibility that researchers can perform the kind of family reconstitution studies that have proved so valuable in reconstructing the social milieu of nonliterate peoples. Bit by bit, it will be possible to capture larger and larger fragments of the varied paths that former slaves traversed as they adjusted to life in freedom.

In the absence of general land reform, electoral politics offered freedmen their best opportunity to redress the inequitable balance of forces that confronted them. As was the case with newly gained educational opportunities, the record shows conclusively that freedmen voted with avidity for as long as it remained physically safe to do so.[48] The Union Leagues served as one of the most important agencies for politicizing newly enfranchised black voters. Scholars know far too little about these leagues, although they existed across the South and played a major role in the initial stages of Republican politics in the Reconstruction governments of a number of states.[49] Research into the development of the leagues may provide information about the emergence of leadership cadres within the freed community. Such information would complement the research already available on the activities of blacks elected to local, state, and national offices during Reconstruction.[50] Out of this attention to the process of politicization should emerge a much clearer picture of the development of interest and factional rivalries among blacks, particularly those who lived in urban areas.

The history of southern urbanization remains to be written, particularly

48. Allen W. Trelease, *White Terror: The Ku Klux Klan Conspiracy and Southern Reconstruction* (New York: 1971), xv–xlviii.
49. E. Merton Coulter, *The South During Reconstruction, 1865–1877* (Baton Rouge, 1947), 127–28.
50. Thomas C. Holt, *Black Over White: Negro Political Leadership in Reconstruction South Carolina* (Urbana, Ill., 1977); Howard N. Rabinowitz (ed.), *Southern Black Leaders of the Reconstruction Era* (Urbana, Ill., 1982); Charles Vincent, *Black Legislators in Louisiana During Reconstruction* (Baton Rouge, 1976).

insofar as postwar urban growth affected the first generation of freed-people.[51] The black population of most southern urban centers grew very rapidly after the war.[52] It would be enormously helpful to know who these "pioneer urbanites" actually were, where they came from, whether they were seasonal migrants who came to the cities between farming seasons or permanent urban dwellers, and how these different migratory streams fared in the southern "urban crucible."[53] Still-scattered data from existing studies suggests that exposure to the harsh challenges of urban life precipitated a process of social class differentiation.[54] Although some former slaves fared extremely well, opening businesses and accumulating property, most others experienced urban proletarianization; that is, they existed at the margins of the economy as chronically underemployed day laborers without a permanent foothold. However, in several important instances, former slave workers managed to create effective alliances with white wage workers, particularly in the mines and along the docks.[55] These early examples of the integration of freedmen into the emerging southern working class warrant close attention, as do the more prevalent examples of bitter interracial strife.

The development of an urban-based black middle class merits careful study. How these men and women managed to accumulate and hold property is as intriguing as the uses to which they put the social and political power that sprang from their affluence. For example, a former slave from Memphis, Tennessee, Robert Reed Church, served as a cabin attendant on a Mississippi River steamer prior to emancipation. With an initial boost from his wealthy white father, Robert Church managed to accumulate a very substantial fortune in real estate and thereby propel himself into a position of enduring social prominence as well as enduring influence within the local, state, and national Republican party. In fact, his son, Robert Reed Church, Jr., carried on the family tradition of "black and

51. Blaine A. Brownwell (ed.), *The City in Southern History: The Growth of Urban Civilization in the South* (Port Washington, N.Y., 1977).

52. Coulter, *The South During Reconstruction*, 261.

53. Douglas H. Daniels, *Pioneer Urbanites: A Social and Cultural History of Black San Francisco* (Philadelphia, 1980); Gary D. Nash, *The Urban Crucible: Social Change, Political Consciousness, and the Origins of the American Revolution* (Cambridge, 1979).

54. Robinson, "Plants Dat Comed from God."

55. Paul B. Worthman and James R. Green, "Black Workers in the New South, 1865–1915," in Huggins, Kilson, and Fox (eds.), *Key Issues in the Afro-American Experience*, II (New York, 1972), 47–69.

tan" political activity so assiduously that he functioned as "Boss Crump's" emissary to Memphis blacks throughout the life of the Crump machine.[56]

Research into the social origins of the black urban middle class should spark interest in the parallel story of the emergence of a class of rural black landowners. For despite all of the hardships endured by the newly freed, the fiftieth anniversary of emancipation found more than 200,000 black landowners listed by the United States census. Although these statistics require careful scrutiny, the roughly 15 million acres under black proprietorship cannot be dismissed.[57] Both the numbers of landowners and the amount of acreage they held suggest that a significant number of freedmen managed to acquire and hold onto farms during an era when many white family farmers were losing their land. This process of class differentiation would have major implications not only for postemancipation social developments but also for southern and national politics.

Because the Republican party tended to draw its black leadership cadres from the emerging strata of urban and rural middle-class blacks, an intriguing area of inquiry awaits scholars interested in the history of black Republicanism. In the same way that "black and tan" alliances played a major role in electing a series of post–Civil War Republican presidents, so too did alliances of convenience between southern black Republicans and southern white Democrats play a significant part in southern state and local politics.[58] Furthermore, it would appear that there was a direct link between the social basis of black Republicanism and the origins of Booker T. Washington's "Tuskegee Machine." Washington drew his supporters from a broad cross section of the national black community, with surprising strength coming from urban professionals both inside and outside of the South.[59] Determining where relatively prosperous blacks thought their political interests lay holds major promise as a contribution to the political history of emancipation, particularly since "black and tan" alliances provoked such heated controversy among both northern and southern blacks.[60]

56. Mary Church Terrell, *A Colored Woman in a White World* (Washington, D.C., 1940).

57. James S. Fisher, "Negro Farm Ownership in the South," *Annals of the Association of American Geographers*, LXIII (December, 1973), 482.

58. Woodward, *Origins of the New South*, 75–106.

59. Louis R. Harlan, *Booker T. Washington: The Making of a Black Leader, 1865–1901*, 254–71.

60. August Meier, *Negro Thought in America, 1800–1915* (Ann Arbor, Mich., 1956), 161–89.

The paradoxical fate of biracial lower-class alliances offers another fruitful arena for research. Unlike the "black and tan" alliances between wealthy southern whites and affluent southern blacks that apparently endured for decades, interracial lower-class political groupings proved consistently unstable. It would appear that alliances of poorer blacks with poorer whites ought to have had a real chance for success during the initial stages of Congressional Reconstruction; a similar situation would seem to have obtained during the heyday of Populism. However, recent research suggests that the Reconstruction alliances collapsed because they could not cope with the complex interpenetration of class and racial tensions between and within various social groups. Although rabid prejudice helped to scuttle biracial southern Republicanism, the primary factors apparently were the hostility of affluent southerners to lower-class politics, the incompatibility of the interests of land-poor yeomen whites and land-hungry freed blacks, and the conflicting priorities of affluent blacks as opposed to their impoverished brethren.[61]

A similar set of constraints contributed to the downfall of southern Populism. However, in this area, unlike the Reconstruction period where scholars know a great deal about the identity of black Republicans, the social basis of black Populism remains shrouded in mystery. Who were the black Populists, why did they join the movement, and why did they leave it? These are questions for which there are at present no satisfactory answers. It would be useful to know how the emerging class of rural black landowners responded to the blandishments of the Colored Farmers' Alliance and then to the appeals of the Populists. Since much of the rhetoric of white Populist leaders seemed directed at black tenants, sharecroppers, and wage laborers, it may well be that independent black landowners saw little of interest in the Populist formula. It would also be useful to know from whom these black landowners were acquiring their property. The probability that some of this land came on the market as a result of post–Civil War debt and tax sales raises the possibility that white Populists resented associating with relatively affluent rural blacks who appeared to be profiting from their dispossession. The question of how much

61. J. Mills Thornton III, "Fiscal Policy and the Failure of Radical Reconstruction in the Lower South," in Kousser and McPherson (eds.), *Region, Race, and Reconstruction: Essays in Honor of C. Vann Woodward* (New York, 1982), 349–94; Robinson, "Beyond the Realm of Social Consensus," 296–97.

influence these class-based tensions exerted during the Populist Movement deserves careful attention, both because these tensions are often misinterpreted as being essentially racial and also because an analysis of these tensions may add depth to our appreciation of the centrifugal tendencies that ripped the Populist alliance asunder.[62]

Although the identity of black Populists remains unclear, there is very little doubt that calls for biracial lower-class political activity provoked a major schism among black political and social leaders. Booker T. Washington took a not altogether unexpected stance opposing such alliances.[63] However, T. Thomas Fortune, a former slave and editor of the *New York Age*, warmly supported the notion. Writing in 1884, Fortune argued strenuously for the identity of interests between impoverished blacks and poorer whites. After taking a hard look at the first two decades of freedom, Fortune concluded that the transformations undergone by the former slaves closely resembled an abortive journey that moved the freedpeople from "*chattel slavery . . .* to *industrial slavery*; a slavery more excruciating in its exactions, more irresponsible in its machinations than the other slavery, which I once endured." Fortune could find but one answer for this dilemma: a permanent alliance of the black and white poor. At the core of this strategy lay Fortune's fervent conviction that "the condition of the black and white laborer is the same, and . . . consequently their cause is common."[64]

Exploring the social origins and the political consequences of class differentiations among southern blacks may help clarify the origins of the Du Bois–Washington controversy that loomed so large in the internal politics of many late-nineteenth-century black communities. These explorations will require renewed interest in biographical studies of persons who played significant roles in black community politics both North and South. Careful analysis will almost certainly reveal the important contributions made by hitherto little-known men and women to the active political debates that blacks carried on within their ranks, debates focused on the task of developing strategies that could counteract the turn toward militant ra-

62. Goodwyn, *Democratic Promise*, 276–306; Barbara J. Fields, "Ideology and Race in American History," in Kousser and McPherson (eds.), *Region, Race, and Reconstruction*, 143–77.

63. Harlan, *Booker T. Washington*, 291–92.

64. Timothy Thomas Fortune, *Black and White: Land, Labor, and Politics in the South* (New York, 1884), 235–36.

cialism characteristic of the age of Jim Crow. Only by identifying the often conflicting social bases of the interests to which different black community leaders saw themselves responding can scholars make analytic sense of the fierce debates that continued to erupt between partisans of Du Bois and Washington.

III

Once scholars develop a more acute sense of the varied patterns of postslavery social development among southern blacks, the most significant challenge confronting students of emancipation will be the task of defining the social parameters of the linkages between these developmental patterns and the late-nineteenth-century origins of southern blacks' relocation to northern urban centers. These origins are crucial to the full comprehension of the emancipation experience, since the massive migrations characteristic of the World War I era tended to follow paths already laid out by these preexisting migration patterns rather than breaking entirely new ground. It already seems clear that most of this interregional movement involved city-to-city residential transfers rather than direct relocations from southern rural to northern urban settings.[65] Only by tracing the cultural passageways that freedpeople and their descendants traversed during the trek from southern rural to southern urban settings and thence to the urban North can students of emancipation decipher the double transformation that first made former slaves into a regional agrarian proletariat and subsequently incorporated these children of emancipation into the American working class.

A fruitful point of departure lies in careful attention to the different streams of postslavery population movement among the former slaves. If ever there was a people in motion, it most certainly was the freedpeople. For one thing, the Civil War years greatly exacerbated the already massive incidence of involuntary family separations caused by the Peculiar Institution. Furthermore, being free afforded an opportunity many freedpeople used to seek to reknit scattered threads of the fabric of extended kin groups.[66] And finally, the frustrations that generally accompanied the

65. Henri, *Black Migration*, 49–80.
66. Gutman, *Black Family*, 363–431.

emancipation experience gave many blacks additional incentives to seek out a better life somewhere other than where they found themselves.[67] At least initially, these movements were localized and tended to follow changes in the locations where laborers thought they could obtain the best working conditions. In other cases, population shifts represented responses to the impact of new opportunities created by the process of urbanization in booming cities such as Birmingham and Atlanta—urban growth spawned by New South industrialization. Another migration pattern saw black laborers moving so as to follow changes in the geographic regions devoted to the production of specific staple crops, changes such as the westward movement of the cotton belt as well as the relocation of the center of American rice production from South Carolina to Arkansas and Louisiana.[68] Although most postwar black migrants tended to remain within the former slave states, a very significant segment of the freed population chose to leave the South in order to move to other areas such as all-black communitarian settlements on the Great Plains or even to devise plans to return to Africa.[69]

Students of emancipation need to know much more about the factors that differentiated these streams of postslavery black migration. The answers to these questions probably lie in detailed studies of the emigrants and of the movements with which they were associated. By carefully studying the push/pull factors that both detached former slaves from their particular social contexts and also differentiated emigrants into the separate streams of post-slavery migration, emancipation studies will begin to establish the direct linkages between adjustments to the demise of slavery and the advent of waves of migration that periodically swept the post–Civil War South.

The recollections of a former slave named Andrew Boone are quite suggestive in this regard. Born in North Carolina in 1847, Boone retained vivid recollections not only of slavery but also of emancipation and its af-

---

67. Du Bois, *Black Reconstruction in America*, 670–709.

68. Stanley L. Engerman, "Economic Adjustments to Emancipation in the United States and the British West Indies," *Journal of Interdisciplinary History*, XIII (Autumn, 1982), 191–220; United States Department of the Interior, Census Office, *Twelfth Census of the United States, 1900, Agriculture*, Vol. II, 94, 425, 528–29.

69. Nell Irvin Painter, *Exodusters: Black Migration to Kansas After Reconstruction* (New York, 1976); William Bittle and Gilbert Geis, *The Longest Way Home: Chief Alfred C. Sam's Back to Africa Movement* (Detroit, 1964).

termath. Having moved north from Raleigh after failing to find the kind of life in freedom that he desired, he worked in New York City for a number of years, mainly as a drummer for an urban circus; Boone proudly recalled living the life of a self-described dandy. Although he married and had a family in New York, he chose to return to North Carolina in order to spend his final years at home in the South. A WPA interviewer asked him at age ninety to assess his personal experience with emancipation. From a perspective embittered by the federal government's refusal to declare him eligible for relief during the Great Depression, Boone critiqued his intro-duction into freedom: "In slavery times, they kept you down an' you had to wuk, now I can't wuk, an' I'm still down. Not allowed to wuk an' still down. It's all hard, slavery and freedom, both bad when you can't eat. The old bee makes de honey comb, the young bee makes the honey, niggers make de cotton an' corn an' de white folks gets de money. Dis wus de case in Slavery times an' it de case now an' de white folks still git de money dat de nigger's labor makes."[70]

As the reminiscences of Andrew Boone make clear, some former slaves managed to escape from the South, despite the strategy of regional racial containment employed by southern Bourbon Democrats. What remain obscure, however, are the social factors that made escape possible for some former slaves like Andrew Boone while keeping most others effec-tively bottled up. His being young and also single obviously made rapid long-distance movement much easier to contemplate and also to achieve than it might have been for an older person or for a head of household, particularly for someone burdened with responsibilities to a multigenera-tional extended family. It may turn out that black urbanization conformed to patterns evident among other groups of nineteenth-century urban migrants, patterns that saw single young adults take the leading role in making the break toward this new way of life.

It appears that gender will be a critical factor in the differentiation of various migratory streams. A recent study comparing black urban migra-tion to the movement of European immigrants outlines some of the meth-ods that young southern males used to gain employment in the urban North. In heavy industry, most jobs could be taken seasonally; this en-abled many southern black heads of household to use the fall and winter

70. Andre Boone in *North Carolina Narratives*, in Rawick (ed.), *American Slave*, XIV, 137.

to earn badly needed cash income, supplements of particular importance either when crops failed or when commodity prices plummeted precipitously. Strike breaking also offered another source of extra income, although such interludes were by their very nature both temporary and dangerous. Work on railroads and steamship lines also provided temporary access to the urban North.[71] Taken together, these strategies expanded the numbers of southern blacks with sufficient exposure to the rhythms of life in the urban North to be able to take advantage of the opportunities created by the sudden advent of World War I.

Education was apparently of major importance in directing the migratory paths undertaken by younger southern black women. Particularly for the female graduates of "normal" schools, there generally seemed to be a healthy market in segregated schools, both North and South. Graduates of southern "normal" schools such as Mary McLeod Bethune and Nannie Burroughs made careers for themselves working in and building black-controlled educational institutions in predominantly rural areas of the Deep South. Other children of the freedpeople, such as Mary Church Terrell and Ida Wells Barnett, moved northward after concluding that the Deep South was inhospitable to black female social activism. The work of these social activists proved quite significant, since they played leading roles in creating the black-controlled infrastructure of urban social and benevolent institutions that helped ease the transition to northern urban life for succeeding groups of southern immigrants.[72] In fact, the dispersion of these young women into a number of different urban areas created a network of urban pioneers, a network that provided succeeding waves of black emigrants with introductions to the intricacies of urban life that often spelled the difference between success and failure.[73]

71. John Bodnar, Roger Simon, and Michael P. Weber, *Lives of Their Own: Blacks, Italians, and Poles in Pittsburgh, 1900–1960* (Urbana, Ill., 1982), 30–40.

72. Alfreda M. Duster (ed.), *Crusade for Justice: The Autobiography of Ida B. Wells* (Chicago, 1970); Kathleen C. Berkeley, "Southern Normal Schools and the Creation of Black Female Networks, 1865–1910," paper, Southern Historical Association annual meeting, 1981.

73. Vincent P. Franklin, *The Education of Black Philadelphia: The Social and Educational History of a Minority Community, 1900–1950* (Philadelphia, 1979); Allan H. Spear, *Black Chicago: The Making of a Negro Ghetto, 1890–1920* (Chicago, 1967).

IV

If the historic task of emancipation involved the incorporation of freed black laborers into the post–Civil War American industrial economy, then scholars will create a viable synthesis only by connecting the study of emancipation to the social processes that were simultaneously leading to the making of an American working class. The same sets of push/pull factors that transformed the children of the freedpeople into a pool of surplus labor also worked to detach native-born white Americans and European immigrants from their agrarian roots and then to direct them toward the industrial economy. To discover that urban pioneers from every racial and ethnic group employed parallel strategies to cope with the challenges of urbanization is to reveal the commonality of their experiences. And the black encounter with urban racism bears comparison to the discrimination leveled at other immigrant groups, since only through such comparisons can scholars accurately assess the impact of discrimination.

These conceptual schemata represent a significant departure from the general tendency to view emancipation as an experience separate and apart from the main currents of American social development. Yet no comprehensive analysis of processes of social change within postslavery Afro-American communities can possibly emerge unless that analysis comes to grips with the revolutionary transformations that post–Civil War industrialization brought to the whole of American society. Only by writing with an eye toward this larger social dynamic can students of emancipation give meaning to the varied contexts through which social dynamics within the black community mediated the evolution of the main lines of social development in postslavery Afro-American life.

COMMENT

ERIC FONER

I commend Armstead Robinson for an excellent examination of the issues facing those now studying the crisis of emancipation and its impact upon American society. Not only has he managed in a brief compass to summarize a good deal of the most recent historical literature, but he has also identified some of the crucial areas in which more work needs to be done before we can arrive at a fully satisfying understanding of emancipation and its legacy, a legacy in some ways still unresolved in America today. My comments, therefore, are more in the way of elaborations on some of Robinson's themes than criticisms of his approach or conclusions. They focus on the period that has for some time now engaged my own attention: Reconstruction.

I fully endorse Robinson's contention that the emancipation of the slaves did make a difference to blacks and whites alike in nineteenth-century America. If this remark seems to belabor the obvious, it is merely because so much of the historical literature of the past decade has tended to belittle the impact of the Civil War, Reconstruction, and emancipation. Studies of national politics have insisted that the postwar constitutional amendments and civil rights laws in no way altered the fundamentally state-oriented nature of the federal system. Investigations of southern social structure have stressed how the planter class retained control of its land and social prestige; the social revolution envisioned by blacks and white radicals like Thaddeus Stevens did not take place. Historians transfixed by theories of "plantation society" have posited an unchanging southern social order based upon plantation agriculture, lasting from the eighteenth into the twentieth century, in which whether labor was slave or free made very little difference. Thus, continuity rather than change has been the theme of much recent writing. Robinson—rightly, I am convinced—is trying to bring us back to the notion that in many ways emancipation did indeed constitute a revolution, one whose full dimensions can be understood only by placing the experience of blacks within the broadest context of the social and economic transformation of the American and, indeed, world political economy.

As Robinson points out, the sources for exploring the black experience in these pivotal years are indeed abundant, so abundant in fact that they have not yet been fully tapped by scholars. Indeed, the contemporary sources for Reconstruction are so rich and so abundant that there is no necessity to rely heavily on interviews and recollections gathered many decades after the period. To the underutilized archives he has mentioned, let me add a few others that enable us to view in all their complexity the aspirations and attitudes of blacks in the aftermath of freedom.

There are the papers of the governors of the various southern states during Reconstruction, and the papers of other Republican officials, filled with letters from local black leaders and ordinary black folk about events large and small. (Probably the most revealing such collections are the papers of the governors of Alabama, South Carolina, and North Carolina and of Mississippi's Adelbert Ames during his senatorship. Unfortunately, the governors of Georgia and Louisiana appear to have destroyed most of their papers, and after examining the financial machinations of their state governments, I can't say I blame them.) There are the voluminous records of the congressional Ku Klux Klan and disputed election investigating committees, which interviewed scores of blacks whose testimony provides vital insights not simply into Klan violence and election fraud but virtually every aspect of local social, economic, and political life. Even the papers of the American Colonization Society constitute a neglected source, for they reflect the ebb and flow of emigrationist sentiment among southern blacks. Finally, there are the proceedings of black political gatherings, local and statewide, and even the neglected records of the various constitutional conventions of 1867/68 that sought to create the political framework for a South in which the rights of all individuals, regardless of color, would be fully protected.

From sources such as these a convincing new portrait of the role of blacks in shaping emancipation and Reconstruction can be constructed. Rather than trying to touch on all the multifaceted ways in which emancipation affected the nature of the black experience, let me briefly turn to one area that, as Robinson suggests, is indeed crucial to understanding the inner workings of black life in this period: politics. It may seem unfashionable in this age of social history to propose that an emphasis on the politics of Reconstruction can bring rewards, but I am convinced that it was through politics that many of the deepest aspirations and values of the black community were articulated. It should be possible to explore how politics provided the forum for a new class of black leaders that combined the elite of slavery days (free blacks, preachers, etc.) with new men seizing the opportunity afforded by the Union Leagues and Republican party to establish their own claims to leadership.

It was politics that allowed blacks to define their distinctive vision of republican citizenship, to seize, as Vincent Harding has shown, upon traditional American values and forge from them a means of expressing their own ambition to transform American society. It was in politics that blacks articulated a new vision of the American state, calling upon government, both national and local, to take upon itself new and unprecedented responsibilities for protecting the civil rights of individual citizens, and to address, despite the failure of land reform, the economic plight of black labor. Indeed, in my view, the failure to distribute land has blinded many students of the period to the less drastic but nonetheless creative and subtle ways black leaders on the local and state levels sought to use political power to respond to the economic aspirations of their constituents.

A reexamination of Reconstruction black politics might also lead us into realms barely touched upon in the existing literature on emancipation. What was the effect on relations of black men and women of the achievement of suffrage by men, thus institutionalizing the distinction between the public sphere of men and the private sphere of women that had defined gender roles in white society but had little relevance to the slave experience? And it was in politics that relations between blacks and poorer whites were worked out, although here I am slightly less sanguine than Robinson about how possible long-term cooperation may have been. Many whites—more than we perhaps imagine—were willing to use the black vote for their own purposes (generally defined as keeping "rebels" out of power), but most were far less able to accept black officeholding and black self-assertiveness in political affairs. Indeed, the range of black-white political bargaining on such issues as homestead exemptions, tax and lien laws, the disenfranchisement of former Confederates, and school segregation remains to be studied.

Let me conclude by reiterating Robinson's insistence that the full meaning of emancipation can only be grasped by examining the two Reconstructions that occurred in the late nineteenth century, for the political economy of the North was transformed no less than that of the South. Just as southerners, black and white, were attempting to come to terms with the meaning of freedom in a postemancipation society, the evolution of capitalism in the North was fatally undermining an old ideal of economic independence for the laborer. The autonomy blacks demanded for themselves was enjoyed by fewer and fewer whites in the North, which may help to explain why northern support for black aspirations evaporated so quickly. The freedman, as one observer noted in 1865, wanted to dwell on his own land, to engage in the marketplace only to the extent that he desired, and "to be able to do that free from any outside control." Yet how many whites in Reconstruction America still enjoyed this kind of economic autonomy? In a sense the debates unleashed by emancipation may have forced Americans finally to appreciate how far they had traveled from the Jeffersonian definition of a republic resting on economically autonomous citizens.

I cannot close without making a final remark. It is that Professor Robinson's paper reinforces a conviction I have long held, namely that the starting point for all studies of emancipation remains that classic of American historical literature, *Black Reconstruction in America* (1935) by W. E. B. Du Bois. This monumental work is replete with insights, revolutionary in their implications for the scholarship of the 1930s, that have since become commonplace: that slavery was the fundamental cause of the Civil War, that blacks played a central part in that conflict and its aftermath, that the land issue was crucial to the fate of Reconstruction, and that an account of the emancipated based only upon the testimony of whites must be hopelessly flawed. Other insights have yet to be assimilated into the study of the period, particularly Du Bois' insistence that a full understanding of emancipation and its legacy can emerge only from a comprehensive examination of social classes both North and South and that the rise and fall of slavery must be considered within the broad context of the international expansion of capitalist social relations. *Black Reconstruction*, in other words, raised the questions that must be answered before a comprehensive portrait of the emancipation experience can be arrived at.

COMMENT

NELL IRVIN PAINTER

Every other year I teach a seminar for graduate students on recent writing in Afro-American history. And after three different seminars, I'm still amazed by the growth and change in the field. My book list is limited to publications no more than three years old, and even though we deal with thirty to forty books per semester, I seldom use more than one or two books repeatedly. In the late 1970s few local studies were published, as though limiting a book in terms of both race and geography meant automatic loss to the publisher. But in the fall of 1983, we noticed that many books in the field were local studies, and many were very valuable. Seeing how quickly the field has grown, I'm pleased to comment on Armstead Robinson's wide-ranging and thoughtful paper on the future of black history.

Robinson's essay sets forth three important topics for investigation: the Civil War origins of the systems of labor that prevailed after the war; the process of class formation among blacks in the second half of the nineteenth century; and migration within and out of the South. Each of these is a large subject well worth studying.

The first is Armstead Robinson's own specialty, and the most current work in the field is his own, notably the forthcoming *Bitter Fruits of Bondage*. The second topic, class formation, is far more fundamental and harder to analyze. Only recently have historians been willing to recognize class differences among blacks, and consequently investigation of class differentiation has hardly begun. The pioneering study dealing with the effects of class and color stratification in politics is Thomas Holt's *Black Over White* (1977). So far, no booklength historical study has concentrated on class differentiation alone. I concur fully with Robinson's estimation of the importance of the topic, and, in addition, I would stress the need to keep urban-rural and regional differences in view.

Migration, Robinson's third area of concentration, has already attracted scholars working in several fields. The pioneer black sociologist George F. Haynes wrote a number of books and articles on the Great Migration in the 1910s and 1920s. The record continues to grow with contributions such as Florette Henri, *Black Migration* (1970) and Allen Ballard, *One More Day's Journey* (1984). While I agree with Robinson that migration is a central issue in the history of black Americans, I doubt that it still need occupy one-third of our attention, having already proved its enduring attractiveness as a field of study.

Were I designing the research agenda for Afro-American history, I would underline Robinson's second topic and then call for a concentration not so much on events or trends, but on habits of mind to be broken. First, I would break the customary substitution of race for all other social and economic categories in Afro-American history, and in southern history as well. No longer would all southern whites be assumed to be the sons of planters and all southern blacks the children of slaves. This habit tends to see southern society in dichotomous terms of black versus white, in which all blacks represent powerlessness and poverty and all whites, wealth and power. By setting two opposing blocks against one another, this vision overlooks complexities and eschews the subtleties that mark good historical writing in all fields.

In large part, I suspect that the reluctance with which many of us juggle variables in addition to race is rooted in a conviction, not always mistaken, that the addition of class, gender, or regional considerations to race is less an honest attempt to write history more sensitively than a subterfuge, a way of downplaying racial oppression and mitigating its severity. Adding other considerations to race is often interpreted as saying that racial oppression was not really very bad. Although this skepticism may make sense politically, it stifles the careful analysis of what Afro-Americans did and thought in the past.

The indisposition to see black women's history as a legitimate field is weakening considerably, and today black women's history is seldom seen as undermining essential black unity. Yet some recent writing includes passages that seem to pit black women against black men in a contest for the claim of the most oppressed. Even now, concentration on the history of black women is sometimes seen as a veiled attack on black men, or on "the black man." This is regrettable, because men and women are neither at war nor identical entities. In the immediate post–Civil War years, for example, educated northern black women, Linda Perkins has shown, came south to teach the freedpeople, whom they saw as their people. These women were subject to the pressures of the role of lady, with its emphasis on respectability, refinement, and fragility, and with that of missionary workers, with imperatives of strength and hard work. As Frances Ellen Watkins Harper and Anna Cooper showed, black women in the South after the Civil War were ladies and workers, teachers and pupils, agents of elevation and means of subsistence.

During Reconstruction, black women did not have the vote, and they could not act politically as men could. Although the evidence shows that women attended political rallies and took a lively interest in politics, their part as political actors in that most political period could not be the same as men's. While they could not vote, large numbers of nineteenth century black women worked for wages, and their roles as workers often conflicted with their roles as mothers. Paid less than men, working women have nevertheless played an important economic part in the history of black people in this country.

Afro-Americans, both men and women, have been working people; when we speak generally of blacks, we assume, usually with justification, that we speak of workers. Yet there exists a reluctance to see black workers as part of American labor history, for several reasons. First, American labor history has long concentrated on unions and unionized workers, both of whom have a long past deeply marred by racism. Second, American labor historians have tended to study industrial labor, from which blacks were largely barred until the 1940s.

From the black side, many historians hesitate to compare black workers with white workers, who have only occasionally extended class solidarity across racial lines. In the context of the South, the issue of class-based politics among the poor is generally accompanied by the assumptions that poor whites are uniquely racist and that racism overshadows every other social and economic consideration. These assumptions ignore the usual but nevertheless actual instances of intraracial cooperation, such as the general strike in New Orleans of 1892. More than that, the assumption that racism ruins class-interest politics among poor blacks and whites ignores the dismal history of lower-class politics in this country in general. Even when unburdened by the issue of race, American workers have not succeeded in sustaining class politics. The Workingmen's and Knights of Labor parties of the mid-1880s fell apart within a few years, despite capturing local governments in several states. And in the 1890s, the People's party succumbed to violence and cooptation, much as had the Republican parties in the South in the 1870s, after enjoying a heyday of only about five years. In short, the conclusion that poor blacks and poor whites cannot collaborate politically in the South simply because of racial tensions is an assumption that ignores the difficulty that poor people in this country have always faced in politics.

Despite the racism of poor whites, whether industrial workers or southern tenant farmers, black working people still share economic disabilities and vulnerabilities with them. The history of most blacks is a history of workers, and seeing blacks as people subject to the treatment meted out to members of the working classes enriches and broadens the writing of black history.

Class has been taboo in Afro-American history in another area as well, that of intraracial conflict. Yet every historian who has worked in the sources generated during the late nineteenth and early twentieth centuries, also the era of segregation, is familiar with what a prominent nineteenth-century Afro-American called "complexional distinctions." But few historians have dealt with the obvious, for fear of opening a Pandora's box of racial disunity. If we are to delve the process of class differentiation, however, we must come to terms with color distinctions intimately tied to class. In the 1865 to 1920 period, light color connoted wealth and education in men and beauty and refinement in women, indicators of class standing too important to be ignored. Regional origins sometimes carried greater or lesser prestige in the reckoning of class standing, but beyond class, regions have had their own significance.

Frederick Douglass, originally from Maryland, had to interpret southern mores to a Pennsylvania Negro in the South. The black carpetbagger had been alarmed by the freedmen's practice of going about armed. Carrying guns, Douglass explained, was a southern tradition that antedated the Civil War. The only change was that after the war black as well as white men carried guns. This is only one example of regional differences among blacks during the period of Reconstruction. Despite the southern roots of virtually all black people in the middle of the nineteenth century, men and women born and raised in the South differed culturally from men and women born and raised in the North. The tensions between northern black families and southern migrants in the era of the Great Migration are familiar to students of Cleveland, Detroit, and Topeka. But the tensions between freedmen and black carpetbaggers are less well known and deserve attention, as part of the investigation of mobility and class formation.

Holding office was recognized immediately as an avenue toward relative power and wealth during Reconstruction, and rightly so. Not surprisingly, there was competition for offices, and groups of constituents tried to reserve as many as possible for themselves. In South Carolina this meant that black South Carolinians preferred to elect their peers rather than men from outside their neighborhoods, state, or region. Northerners had generally enjoyed more advantages than southerners, and by dint of education, the former were better placed to win elective and appointive offices. But as early as 1870, Martin Delany complained that black southerners tarred northern blacks with the carpetbagger label and publicly expressed preference for black southern rather than northern officeholders. A black carpetbagger himself, Delany called such sectional feeling "preposterous," and other prominent black men agreed. But his grievance endured, as southern blacks understandably sought to keep choice plums for themselves. Future Reconstruction studies will need to take cognizance of such sectional differences among Afro-Americans in order to understand what now seem like nuances. This is true of class and gender as well.

If Afro-American history is to continue to flourish as an intellectually challenging field, its practitioners must continue to refine their analytic tools and sharpen their terms of discussion. By definition, Afro-American history must give racial considerations a great deal of attention—the field is defined by race. But Afro-American history cannot stop with race. I have mentioned three large categories that must qualify racial generalizations, but several other themes need to be looked at as well, such as rurality, cultural exchanges with Native Americans and Irish immigrants,

Christianity as a cultural style, and the diffusion of patterns of music and language.

In setting out an agenda for future study in Afro-American history, I would not only add other factors to race, but I would also examine how racist stereotypes have influenced historians' interpretations of black people's actions and words. I would have historians scrutinize stereotypes, recognize their force, then try not to let stereotypes distort their use of sources. This is difficult, as Barbara J. Fields has shown in her excellent essay "Ideology and Race in American History" (in J. Morgan Kousser and James M. McPherson [eds.], *Region, Race, and Reconstruction* [1982]). Fields rightly stresses the ways in which historians reinforce pernicious stereotypes by using sources thoughtlessly. I would complement her message by asking historians not to modify their sources by trying to downplay stereotypes.

A racist society uses racial stereotypes to reinforce racial subordination, so it is hardly surprising that many current historians try to avoid using examples or drawing conclusions that seem to feed unfortunate stereotypes. But this kind of censorship can obscure the significance of controversies in the past. Using my own research on South Carolina during Reconstruction, I would like to reconsider the stereotype of blacks in political life that holds that Afro-Americans are politically inept.

This stereotype goes back to the nineteenth century, to the justification for European colonialism in Asia and Africa, and, in this country, to the period of the Spanish-American War, when the United States became a colonial power. The argument that colored peoples were not able to govern themselves was applied to Filipinos and Cubans at the turn of the century, but for domestic history, black Americans were the main target of the charge. Disfranchisement, segregation, and extralegal violence were all justified in the late nineteenth and early twentieth centuries because blacks purportedly could not exercise political power responsibly. Part of the proof was the charge that Reconstruction and Negro rule had produced an unprecedented tide of corruption in the South. This interpretation was scarcely challenged until the middle of the twentieth century. Since then, historians revising the racist Dunning school of Reconstruction history have downplayed or explained away the issue of black corruption in Reconstruction. Instead of examining it closely, they have swept it under the rug.

Our usual conclusions about Reconstruction are now that the central issue was race, more specifically, whether or not white supremacy would prevail. And second, we believe that antiblack violence coupled with a refusal of the federal government to protect blacks from it (and a corrupt bargain with railroad executives) brought Reconstruction to an end. This is part of the story, a very large part, of course. But it seems to me that the history of Reconstruction is far more interesting and complicated if we look more carefully and confront the import of the issue of corruption at the time.

My example comes from South Carolina and features Martin Delany, who is now known as the father of black nationalism. Delany, in the antebellum period, had been an abolitionist and a leading emigrationist. He had worked with Frederick Douglass in the 1840s; then, despairing of significant improvement in American race relations, he had journeyed to what is now Nigeria shortly before the war and signed a treaty to permit the immigration of free blacks. Toward the end of the Civil War he was commissioned a major in the Union army and was stationed in Charleston. Having served as an officer in the Freedmen's Bureau until 1868, Delany remained in Charleston as a businessman. In the early 1870s Delany began to harbor misgivings about the Republican regime in South Carolina. In 1874 he ran for lieutenant governor with a Democratic running mate on the Independent Republican ticket, in the absence of Democratic opposition.

Delany was not alone among prominent blacks in doubting the viability of Republican Reconstruction, despite its massive black support. He and several others in South Carolina, the Reverend Richard H. Cain, Robert B. Elliott, Francis L. Cardozo, and Joseph H. Rainey, as well as P. B. S. Pinchback of Louisiana and W. A. Pledger of Georgia, began publicly to deplore the corruption associated with southern Republicanism.

Moving away from the espousal of simple democracy, which in South Carolina had empowered the black majority, most of whom were recently emancipated, Delany increasingly spoke of intelligence (i.e., education), respectability (usually associated with relative wealth), and honesty (said to reside with natural aristocrats) as the proper qualifications for political officeholding. Delany advised freedmen to ally themselves with the wealth of the South—planters and other former Confederates who were to be found in the Democratic party—and to turn away from the poor white southerners and white carpetbaggers whom, he said, had done nothing whatever for freedmen and had split South Carolina along racial lines.

By 1876, when the Democratic party fielded a slate of candidates, Delany supported Wade Hampton III, a former Confederate general and wealthy planter. Having been one of the blackest men in America, Delany was now an apologist for the Redeemers of South Carolina. He always opposed violence and insisted on the respect of black civil rights, but by 1876 he thought the interests of the blacks of the state lay with the better class of local whites. Agreeing with Wade Hampton that a planter- and business-led Democratic party could serve the interests of all the people at once, he thought that such a government would govern honestly, attract northern capital, and, in the midst of the depression of the 1870s, restore prosperity.

For Delany, this reasoning represented the only salvation of the race, but he learned in October that his views clashed with those of poor black South Carolinians who worked for the very sort of people he was supporting. To a hostile black audience in the Sea Islands, Delany protested in vain that he was their friend and only wanted to teach them what was best, for their own sakes. At another failed political meeting a few days later, black Republicans fired on him and his white colleagues.

Delany learned the hard way that what he saw as the best interests of the race was not always acceptable to other blacks, particularly those who were poor. Without realizing it, Delany thought like people who were comfortably situated, not like the poor. Prizing harmony and the ideal of an identity of interest across class lines—rather than that of standing up to one's employers during hard times—Delany's criticism of Reconstruction was nearly identical to that of white Democrats of the better classes. His concern for reducing corruption and reestablishing respectability in government replicated the hallmarks of conservative government throughout the country.

The point here, however, is not that Delany was somehow a traitor to his race or a man who had been whitewashed, for he believed sincerely that he held the interests of black people paramount. He had not been bribed or misled, and he was not alone among his black peers. Recent scholarship stresses the gap between the material circumstances of black officeholders and their constituents—the officeholders were better off than ordinary black voters in the Reconstruction South. These officeholders,

with educated, self-employed men like Delany, were more likely to suc-
cumb to Redeemer rhetoric stressing honesty and economy in government
than were their constituents. At this point I do not know how many hundreds of blacks in South Carolina supported Wade Hampton, like Delany,
out of conviction. It is already clear, however, that violence and intimidation do not tell the entire story of the end of Republican Reconstruction in
South Carolina.

Historians have all too often lumped several categories of people together as though they were interchangeable, here, black = Republican =
worker. And we have downgraded the power of corruption as an issue, as
though the charge were universally recognized as mere racism at the time.
While the equation holds for large numbers of South Carolinians in the
1870s, it does not hold for all, particularly those in leadership positions.
In seeking to understand as important an event as the end of Reconstruction, we ought not have recourse to generalizations that obscure the finer
points and blur the focus of events.

To the extent that prominent individuals like Delany, Cain, Pinchback,
and Pledger influence history, their reasoning, even when they took minority positions, needs to be reckoned with. Arguing that black reconstructionists stole rather little in comparison with white reconstructionists, that
there was far more stealing going on in New York and Washington, where
there was more to steal, or that the Redeemers stole a great deal more in
their turn does not substitute for a careful attempt to understand what
happened in 1876. Just as corruption opened the way for the civil service
reform campaign and the restriction of democracy in the North, so the
issue of corruption in the South also paved the way for the return to power
of the so-called wealth and intelligence of the South, with the support of
prominent blacks who shared the values of the better classes.

This is one small example of the way a taboo subject can illuminate
events; doubtless hundreds more exist. If I were to outline the future shape
of Afro-American history, I would try to get historians to transcend the
weight of stereotype and to bravely investigate black life fully, even when
the evidence shows angry, violent, disorderly black people. After all, anger,
violence, and disorder are thoroughly human emotions and actions. By
sanitizing blacks who lived in the past, historians make them less than
complete human beings.

IV URBAN STUDIES

The Black Urban Experience in American History

KENNETH L. KUSMER

In marked contrast with such traditional areas of research as slavery and emancipation, the subject of black urban history has only recently begun to engage the interest of historians in a serious way. As a topic of historical research, the field can scarcely be said to have existed prior to the mid-1960s. However, the number of dissertations and books in black urban history has increased dramatically during the past decade, and this literature has reached a point in both quantity and variety that a summation of its import and direction is now a necessity. My purpose in surveying this literature is threefold: first, to provide an overview of the historiography in the field; second, to offer a theoretical framework or scaffolding for research in black urban history; finally, utilizing this theoretical framework, to assess and critique the most recent trends in the literature of this field and to offer suggestions for future research.

With few exceptions, the first studies of black urban communities in the United States were written by sociologists or concerned reformers, not by historians.[1] Between 1899, when W. E. B. Du Bois published *The Philadelphia Negro: A Social Study*, and 1948, when the man who would later become the nation's first black cabinet officer, Robert Weaver, produced his study *The Negro Ghetto*, a number of important inquiries into various as-

---

1. The first strictly historical article in black urban history was Carter G. Woodson's "The Negroes of Cincinnati Prior to the Civil War," *Journal of Negro History*, I (1916), 1–22.

pects of black urban life appeared. These included significant works by George Edmund Haynes, Monroe N. Work, R. R. Wright, Jr., Ray Stannard Baker, Mary White Ovington, Louise V. Kennedy, E. Franklin Frazier, and others.[2] In 1945 the appearance of St. Clair Drake and Horace R. Cayton's masterly study of Chicago's South Side ghetto, *Black Metropolis*, marked the pinnacle of achievement within the sociological genre.[3] Few sociologists of that era recognized the potential value of history to their discipline. It is not surprising, then, that most of these early studies took a fundamentally ahistorical view of the Afro-American urban experience. Frazier and Drake and Cayton were exceptions in this regard; they were very much concerned with providing a historical milieu for their studies. Considering his historical training, however, it is surprising how little interest Du Bois took in the evolution of the urban black community. A paltry thirty-five pages of *The Philadelphia Negro* is devoted to historical background. Du Bois was typical in this respect. However brilliant or innovative, these early sociological works were primarily concerned with current conditions or with the recent past. They left a rich legacy of information about the nature of black class and occupational patterns, race relations, institutions, and political life, but they revealed little about changes that occurred over the long run.

Another tendency of early investigations of black urban life was to focus either directly or indirectly on the migration of black peasants to the North, especially the legendary "Great Migration" of 1916 to 1919. A number of volumes, such as Emmett J. Scott's *Negro Migration During the War* (1920), dealt exclusively with the causes and consequences of black migration from the South.[4] Other studies surveyed the impact on specific

2. W. E. B. Du Bois, *The Philadelphia Negro: A Social Study* (Philadelphia: 1899); Du Bois, *The Black North in 1901* (New York, 1970 reprint); Monroe N. Work, "Negro Real Estate Holders of Chicago" (M.A. thesis, University of Chicago, 1903); George Edmund Haynes, "Conditions Among Negroes in the Cities," *Annals of the American Academy of Political and Social Science*, XLIX (1913); R. R. Wright, Jr., *The Negro in Pennsylvania* (Philadelphia, 1909); Mary White Ovington, *Half a Man: The Status of the Negro in New York* (New York, 1911); Louise V. Kennedy, *The Negro Peasant Turns Cityward* (New York, 1930); E. Franklin Frazier, *The Negro Family in Chicago* (Chicago, 1932); Clyde V. Kiser, *Sea Island to City: A Study of St. Helena Islanders in Harlem and Other Urban Centers* (New York, 1931); Robert Weaver, *The Negro Ghetto* (New York, 1948).

3. St. Clair Drake and Horace R. Cayton, *Black Metropolis: A Study of Negro Life in a Northern City* (New York, 1945).

4. Studies dealing with the World War I migration and its immediate effects include

communities. George Edmund Haynes studied Negro newcomers to Detroit, Abraham Epstein and Ira Reid investigated the social conditions of blacks in Pittsburgh, Abram Harris surveyed the black population of Minneapolis, and Clyde V. Kiser produced an important volume on St. Helena Islanders in New York City. The 1922 report of the Chicago Commission on Race Relations and E. Franklin Frazier's *The Negro Family in Chicago* (1932) also viewed the movement of southern newcomers into the northern metropolis as a major factor in understanding racial conditions in the city.[5] By the 1930s most scholars had come to perceive the mass migration of the World War I period, and the accompanying problems of adjustment and conflict that it engendered, as the most significant and dramatic event influencing black urban life in the United States.

A later generation of historians and history-minded sociologists would draw upon these early works in formulating their own views of black urban development. The strength of the early scholarly studies was their analytical approach to class structure, organizations, and numerous other aspects of black life. They also contained astute and detailed discussions of race relations in many cases, and it was in this area, if anywhere, that a historical approach was most often used. Some of the volumes by reformers or amateur sociologists, such as Ray Stannard Baker's *Following the Color Line* (1908), Mary White Ovington's critical 1911 assessment of the status of blacks in New York, and John Daniels' 1914 study of Boston Negroes, also provided a wide range of information on patterns of discrimination and racial interaction, much of which is still useful to scholars today.[6]

Unfortunately, however, these early studies had certain weaknesses and biases. Not only did they focus almost exclusively on conditions in the

---

Emmett J. Scott, *Negro Migration During the War* (New York, 1920); U.S. Department of Labor, *Negro Migration in 1916–17* (Washington, D.C., 1919); and Thomas J. Woofter, *Negro Migration* (New York, 1920). A recent general survey is Florette Henri, *Black Migration: Movement North, 1900–1920* (New York, 1975).

5. George Edmund Haynes, *Negro Newcomers in Detroit, Michigan* (New York, 1918); Abraham Epstein, *The Negro Migrant in Pittsburgh* (Pittsburgh, 1918); Ira D. A. Reid, *Social Conditions of the Negro in the Hill District of Pittsburgh* (Pittsburgh, 1930); Abram L. Harris, *The Negro Population in Minneapolis: A Study of Race Relations* (Minneapolis, 1927); T. Earl Sullenger and J. Harvey Kerns, *The Negro in Omaha* (Omaha, 1931).

6. For full documentation, see the bibliographical footnote in Kenneth L. Kusmer, *A Ghetto Takes Shape: Black Cleveland, 1870–1930* (Urbana, 1976), 55n.

North, but they established the notion that a few large black communities there—especially Chicago's South Side and Harlem—were typical. A corollary was the tendency to use the Great Migration as the beginning point for the discussion of the development of black ghettos. This emphasis ensured that the first modern historical studies of black urban communities published in the 1960s would deal with New York and Chicago, and that they would focus on the early twentieth century. (An earlier exception to this was Robert Austin Warner's *New Haven Negroes: A Social History* [1940], which did not focus on the Great Migration period. Warner's discursive approach to the subject matter, however, did not provide a useful model for later research.)[7]

The early studies of blacks in cities also tended to present the adaptation of life-styles of migrants in negative terms. There was a decided emphasis upon the "pathological" effects of racism and the inability of the newcomers to adapt to urban life successfully. E. Franklin Frazier was particularly influential in formulating this type of analysis. In *The Negro Family in Chicago* (1932), he focused on the debilitating effects of the urban environment on black migrants. The migrant in the northern metropolis, Frazier concluded, was all too often "the prey of vagrant impulses and lawless desires." Frazier viewed the black nationalist movement of Marcus Garvey as a product of the alienation of an uprooted black peasantry.[8]

Frazier has been an easy target for critics because of his emphasis on the supposed instability of many black migrant families.[9] In fairness to Frazier (whose works have often been used as an ideological foil), it should be pointed out that he never claimed that the "matriarchal" family system was typical among blacks. Insofar as he did see this as an important characteristic of a sizable portion of the black lower class, he certainly was not alone. In *The Philadelphia Negro*, Du Bois was as critical as Frazier of the marital and sexual practices of lower-class blacks in the new urban environment. Many, he said, had "little home life, rather a sort of neighborhood life, centered in the alleys and on the sidewalks, where the children are educated." This intriguing statement could have served as a prelude to

7. Robert Austin Warner, *New Haven Negroes: A Social History* (New Haven, 1940).
8. Frazier, *The Negro Family in Chicago*, 75–76, 147; Frazier, "The Garvey Movement," *Opportunity*, IV (1926), 346–48.
9. See, for example, Herbert Gutman, *The Black Family in Slavery and Freedom* (New York, 1976).

a sympathetic inquiry into the nature of black kinship systems in the metropolis, but instead Du Bois closed the subject abruptly on a moralistic note.[10] Drake and Cayton, for all their sensitivity, also argued that "the roving masses of Negro men has been an important factor . . . in preventing the formation of stable, conventional family units" among lower-class blacks.[11] The perspective of these black scholars must be viewed in the context of their time. They were attempting to overcome both popular prejudice and the theories of some white racist sociologists, which commonly presented blacks as innately inferior and immoral. These black sociologists thus often interpreted the pathologies of the ghetto as the product of racial and class discrimination. Drake and Cayton, for example, directly connected black family patterns to irregular employment and job discrimination. Nevertheless—even if for the best of reasons—there was a strong tendency in the early literature to portray black urban life as a world warped by prejudice and disordered by the impact of urbanization.

Exceptions to this approach did exist, primarily among popular writers unschooled in sociological theories. James Weldon Johnson's *Black Manhattan* was unusual not only in its emphasis upon the unique cultural achievements of blacks in music, sports, and theater, but also in its strong historical orientation. Johnson's book and Alain Locke's edited volume *The New Negro* were prophetic in their attempt to look beyond the haze of pathology and disorienting effects of ghetto life to find shared cultural values and a continuity of identity with previous generations. But their concerns were definitely a minority view at the time. A more typical approach was indicated by the title of a book by Thomas J. Woofter that came out in 1928, *Negro Problems in Cities*.[12]

Most of the seminal literature in black urban studies appeared before 1940. The lack of interest in the subject by historians of that era is partly explained by the fact that urban history of any sort attracted little attention at the time. The first significant scholarly study in urban history, Arthur Schlesinger, Sr.'s *The Rise of the City*, did not appear until 1933.[13]

10. Du Bois, *Philadelphia Negro*, 193.

11. Drake and Cayton, *Black Metropolis*, 583.

12. James Weldon Johnson, *Black Manhattan* (New York, 1930); Alain Locke (ed.), *The New Negro* (New York, 1925); Thomas J. Woofter, *Negro Problems in Cities* (New York, 1928).

13. Arthur M. Schlesinger, Sr., *The Rise of the City, 1878–1898* (New York, 1933).

There was also, of course, a definite racial bias in the history profession, as evidenced in the works of U. B. Phillips and the Dunning school of Reconstruction historiography. Thus, black urban history labored under a double burden. Between 1920 and 1950 there were a number of unpublished M.A. theses written by students at Columbia and the University of Chicago.[14] Among scholarly periodicals, however, only the *Journal of Negro History*—hardly an establishment journal at the time—published occasional articles dealing with blacks in cities.[15]

What is more difficult to understand is that the enlarged black migration that began during World War II and reached flood proportions during the 1950s and early 1960s also failed to stimulate historical inquiry. It is ironic that, at a time when black ghettos were expanding at a faster rate than at any previous period in American history, the attentions of historians of black America were riveted not on the origins and significance of the ghetto but on the institution of slavery.[16]

Again, there were exceptions. Emma Lou Thornbrough's *The Negro in Indiana* provided considerable insight into the conditions of Afro-Americans in the cities of one state. August Meier's studies of racial leadership and ideologies exhibited an awareness of differences between various cities. He and David L. Lewis researched the class structure of black Atlanta, and Clarence Bacote contributed an original article on the black politics of that city. Articles by Richard Wade (on Cincinnati's black population before 1830) and Louis Harlan (on New Orleans during Reconstruction) and Leon Litwack's pioneering history of antebellum northern

---

Note the ridiculous early effort (or requirement) to fit urban history into a national political framework. The years 1878 and 1898 are of no particular significance to urban history.

14. See Gilbert Osofsky, *Harlem: The Making of a Ghetto* (New York, 1966), 193, for a listing of these.

15. See Arnett G. Lindsay, "The Economic Condition of Negroes in New York Prior to 1861," *Journal of Negro History*, VI (1921), 190–99; Leo H. Hirsch, Jr., "New York and the Negro, from 1783 to 1854," *ibid.*, XVI (1931), 382–473; and E. Horace Frichett, "The Traditions of the Free Negro in Charleston, South Carolina," *ibid.*, XXV (1940), 139–52.

16. Two valuable surveys are Reynolds Farley, "The Urbanization of Negroes in the United States," *Journal of Social History*, II (1968), 241–58, and Richard Morrill and O. Fred Donaldson, "Geographical Perspectives on the History of Black America," in Robert T. Ernst and Lawrence Hugg (eds.), *Black America: Geographical Perspectives* (New York, 1976), 9–33.

blacks, *North of Slavery*, also provided information on urban conditions.[17] But these studies were quite scattered and certainly represented no historiographical trend. The idea of studying a single black community intensely scarcely existed. So, for example, when Leslie Fishel produced a seminal article on northern black politics in the post–Civil War era, he took a broadly national perspective rather than examining any particular local circumstances that produced black politicians. Not until 1973, with the publication of David Katzman's history of black Detroit in the nineteenth century, would we have a thorough case study of black politics in a northern city during this period.[18] Slavery and abolition dominated black historiography in the 1950s and early 1960s. Not surprisingly, then, one of the first major historical studies to deal specifically with black urban conditions also doubled as a contribution to the literature on the Peculiar Institution—Richard Wade's *Slavery in the Cities*.[19]

The first half of the 1960s was a transition period, however, because a number of scholars were focusing more specifically on aspects of black urban history. Elliott Rudwick's study of the East St. Louis race riot of 1917 and Seth Scheiner's history of Harlem, *Negro Mecca* (1965), were pathbreaking works, as were the comparative demographic studies of Stanley Lieberson and Karl and Alma Taeuber. Sympathy for the Civil Rights Movement played an important role in promoting research in black urban history in the late 1950s and early 1960s. The authors of the first genuinely historical studies of black urban communities were racial liberals, deeply concerned about the plight of blacks, and in turning to the study of black urban history they combined this concern with an interest in ur-

17. Emma Lou Thornbrough, *The Negro in Indiana: A Study of a Minority* (Indianapolis, 1957); August Meier, *Negro Thought in America* (Ann Arbor, 1963); August Meier and David L. Lewis, "History of the Negro Upper Class in Atlanta, Georgia," *Journal of Negro History*, XLIV (1959), 130–39; Clarence Bacote, "The Negro in Atlanta Politics," *Phylon*, XVI (1955), 333–50; Richard C. Wade, "The Negro in Cincinnati, 1800–1830," *Journal of Negro History*, XXXIX (1954), 43–57; Louis Harlan, "Desegregation in New Orleans Public Schools During Reconstruction," *American Historical Review*, LXVII (1962), 663–75; Leon Litwack, *North of Slavery: The Negro in the Free States, 1790–1860* (Chicago, 1961).

18. Leslie Fishel, "The Negro in Northern Politics, 1870–1900," *Mississippi Valley Historical Review*, XLII (1955), 466–89; David M. Katzman, *Before the Ghetto: Black Detroit in the Nineteenth Century* (Urbana, 1973).

19. Richard C. Wade, *Slavery in the Cities: The South, 1820–1860* (New York, 1964).

banization. In 1966 Gilbert Osofsky published his engagingly written volume, *Harlem: The Making of a Ghetto*, and the following year Allan H. Spear's *Black Chicago: The Making of a Negro Ghetto, 1890–1920* appeared.[20] The ghetto riots of the mid- and late 1960s helped make these books scholarly best sellers and intensified interest in the field among researchers.

Osofsky's book commanded the greater attention at the time, although in retrospect it appears less significant. Both in its subject matter and organization, it had more in common with the impressionistic social history of the 1950s than with the emerging, analytical "new social history" of the 1960s and 1970s. Crammed with interesting facts, Osofsky's history of Harlem between 1890 and 1930 focused upon discrimination, the growth of slum conditions, and the "tangle of pathology," whereas Spear's volume, though less sprightly in style, offered a more comprehensive approach that successfully correlated changes in residential patterns, black occupations, organizational activities, and politics. One of Osofsky's most original contributions was his discussion of how Harlem, a "genteel" middle-class white community in 1890, underwent such a rapid change in racial composition, especially the role played by real estate dealers of both races. For a case study of contested neighborhoods and the role of real estate interests, however, Thomas Philpott's comparative study of immigrant and black housing conditions in Chicago now presents a more authoritative account.[21]

In his influential article "The Enduring Ghetto," Osofsky stressed the damaging effects of poverty and segregation on black urbanites. He argued forcefully that "the essential structure and nature of the Negro ghetto have remained remarkably durable since the demise of slavery in the North. There has been an unending and tragic sameness about Negro life in the metropolis over the two centuries."[22] Surely, to prove this contention

20. Elliott Rudwick, *Race Riot at East St. Louis, July 2, 1917* (Carbondale, 1964); Seth Scheiner, *Negro Mecca* (New York, 1965); Stanley Lieberson, *Ethnic Patterns in American Cities* (Glencoe, Ill., 1963); Osofsky, *Harlem*; Allan Spear, *Black Chicago: The Making of a Negro Ghetto, 1890–1920* (Chicago, 1967); Karl and Alma Taeuber, *Negroes in Cities* (Chicago, 1965).

21. Thomas Philpott, *The Slum and the Ghetto: Neighborhood Deterioration and Middle-Class Reform, Chicago, 1880–1930* (New York, 1978).

22. Gilbert Osofsky, "The Enduring Ghetto," *Journal of American History*, LV (1968).

one would have to examine the histories of many black communities, carefully studying a range of variables at different points in time. Osofsky did none of these things, and he relied largely upon information drawn from New York and Philadelphia, two cities that he apparently felt could be used interchangeably. From the very beginning, racism has run like a dark thread through American history, and it has repeatedly scarred the lives of black city dwellers. Yet racial antagonism has varied in intensity over both place and time; its effects have been channeled in distinctive ways in different types of communities; and it has impacted upon various elements of the black community in different ways.

In the nineteenth century in particular, many urban blacks (especially in the North) lived in smaller cities, and conditions in these communities may have varied considerably. Surveying two New Jersey cities during the antebellum period, Spencer Crew found that racism "was more openly expressed in Elizabethtown than in Camden, blacks had fewer social outlets, and black Elizabethtown workers suffered greater competition for jobs from newly arrived immigrant groups." These differences continued into the late nineteenth and, to some extent, the early twentieth century.[23] Even without comparing northern and southern cities, it is evident that there has been considerable variation in levels of discrimination and the quality of life in general for black Americans living in different communities. Although it is not primarily a study in urban history, David Gerber's *Black Ohio and the Color Line, 1865–1915* offers a great deal of information on different types of communities throughout one state. He shows that, especially before 1900, in the North there was considerable variation in discrimination, residential segregation, and the black response to these developments.[24]

The treatment of black students and teachers in the public school systems of northern cities in the early twentieth century illustrates one weakness of the "tragic sameness" theme. All types of conditions existed, from high levels of integration in Boston, New Haven, and Cleveland to segregated or quasi-segregated facilities in Indianapolis, Gary, and most parts

---

23. Spencer Crew, "Black New Jersey Before the Civil War: Two Case Studies," *New Jersey History*, XCIX (1981), 67–86; Crew, "Black Life in Secondary Cities: A Comparative Analysis of the Black Communities of Camden and Elizabethtown, New Jersey, 1860–1920" (Ph.D. dissertation, Rutgers University, 1978), Chaps. 3–4.

24. David Gerber, *Black Ohio and the Color Line, 1865–1915* (Urbana, 1976).

of southern and central Ohio, Indiana, and Illinois. The situation in most cities lay somewhere between these alternatives, with integration limited by both school board policies and, increasingly after 1917, by de facto segregation due to the growth of ghettos.[25] The treatment of black educational professionals in two very similar cities, Cleveland and Pittsburgh, shows the wide variation that could exist at the local level. In the 1920s in Cleveland black teachers increased substantially in numbers, taught at both the high school and elementary school level, and remained fairly well integrated within the system; in 1929 most black teachers there taught in predominantly white schools. In Pittsburgh, however, no black teachers at all were hired between 1881 (when black schools were abolished) and 1933, and until the 1950s black teachers were restricted almost entirely to the predominantly black schools of the ghetto Hill District.[26] Judy J. Mohraz, in comparing Indianapolis, Philadelphia, and Chicago during the 1900 to 1930 period, found significant differences in both the patterns of segregation in schools and in the response of the respective black communities to their particular local circumstances, with Indianapolis blacks at one extreme adopting an accommodationist stance on the school issue and Chicago blacks, at the other extreme, taking a more militant, integrationist position.[27]

From another point of view, the idea of "tragic sameness" makes the study of black urban history too much an exercise in negativity, because it ignores the positive ways in which black urbanites have responded to their environment. Herbert Gutman has explicitly criticized Osofsky for his statement that "the slave heritage, bulwarked by economic conditions, continued into the twentieth century to make family instability a common factor in Negro life." In contrast to Osofsky, he found that in New York in

25. John Daniels, *In Freedom's Birthplace* (Boston, 1914), 185; Warner, *New Haven Negroes*, 174–75; Mame Charlotte Mason, "The Policy of Segregation of the Negro in the Public Schools of Ohio, Indiana, and Illinois" (M.A. thesis, University of Chicago, 1917); Du Bois, *Philadelphia Negro*, 88–89, 349–50; Thornbrough, "Segregation in Indiana during the Klan Era of the 1920s," *Mississippi Valley Historical Review*, XLVII (1961), 600, 604; Michael W. Homel, *Down from Equality: Black Chicagoans and the Public Schools, 1920–41* (Urbana, 1984).

26. Kusmer, *A Ghetto Takes Shape*, 182–83; Ralph Proctor, Jr, "Racial Discrimination Against Black Teachers and Black Professionals in the Pittsburgh Public School System, 1834–1973" (Ph.D. dissertation, University of Pittsburgh, 1979).

27. Judy Jolly Mohraz, *The Separate Problem: Case Studies of Black Education in the North, 1900–1930* (Westport, Conn., 1979).

the early twentieth century, "large numbers of lower-class southern black migrants" were able to adapt "familial and kin ties . . . to life in the emerging ghetto."[28] To speak of the northern black ghettos of the 1920s mainly in negative terms also ignores the advances in occupational status, social freedom, and racial unity that the migrants experienced in the North.[29]

Recently other scholars have more sharply criticized the traditional approach to black urban history that focuses heavily upon the ghetto as slum. James O. and Lois E. Horton's *Black Bostonians: Family Life and Community Struggle in the Antebellum North* is suggestive of the new view. "Poverty and discrimination," the authors say, "did not force disorganization [among black Bostonians], but often actually encouraged organization." The focus of the book is on black cooperation through mutual aid. "Where possible, blacks established institutions to serve their needs, supplementing the family's role and binding black people into a community of shared disadvantage."[30] Albert S. Broussard, in studying San Francisco's black community in the early twentieth century, also stresses the importance of community organizations. Douglas Daniels, in his episodic social history of blacks in the same city, has objected to the type of history which "titillates the reader with the squalor of ghetto life"; he is more concerned with black leaders and variations in life-styles.[31] Lawrence De Graaf, in his seminal article on the Los Angeles black community before 1930, and Daniels imply that economic and social conditions for blacks on the West Coast were generally superior to the rest of the country.[32] Finally, in *Alley Life in Washington*, James Borchert goes a step further, shifting analysis of black urban conditions completely away from social structure, race relations, and black leadership to explore black lower-class

28. Gutman, *Black Family*, 455; Osofsky, *Harlem*, 133–34.

29. Kusmer, *A Ghetto Takes Shape*, Chaps. 9–10; Joe William Trotter, Jr., *Black Milwaukee: The Making of an Industrial Proletariat, 1915–1945* (Urbana, 1985).

30. James Oliver Horton and Lois E. Horton, *Black Bostonians: Family Life and Community Struggle in the Antebellum North* (New York, 1979), 25.

31. Douglas Daniels, *Pioneer Urbanites: A Social History of Black San Francisco* (Philadelphia, 1980), viii; Albert Broussard, "Organizing the Black Community in the San Francisco Bay Area, 1915–1930," *Arizona and the West*, XXIII (1981), 335–54. See also Quintard Taylor, "The Emergence of Black Communities in the Pacific Northwest: 1865–1910," *Journal of Negro History* LXIV (1979), 342–54.

32. Lawrence De Graaf, "The City of Black Angels: Emergence of the Los Angeles Ghetto, 1890–1930," *Pacific Historical Review*, XXXIX (1970), 328–50.

folklore, religion, and family life. In the process he mounts the most concerted attack yet on what he calls the "breakdown thesis." Examining in a highly original manner the communal aspects of black alley dwellers, he argues that "the migrants demonstrated considerable ingenuity in modifying and adapting their rural folk culture to the new environment without, for the most part, either rejecting or dismissing those traditional patterns of behavior." Far from being disordered by their new environment, the migrants "remade" it, "both physically and cognitively, to fit their needs."[33] Borchert's approach thus stands at the polar opposite to the work of Osofsky, as well as to the older sociological tradition.

The past dozen years have witnessed an outpouring of studies dealing with the black urban experience, and they have increased our knowledge from the relatively limited chronological framework of Osofsky and Spear to a time span of almost two centuries. We now have books on Boston and Providence for the antebellum period, as well as Leonard P. Curry's survey, *The Free Black in Urban America, 1800–1850*.[34] David Katzman, Elizabeth Pleck, and Thomas Cox have examined Detroit, Boston, and Topeka for the period between the Civil War and the early twentieth century; August Meier and Elliott Rudwick, Richard W. Thomas, Christopher Wye, and Joe William Trotter, Jr., have extended our knowledge of Detroit, Cleveland, and Milwaukee into the 1930s and early 1940s. Arnold Hirsch's book on Chicago, *Making the Second Ghetto*, is the first significant case study of the emergence of the "new ghettos" that accompanied the black migration of the 1940s and 1950s. Like Philpott, Hirsch focuses exclusively on the issue of housing.[35] Although it is by no means comprehensive,

33. James Borchert, *Alley Life in Washington: Family, Community, Religion, and Folklife in the City, 1850–1970* (Urbana, 1980), xii.

34. Katzman, *Before the Ghetto*; Horton and Horton, *Black Bostonians*; Robert J. Cottrol, *The Afro-Yankees: Providence's Black Community in the Antebellum Era* (Westport, Conn., 1982); Leonard P. Curry, *The Free Black in Urban America, 1800–1850* (Chicago, 1981).

35. Elizabeth Pleck, *Black Migration and Poverty: Boston, 1865–1900* (New York, 1979); Thomas C. Cox, *Blacks in Topeka, Kansas, 1865–1915* (Baton Rouge, 1982); August Meier and Elliott Rudwick, *Black Detroit and the Rise of the UAW* (New York, 1979); Richard W. Thomas, "The Black Urban Experience in Detroit, 1916–1967," in Homer C. Hawkins and Richard W. Thomas (eds.), *Blacks and Chicanos in Urban Michigan* (East Lansing, 1979), 56–80; Christopher Wye, "The New Deal and the Negro Community: Toward a Broader Conceptualization," *Journal of American History*, LIX (1972), 621–39; Wye, "Midwest Ghetto: Patterns of Negro Life and Thought in Cleveland, 1929–1945" (Ph.D. dissertation, Kent State University, 1973); Trotter,

Harold X. Connolly's history of blacks in Brooklyn is one of the few sustained attempts to study the development of a black community over the entire span of the nineteenth and twentieth centuries, and the comparative histories of Theodore Hershberg and others on Philadelphia, John Bodnar, Roger Simon, and Michael Weber on Pittsburgh, and Olivier Zunz on Detroit have also added significantly to our knowledge about black adjustment to urban life.[36]

Despite the great concern with race that dominates southern historical writing, works specifically dealing with black urban conditions in that section have been far fewer in number than those focusing on the North. The early sociological tradition militated against exploring the nature of southern urban life. John Blassingame's *Black New Orleans, 1860–1880* and the studies of Savannah in the late nineteenth century by Blassingame and Robert Perdue broke new ground; and they centered much more on the black community itself than had such previous studies as Constance M. Green's history of race relations in Washington, D.C.[37] Recent studies of the Houston race riot of 1917 and the Tulsa race riot of 1921 by Robert V. Haynes and Scott Ellsworth place their subjects in a broad historical context that helps explain the plight of southern urban blacks during a period of hysteria.[38] A few historians of the South have gone beyond the study of a

---

Black Milwaukee: The Making of an Industrial Proletariat; Dominic J. Copeci, Jr., *The Harlem Riot of 1943* (Philadelphia, 1977); Copeci, *Race Relations in Wartime Detroit: The Sojourner Truth Housing Controversy of 1942* (Philadelphia, 1984); Arnold Hirsch, *Making the Second Ghetto: Race and Housing in Chicago, 1940–1960* (Cambridge, England, 1983); Adrienne L. Jones, "The Central Avenue Community, 1930–1983," in Edward Miggins (ed.), *The People and Neighborhoods of Cleveland* (forthcoming).

36. Harold X. Connolly, *A Ghetto Grows in Brooklyn* (New York, 1977); Theodore Hershberg (ed.), *Philadelphia: Work, Space, Family, and Group Experience in the Nineteenth Century* (New York, 1981)—see especially the article "A Tale of Three Cities," pp. 461–91; John Bodnar, Roger Simon, and Michael Weber, *Lives of Their Own: Blacks, Italians, and Poles in Pittsburgh, 1900–1960* (Urbana, 1982); Olivier Zunz, *The Changing Face of Inequality: Urbanization, Industrial Development, and Immigrants in Detroit, 1880–1920* (Chicago, 1982).

37. John Blassingame, *Black New Orleans, 1860–1880* (Chicago, 1972); Blassingame, "Before the Ghetto: The Making of the Black Community in Savannah, Georgia, 1865–1900," *Journal of Social History*, VI (1973); Robert Perdue, *The Negro in Savannah, 1865–1900* (New York, 1973); Constance M. Green, *The Secret City* (Princeton, 1967). A specialized study of some interest is Arthe Agnes Anthony, "The Negro Creole Community of New Orleans, 1880–1920: An Oral History" (Ph.D. dissertation, University of California/Irvine, 1978).

38. Robert V. Haynes, *A Night of Violence: The Houston Race Riot of 1917* (Baton

single community and have looked at black urban conditions in the region as a whole. In particular, Ira Berlin's incisive history of the free Negro in the antebellum South, Howard Rabinowitz' exhaustive survey *Race Relations in the Urban South, 1865–1890* (which goes well beyond its title in providing information on black communities) and Zane Miller's comparative analysis of data on five southern cities for the 1865 to 1920 period have expanded our knowledge considerably.[39] Strictly speaking, Berlin's book is not urban history, but one of his main points is that the free Negro population was much more urbanized than that of white southerners. In the South and, to a lesser degree, in the North as well at that time, free blacks were among the first Americans to have a genuine commitment to an urban way of life; especially in the Deep South, free Negro culture was essentially forged in cities.

However enlightening particular monographs have been, there has been little attempt at broad generalization in black urban history. The historiography of the field is strikingly different from that of slavery, in which scholars from U. B. Phillips to John Blassingame to Eugene Genovese have repeatedly tried to capture the meaning of involuntary servitude through a holistic approach; small-scale studies of the Peculiar Institution have been few and far between. In marked contrast, the field of black urban history has developed chaotically in a series of community studies that sometimes deal with common historical issues but just as often do not.[40]

Certainly we need many more studies of specific communities, as well as works that deal with particular aspects of black migration and urbaniza-

Rouge, 1976); Scott Ellsworth, *Death in a Promised Land: The Tulsa Race Riot of 1921* (Baton Rouge, 1982). An outstanding study of a northern riot is William Tuttle, Jr., *Race Riot: Chicago in the Red Summer of 1919* (New York, 1970).

39. Ira Berlin, *Slaves Without Masters: The Free Negro in the Antebellum South* (New York, 1974); Howard Rabinowitz, *Race Relations in the Urban South, 1865–1890* (New York, 1978); Zane Miller, "Urban Blacks in the South, 1865–1920: An Analysis of Some Quantitative Data on Richmond, Savannah, New Orleans, Louisville, and Birmingham," in Leo Schnore (ed.), *The New Urban History* (Princeton, 1975), 184–204.

40. Two previous surveys of the literature of the field are Allan Spear, "The Origins of the Urban Ghetto, 1870–1915," in Nathan I. Huggins, *et al.* (eds.), *Key Issues in the Afro-American Experience* (New York, 1971), II, 153–66, and Zane L. Miller, "The Black Experience in the Modern American City," in Raymond Mohl and James Richardson (eds.), *The Urban Experience* (Belmont, Cal., 1973), 44–60. See also Hollis Lynch (ed.), *The Black Urban Condition* (New York, 1973).

tion. Historians should, however, resist the tendency to focus on too narrow a time period or subject matter. Badly needed are more studies that either deal comprehensively with many aspects of black urban life or, if they cannot be so comprehensive, cover a very substantial time period or compare a number of different cities over a shorter time period. There is a danger in generalizing from too limited a chronological framework or from only a single community. Scholars working in this area have recently become more aware of the need to place the history of a particular community in a larger context by comparing it with other communities. They are less prone to fall into the trap of claiming that the city they are studying is representative in every respect. Going a step further, however, we need to begin to compare and contrast blacks in a variety of cities in a more systematic way—to move beyond the community studies format, in other words.

The literature of black urban history is extremely diverse in scope, subject matter, and analytical depth. Even so, is there a way of ordering the information derived from these various histories so that, in a preliminary fashion, we can begin the process of creating a theoretical foundation for future work in the field? Such an overall theoretical framework, I think, must be based on a recognition that there are three general forces that have shaped the black urban experience:

(1) *External forces.* These refer very generally to the attitude of whites toward blacks, and more particularly to the manner in which the behavior of whites impinges upon blacks. The degree of white hostility toward blacks, levels and types of discrimination, the limits that the white population sets to acceptable racial contact, the existence or lack of violence directed against blacks—all these count as external forces.

(2) *Internal forces.* These refer to the ways in which black urban dwellers have responded to their circumstances, either through the retention or creation of cultural values or institutions that are indigenous to the black community. Religious institutions, folk culture, and distinctive family patterns are examples of internal forces at work in the black community; so too are secular institutions of various sorts and black-based businesses. In addition, the attitude of blacks toward whites, and the behavior that results from such attitudes, also falls under the heading of internal forces.

(3) *Structural forces.* These refer to fundamentally nonracial forces at

work in the urban system that affect the black community in some manner. The type and quantity of various housing stocks, the kind of transportation and communication systems available in a particular city, the general economic structure of a metropolis (commercial, manufacturing, etc.), and numerous other aspects of urban society can, at any given time, impinge upon black urban dwellers in distinctive ways.

In examining the influence of these factors, it is essential to recognize that none of them, under most circumstances, operates completely independently of the other two. External forces or pressures from the white population (or a segment of it) can cause black organizations, leadership, even family patterns, perhaps, to undergo change. There was a tendency, for example, for black leadership in northern cities to shift in an accommodationist direction in the early twentieth century, as segregation and white hostility generally became more common. Conversely, the more militant stance of both the New Negro leaders and the Garveyites of the post–World War I era illustrates how internal factors can, to some extent, resist external threats even when the latter are quite substantial—for clearly there was no discernible decline in the racism of white city dwellers in the 1920s. But the much enhanced size of the black population plus the increasingly frequent reliance of black professionals (who made up most of the New Negro group) upon a predominantly black clientele (thereby emancipating them from white influence to a degree) created the basis for a more militant leadership in fighting racism.[41]

Before returning to a discussion of internal forces in the black community, I want to stress the significance of structural factors, because few scholars have recognized their importance. The lack of development of an independent black theatrical tradition in urban America (especially Harlem) during the first thirty years of the twentieth century is an interesting case. "The demise of the Black theater during the early years of the century," sociologist Arthur Paris argues, "was not due to any cultural rejection by the Black bourgeoisie or an abdication of its economic prerogatives nor to any treason on the part of Black artists and intellectuals. Doubtless there was some of that, but it made no difference." The failure was exacerbated, indirectly, by racial discrimination (in the sense that few blacks had either the capital to establish theaters or even the price of a

41. See, for example, Kusmer, *A Ghetto Takes Shape*, Chaps. 6, 8, and 11, and Tuttle, *Race Riot*, on the militant "New Negro."

ticket to go to one), but a major proximate cause was the centralization and standardization of theatrical productions, along with a vast increase in their cost and the growth of the movies, all of which "operated to push live entertainment out of Harlem altogether." Thus "the failure of an incipient Black live dramatic tradition is a particular instance of a general decline in live theater that occurred after the turn of the century."[42]

At any given time the effect of structural forces may be great or small, depending upon the relative strength of internal or external forces. One example is the development of segregated streetcars in the South. As Howard Rabinowitz points out, the lack of segregation in these accommodations in the 1870s and 1880s was not necessarily due to relatively liberalized racial attitudes of whites (although that may have been a factor) as much as it was a result of constrictions inherent in the technology of transportation.[43] Segregation was difficult because it required a separate horse and car for blacks or the opening of a part of the small, already crowded cars that whites used. Steam-driven or electric trolleys, introduced at the end of the 1880s or during the 1890s, either had two cars or a single commodious compartment. In both cases, segregation was easier. Rising racism at the turn of the century was obviously a cause of segregation on trolleys, but the new technology facilitated this. The internal forces of the black communities of the South, subjected increasingly to disfranchisement and terrorism after 1900, were not able to overcome the combination of structural and external forces arrayed against them. In a number of cities blacks boycotted streetcars when segregated cars were introduced in the early 1900s, but in every instance their efforts failed.[44] On the other hand, one might argue that the success of the Montgomery bus boycott in the 1950s, while due primarily to the persistence of a black community united under the leadership of Martin Luther King, Jr., was also facilitated by the increasing use of a new and more democratic form of transportation in the South—the automobile, which made car-pooling an alternative to riding the buses.

Perhaps the most significant example of the effect of structural forces,

42. Arthur Paris, "Cruse and the Crisis in Black Culture: The Case of the Theater, 1900–1930," *Journal of Ethnic Studies*, V (n.d.), 51–68.

43. Rabinowitz, *Race Relations*, 192–93.

44. August Meier and Elliott M. Rudwick, "The Boycott Movement Against Jim Crow Streetcars in the South, 1900–1906," *Journal of American History*, LV (1969), 756–75.

however, is in the area of residential segregation. The historical development of residential segregation of black Americans is a more complex process than usually recognized, because in studying single communities, historians have ignored the impact of divergences in urban structure on the growth of ghettoization.

It is becoming increasingly evident that the focus in the early literature on the World War I period is inadequate in explaining the development of black segregation in cities. The ghettos of the 1920s represented a culminating stage in a process long under way. Even in the middle of the nineteenth century, blacks were more segregated than white immigrant groups in American cities. At that time, however, the differences were not nearly as great as they later would become, and certainly no equivalent of the modern ghetto existed. This situation, in most instances, had little to do with racial attitudes; white hostility produced antiblack riots and growing job discrimination against blacks in the decades before the Civil War.[45] Fundamentally, it was the nature of the nineteenth-century city that inhibited ghettoization. Lack of adequate transportation systems, mixed patterns of land use, the rapid growth of cities, and the decentralization of work and residence led to the dispersal of both immigrant and black populations at the time. This was true of cities in both the North and the South. Segregation levels in the South were particularly low, however, due to the greater propensity of southern free Negroes to live in alleys or shacks close to the homes of whites whom they served as domestics.[46] In the North during the Civil War and Reconstruction period blacks tended to live in particular sections of cities, but were seldom highly segregated. In 1860 in Brooklyn, blacks "still lived scattered about," while in Boston, even in areas where the black population was most concentrated, "blacks and whites lived adjacent to one another or shared the same dwellings." In 1875, in Kansas City, "the making of the ghetto did not seem to be an imminent prospect," and most blacks "resided in areas that were only one-eighth black."[47]

By the eve of the Great Migration a considerable change had occurred, and at least in the major northern industrial centers this period witnessed

45. Hershberg (ed.), *Philadelphia*, 368–91; Horton and Horton, *Black Bostonians*.
46. Berlin, *Slaves Without Masters*, 253–58; Hershberg (ed.), *Philadelphia*, 468–70; Sam B. Warner and Colin Burke, "Cultural Change and the Ghetto," *Journal of Contemporary History*, IV (1969), 173–87; Kusmer, *A Ghetto Takes Shape*, 12–13.
47. Horton and Horton, *Black Bostonians*, 3; Connolly, *A Ghetto Grows in Brooklyn*, 7–8; Cox, *Blacks in Topeka*, 33–34.

the formative development of the modern black ghetto. In 1913 George Edmund Haynes found much evidence of this. "New York has its 'San Juan Hill' in the West Sixties, and its Harlem district of over 35,000 within about eighteen city blocks; Philadelphia has its Seventh Ward, Chicago its State Street, Washington its North West neighborhood, and Baltimore its Druid Hill Avenue."[48] A closer examination of residential patterns at this time, however, indicates that this trend was not as uniform as Haynes implied. In Philadelphia, for example, a contemporary noted that between 1890 and 1910 "a very large concentrated nucleus" of blacks had developed in the seventh and thirtieth wards, but that a large fraction of the black population still lived outside this area, scattered over two-thirds of the city. In Cleveland, on the other hand, there were far fewer Negroes living outside the main area of black settlement, but this nucleus was smaller and less well defined prior to the Great Migration. A similar situation prevailed in Boston. In 1914 about 40 percent of the city's Afro-Americans lived within an area one mile wide and one and one-quarter miles long. Within this district, however, blacks still constituted only a third of the population and only a few streets were all-black. Only Chicago had a sharply defined black belt before 1900.[49]

In the South, as two recent studies have shown, segregation also proceeded apace in the late nineteenth century.[50] Nevertheless, there were differences between southern cities and the large northern metropolises at the turn of the century. In the South, the enclaves of blacks were greater in number in any given city and more dispersed. Furthermore, there were substantially more blacks living outside these clusters in southern cities than in the large northern urban areas, although Philadelphia may be a partial exception. Finally, the older, slow-growing southern cities—such as New Orleans, Charleston, and Mobile—retained the traditional pattern of racial intermingling in residency much longer than did New South cities like Atlanta.[51] Unfortunately, specific studies of residential change in southern cities in the twentieth century have not been completed, so it is

48. Haynes, "Conditions Among Negroes," 109.

49. John Emlen, "The Movement for the Betterment of the Negro in Philadelphia," *Annals of the American Academy of Political and Social Science*, XLIX (1913), 84; Daniels, *In Freedom's Birthplace*, 146–47; Pleck, *Black Migration*, 79–80; Philpott, *The Slum and the Ghetto*, 119; Kusmer, *A Ghetto Takes Shape*, 41–43.

50. Rabinowitz, *Race Relations*, 97–116; John Kellogg, "Negro Urban Clusters in the Postbellum South," *Geographical Review*, LXVII (1977), 310–21.

51. Charles S. Jonson, *Patterns of Negro Segregation* (New York, 1943), Chap. 1;

difficult to make a definitive statement. What is clear is that differences in urban structure did influence the rate of ghettoization.

This is equally true of the North, but scholars have failed to recognize the importance of structural factors in the development of segregation in that section because they have focused too exclusively on the largest urban areas, especially Chicago and New York. To gain a fuller understanding of the northern situation, I computed indexes of dissimilarity (a basic measurement of segregation, ranging from 0 to 100) for twenty-nine northern and western cities for the years 1870, 1890, 1910, and 1920. In 1870, the index for all of the cities, with the exception of Chicago, indicated a low or, at most, moderate amount of clustering among the black population. During the next forty years segregation increased everywhere, but in 1910 there were still ten cities with indexes under 40 and only five major industrial centers had indexes high enough (60 to 75) to denote the existence of a nascent black belt. Throughout the entire period, Chicago was far from being typical (as it traditionally has been portrayed); in fact, it had the highest level of segregation of any city in the North.[52]

Prior to World War I—and even, to an extent, afterwards—the level of segregation of blacks in a particular city was closely related to the community's urban structure. Segregation was highest in the fully developed large industrial centers of the North and lowest in the languishing gulf port cities of the South. The variations between these two extremes did not always divide along North/South lines, however. Atlanta had more in common with Philadelphia than with Mobile. On the other hand, there were a number of smaller or medium-sized northern cities, such as Columbus, Ohio, and Indianapolis and Evansville, Indiana, that had relatively low levels of segregation in housing compared to Chicago or Detroit. Finally, the relatively low degree of segregation in such cities as Minneapolis, Denver, Milwaukee, and especially Los Angeles in the early twentieth century resulted from an entirely different situation. These cities, though moderate in size, were still in a state of dynamic growth. There, rapid population

---

Taeuber and Taeuber, *Negroes in Cities*, 189–93. Valuable work in progress on Houston's black community in the early twentieth century is being done by Virginia Bernhard and Barbara Day, of the University of St. Thomas.

52. Kenneth L. Kusmer, "The Origins of Black Ghettos in the North, 1870–1930: A Study in Comparative History" (Paper presented at the University of Chicago Social History Workshop, 1974), 12–14.

turnover, unstable housing markets, and less-developed transportation systems retarded segregation among all groups, including blacks.[53]

Black migration, like the process of ghettoization, has also been much more complex than one would realize by looking only at a few major industrial centers during the World War I period. Black migration northward began before the Civil War; after the war there was a substantial influx of freed slaves into southern, not northern, cities. One result, in Atlanta, was the emergence of ghettoized areas much earlier than in most other southern cities.[54] As Nell Painter has made clear in her book *The Exodusters* (1977), the main thrust of black migration in the late 1870s was westward, not to either the North or South. The impact on the black community of Topeka at that time was no less dramatic than the later Great Migration would be on Chicago; the black population of Topeka increased 400 percent between 1878 and 1880.[55] A lesser influx of blacks into both northern and southern cities in the 1890s preceded the World War I migration. On the other hand, as Richard Thomas has pointed out, there was also a very intense migration cityward during 1924/25, when immigration from abroad declined dramatically following the passage of the National Origins Act.[56] Finally, it must be mentioned that some cities—such as Boston—never were affected much by the Great Migration; migration to Boston occurred much more gradually over a long time period.

By focusing almost entirely upon the Great Migration to a few large northern cities during World War I, conservative theorists have been able to advance the "last of the immigrants" theory as a plausible explanation for retarded black occupational and economic development in the twentieth century. The black migration during and after World Wars I and II, argued one sociologist, "poured so large a Negro population into the cities, and especially the large cities, over so short a period of time that it

53. *Ibid.*, passim; De Graaf, "City of Black Angels," 328–29; Harris, *Negro Population in Minneapolis*, 13–14; Trotter, *Black Milwaukee*, 23–24.

54. Jerry J. Thornberry, "The Development of Black Atlanta, 1865–1885" (Ph.D. dissertation, University of Maryland, 1977), Chap. 2.

55. Nell Irvin Painter, *Exodusters: Black Migration to Kansas after Reconstruction* (New York, 1977); Cox, *Blacks in Topeka*, 42.

56. Richard W. Thomas, "From Peasant to Proletarian: The Formation and Organization of the Black Industrial Working Class in Detroit, 1915–1945" (Ph.D. dissertation, University of Michigan, 1976), 6–7.

made the Negro immigratory stream relatively unassimilable—economically, socially, and politically."[57] Such a theory not only fails to understand the impact of long-term discrimination; it is also based upon a totally unhistorical conception of the migration process.

If closer analysis of segregation patterns and migration patterns indicates less clear differentiation between North and South, much the same can be said for the internal nature of black communities during the period since the Civil War. In her study of Boston in the late nineteenth century, Elizabeth Pleck notes that about half of the black migrants who came there from Virginia had already lived in small cities. She argues that the migrants' higher levels of education and skills, as well as their previous experience with urban conditions, made their adjustment to the northern city smoother than previously believed.[58] This phenomenon was not limited to the late nineteenth century. The classic migration of black peasants to urban centers did occur, but it probably was greatest during the 1916 to 1919 period. A survey of black migrants to Philadelphia in the mid-1920s indicates that 40 percent came from cities over 10,000 in population, and 28 percent from cities of more than 50,000. Furthermore, these migrants were not exclusively the sharecroppers of legend. Over 40 percent of the migrants who came from communities of less than 2,500 had been employed at nonagricultural work; they were drivers, craftsmen, and laborers who worked both in the fields and in nearby towns and villages.[59]

In a similar approach to black migration, Peter Gottlieb also stresses continuity between life in the South and in the northern city, focusing on the first three decades of the twentieth century. Gottlieb plays down the importance of the Great Migration as a watershed. Following the lead of Clyde Kiser's classic study *Sea Island to City*, he finds that southern blacks were increasingly taking part in nonagricultural work through seasonal migration. In an analysis that meshes well with the work of Paul Worth-

57. Philip Hauser, "Demographic Factors in the Integration of the Negro," in Talcott Parsons and Kenneth B. Clarke (eds.), *The Negro American* (New York, 1967), 87. See also Irving Kristol, "The Negro of Today Is Like the Immigrant of Yesterday," in Peter Rose (ed.), *Nation of Nations* (New York, 1972), 37–45; and Nathan Glazer, "Blacks and Ethnic Groups: The Difference, and the Political Difference It Makes," in Huggins, *et al.* (eds.), *Key Issues*, II, 202–203.

58. Pleck, *Black Migration*, IX, 202–203.

59. Fredric Miller, "The Black Migration to Philadelphia: A 1924 Profile," *Pennsylvania Magazine of History and Biography*, CVIII (1984), 315–50.

man and James Green, Gottlieb argues that black southerners were already becoming involved in industrialism, as well as in the migration process, before they began to come north in large numbers in 1916. Through extensive interviews with former migrants to Pittsburgh, Gottlieb discovered that migration often occurred in stages, that in the 1920s the migrants returned frequently to the South for vacations or holidays, and that their ties to family members or churches in the South remained strong.[60]

There is another sense in which the work experience of black migrants may not have been such a dramatic change as we have previously believed. The wages were higher than in the South, and there was unquestionably a breakthrough into industrial jobs in the North during World War I. But as Joe Trotter shows in his forthcoming study of black industrial workers in Milwaukee, the industrial jobs blacks were offered often involved little skill. Black men entered the industrial system at the bottom, doing the hot and dirty work in the steel mills, enduring dangerous fumes and chemicals in the tanneries, and wading through the blood of slaughtered animals in the packing houses.[61]

By far the most provocative study emphasizing the continuity between South and North in the new urban environment is James Borchert's *Alley Life in Washington*, which despite its subtitle deals mostly with the period between 1865 and 1930. Borchert shows convincingly how alley environments intensified the level of communal involvement among black migrants, helping to perpetuate religious rituals and folklore, as well as small-scale mutual benefit societies. In both text and photographs, he has helped us to see beyond the stereotypes of past social investigators—as well as some historians—to the humanistic reality of the lives of the men, women, and children who lived in these environments.[62]

One can only be sympathetic to the concerns of those scholars who wish to give greater emphasis to the internal values of the black community. Yet it is impossible to wholeheartedly agree with the approach or conclusions of some of them. Pleck claims, for example, that southern mi-

---

60. Peter Gottlieb, "Black Migrants and Jobs: The New Black Worker in Pittsburgh, 1916–1930," *Western Pennsylvania Historical Magazine*, LXI (1978), 3–5; Kiser, *Sea Island to City*; Paul Worthman and James Green, "Black Workers in the New South, 1865–1915," in Huggins, *et al.* (eds.), *Key Issues*, II, 47–69.
61. Trotter, *Black Milwaukee: The Making of an Industrial Proletariat*, Chap. 2.
62. Borchert, *Alley Life in Washington*.

grants set themselves apart and managed to avoid "northern" culture. Yet she presents data on organizations that, with the single exception of one black church, seem to indicate the exact opposite—that southern and northern-born Negroes were well "integrated" in most institutions in Boston's black community. Pleck's argument that intermarriage with whites was higher among northern (especially Massachusetts-born) blacks is also dubious when one considers the evidence. During the 1870s, twice as many black menial workers were likely to be married to whites as were grooms not in menial occupations, and breakdown of this data by regional background does not alter the occupational correlation. It appears, then, that "southernness" is actually a spurious variable and that the real determining factor in intermarriage rates was class or occupation.[63]

Gottlieb's analysis is valuable and presents a new, much needed perspective on black migration. Yet as he himself indicates—indeed, or how else could he have interviewed them—these migrants did eventually choose the new urban environment over their former life-style, whatever demurrers they may have had along the way. Furthermore, it remains to be proven whether the type of movement between North and South indicated by Gottlieb was as typical of black newcomers to Detroit and Chicago as it was of those who came to Pittsburgh, which had a greater proximity to the migrants' southern homeland than did many other northern cities. (Much depends, it seems to me, on where the migrant stream to northern cities came from. In Chicago and Detroit, there was a greater number from the Deep South, and it may have been less feasible for migrants to return there.) Conclusions in this area must await further research on a variety of communities.

For all his originality, it is also difficult to accept some of Borchert's conclusions at face value. There is truth in his argument that there is more to the history of black crime than the reports of contemporary middle-class investigators reveal: prostitution, bootlegging, and gambling gave employment to many, and the black poor—shut out of many legitimate occupations—did not necessarily view such activities negatively. But Borchert veers dangerously close to romanticizing the poor when he says that crap games and numbers were "more of a recreational and communal activity

63. Pleck, *Black Migration*, 115; see the footnote, 115n–116n, which presents data that seem to invalidate the conclusions reached in the text.

than a way to win money."[64] As for prostitution and bootlegging, these activities usually involved violence as a matter of course, but Borchert does not focus on this.[65] Borchert also claims that "formal education was often expendable" for alley dwellers and that "alley children [and, by implication, other alley residents] were more comfortable with oral than with written or literary culture."[66] He does not provide statistics on school attendance that would help to prove this, however. Timothy Smith has shown that blacks at the turn of the century kept their children in school longer than most immigrants did, so either the alley dwellers' views were unique among blacks or there is a flaw in Borchert's analysis.[67]

While there is no doubt that urban folk culture is an interesting and little-studied aspect of black urban history, I think it would be a mistake to identify the retention of cultural values totally with that aspect of black society or to claim that "the schools and the media" were somehow subversive of independent black culture and thought.[68] The struggle of black urbanites for literacy (often in the face of segregated or underfinanced schools) has been too great, and the uses of that literacy too diverse, for such judgments to be valid.[69] Overemphasis on oral traditions in urban society may, for example, lead historians to neglect the often important role that black newspapers have played in both shaping and reflecting values in black communities. In 1971, in a pioneering article that surveyed the development of the black press through the 1920s, Nell Painter stated that "no doubt there was tremendous room for improvement in Black journalism during the first hundred years, but its critics never denied the

64. Borchert, *Alley Life in Washington*, 187. For a valuable comparative perspective on "ethnic specialization" in crime, see Mark Haller, "Organized Crime in Urban Society: Chicago in the Twentieth Century," *Journal of Social History*, V (1971–72), 217–23.

65. See the forthcoming book on crime and the Philadelphia black community between the Civil War and World War I, by Roger Lane.

66. Borchert, *Alley Life in Washington*, 146, 150.

67. Timothy Smith, "Native Blacks and Foreign Whites: Varying Responses to Educational Opportunity in America, 1880–1950," *Perspectives in American History*, VI (1972), 309–36.

68. Borchert, *Alley Life in Washington*, 165.

69. It is significant, perhaps, that Carter G. Woodson, in the very first article ever published in black urban history, made the black quest for, and appreciation of, formal education one of the key points in his discussion of Cincinnati's antebellum black community. See Woodson, "The Negroes of Cincinnati," 17–20.

need for 'Race' papers nor the irreplaceable service the Black press had rendered in publicizing" the activities and accomplishments, as well as the oppression, of Afro-Americans.[70]

Considering the rather modest size of many black communities in the late nineteenth century, the number of black newspapers that sprang up was considerable; it is one indication of how important the printed word was to these black communities. Like the black church, newspapers served a purpose that was often much larger in scope than that of parallel white institutions. According to one historian, the many black newspapers of the Reconstruction era were significant "in an effort to achieve certain political ends, promote harmony and good will between whites and blacks, instruct and educate the race, and defend the newly acquired rights of black Americans." By 1890, says a historian who surveyed newspapers after Reconstruction, the black press had become "an indispensable part of the developing black community."[71] Other studies indicate that the black press in the twentieth century has been invaluable as a force for racial advancement and as "the focal point of every controversy and every concern of black people."[72] Unfortunately, however, there has been too little emphasis on the local impact of these newspapers and their relationship to the black community. There are good biographies of some important black journalists and editors: Robert S. Abbott, Robert L. Vann, T. Thomas Fortune, and William Monroe Trotter.[73] A very few scholars have begun exploring the social content of these papers (instead of focusing solely on politics).[74] What is missing, however, are studies of how the

70. Nell Irvin Painter, "Black Journalism, the First Hundred Years," *Harvard Journal of Afro-American Affairs*, II (1971), 30–42 (quote p. 42).

71. Allen W. Jones, "The Black Press in the 'New South': Jesse C. Duke's Struggle for Justice and Equality," *Journal of Negro History*, LIV (1979), 215; Martin E. Dann (ed.), *The Black Press, 1877–1890: The Quest for National Identity* (New York, 1971), 14.

72. Dann (ed.), *The Black Press*, 8. See Charlotte G. O'Kelly, "Black Newspapers and the Black Protest Movement: Their Historical Relationship, 1927–1945," *Journal of Negro History*, LXIII (1982), 1–14, which cites many obscure master's theses dealing with the black press. On the general importance of literacy in the black community, see Horton and Horton, *Black Bostonians*, 13, and Cox, *Blacks in Topeka*, 165, which question the idea that black papers were read only by the middle class.

73. Roy Ottley, *The Lonely Warrior* (Chicago, 1955); Andrew Buni, *Robert L. Vann of the Pittsburgh Courier* (Pittsburgh, 1974); Emma Lou Thornbrough, *T. Thomas Fortune* (Chicago, 1972); Stephen R. Fox, *The Guardian of Boston: William Monroe Trotter* (New York, 1971).

74. See, for example, Bess Beatty, "Black Perspectives of American Women: The View from Black Newspapers, 1865–1900," *Maryland Historian*, IX (1978), 39–50.

black newspaper has functioned historically as a communication device in the urban context.

"Rather than succumbing to mainstream values as propagated by the schools and the media," says Borchert in his study of the Washington alley dwellers, "they largely rejected the former and used only those elements of the latter that supported their own worldview."[75] This may have been true of the alley dwellers, but whether this thesis applies equally well to black urban society as a whole, especially in the twentieth century, is open to question. Structural factors (their enclosed space) may have played an important role in reinforcing communal aspects of life in the alley dwellings. But in most cities few blacks lived in such dwellings, and even in Washington, progressively fewer have lived there during the twentieth century. What about the tenements and row houses that dominated the landscape of other black communities? Studies similar to Borchert's, dealing with different cities, will be necessary to test the hypothesis.

At present, the perspective of Ira Berlin and Lawrence Levine seems more persuasive. While stressing the continuity of black cultural values in urban society, they also note that such values gradually evolve and develop ambiguities. Levine, for example, connects the emergence of the blues with "the rise of a more personalized, individual-oriented ethos among Negroes at the turn of the century." The blues had much in common with West African musical traditions, "with its call and response pattern, its polyrhythmic effects, and its methods of vocal production," but it was more than just a continuation of that tradition under new circumstances. And the rise of a new *mentalité* among blacks, leading to the modification of cultural forms, was closely related to the increasing urbanization of the black population after 1900.[76]

We need very much to consider, on their own terms, the internal values or forces at work in the black community. As Robert L. Harris has recently

75. Borchert, *Alley Life in Washington*, 165. The contrast between Borchert's book and another recent volume, Philpott's *The Slum and the Ghetto*, is instructive. Philpott takes the traditional view of impoverished areas as debilitating slum environments. His book could have been improved by use of the kind of anthropological approach utilized by Borchert, but it remains to be seen whether tenements or the "vertical ghettos" of modern housing projects support communal forms as well as Borchert suggests the alley dwellings did.

76. Berlin, *Slaves Without Masters*, 78; Lawrence Levine, *Black Culture and Black Consciousness: Afro-American Folk Thought from Slavery to Freedom* (New York, 1977), 223–24.

said, mature scholarship in Afro-American history in general now requires "a conceptualization whose starting point is the black population."[77] But we must also recognize that external or structural forces can influence, modify, delimit or, sometimes, reinforce those internal aspects. There seems to be a fear that a recognition of the complexity of forces at work in shaping the black community will lead to a reversion to the traditional sociological point of view. But this need not be true. The history of the black family in urban America is a case in point. There can be little doubt that the black family was undergoing modification at the beginning of the twentieth century, adopting a more augmented and extended family style to meet the difficult circumstances of urban life. But as August Meier and Elliott Rudwick have stated, "while it is customary to look upon the high incidence of such households as a sign of social disorganization among lower-class Negroes, there is another way to view the matter. The matri-focal family pattern can be regarded as a stabilizing influence in the lives of its members, as a creative response to the circumstances under which black people found themselves in the urban ghetto."[78]

Internal forces at work in the black community do not necessarily become more attenuated as time passes. Quite the opposite, I would argue that in many ways internal factors become *more* significant as time passes. Nowhere is this more evident than in the history of black urban politics. At the end of the nineteenth century, the black population of northern cities was usually too small to exercise much influence at the local level, although a few strategically placed black legislators were able to assist themselves, if not their black constituents. The replacement of the convention system by the direct primary at the turn of the century eliminated many of these black politicians.[79] By 1915, however, migration northward and increasing residential segregation in major industrial centers created a base for the beginning of modern black urban politics in the North. These early black politicians were hardly independent, however. They needed

77. Robert L. Harris, "Coming of Age: The Transformation of Afro-American Historiography," *Journal of Negro History*, LXVII (1982), 118.

78. Gutman, *Black Family*, 432–60; August Meier and Elliott Rudwick, *From Plantation to Ghetto* (Rev. ed.; New York, 1976), 251.

79. See, for example, Michael L. Goldstein, "Preface to the Rise of Booker T. Washington: A View from New York City of the Demise of Independent Black Politics, 1889–1902," *Journal of Negro History*, LXII (1977), 81–99; Kusmer, *A Ghetto Takes Shape*, Chap. 6.

support from white politicos as well as from the black electorate, especially if they wished to control the small amount of patronage allotted the black community.

As Martin Kilson has pointed out, a type of patron-client relationship developed between the white (usually Republican) party leaders and black councilmen and ward heelers.[80] As early as the end of the 1920s, however, the growth of the ghetto made possible a degree of black political independence at the local level.[81] (Black Republicans in Chicago were able to exercise considerable influence even before the 1920s, because of their greater cohesiveness and numbers, but also because white mayors and the white-dominated machine were willing to cooperate with blacks for their mutual benefit. One result was that the black faction in the Chicago Republican party was particularly strong in resisting the New Deal tide of the 1930s.)[82] The post-1940 migration further enhanced this trend toward black independence, although it occurred within a context of white domination at the top of the political structure. By the 1970s, of course, the growing strength of the black electorate had resulted in the election of a number of black mayors. Clearly, as the twentieth century has progressed, black urban politics has become increasingly emancipated from local white "machines." Potentially, at least, such a system of politics is much more responsive to the needs and aspirations of the black community than what had been the case half a century ago.

If we look at the black urban church, on the other hand, we see the decline of external influences (from whites) and the emergence of internal

80. Martin Kilson, "Political Change in the Negro Ghetto, 1900–1940s," in Huggins et al. (eds.), Key Issues, II, 167–85. For general discussion, see David A. Gerber, "Politics of Limited Options: Northern Black Politics and the Problem of Change and Continuity in Race Relations Historiography," Journal of Social History, XIV (1980), 235–55.

81. Kusmer, A Ghetto Takes Shape, 269–74; Osofsky, Harlem, 159–78.

82. Harold Gosnell, Negro Politicians: The Rise of Negro Politics in Chicago (Chicago, 1935), should be supplemented by two recent dissertations: Charles Russell Branham, "The Transformation of Black Political Leadership in Chicago, 1864–1942" (Ph.D. dissertation, University of Chicago, 1981), and Christopher Robert Reed, "A Study of Black Politics and Protest in Depression-Decade Chicago: 1930–1939" (Ph.D. dissertation, Kent State University, 1982). Two outstanding case studies of black politics and race relations at the local level are Mark Naison, Communists in Harlem During the Depression (Urbana, 1983), and Paul Kleppner, Chicago Divided: The Making of a Black Mayor (DeKalb, 1985), which surveys the 1955–1983 period.

control at a much earlier stage; still, the gradual progression from external to internal has much in common with later developments in the political realm. Albert Raboteau and Howard Rabinowitz have described well the gradual emergence of independent black religious institutions in the South, both during the slavery era and immediately following emancipation. (The subject is not limited to urban history, but I am referring to it here in the urban context.) At the early stage, as Raboteau points out, black churches were not completely independent of whites, but there was a growing autonomy despite the existence of the slave system, which made any black independent activity suspect to whites.[83] A similar transition occurred somewhat earlier in the North. Robert Cottrol sees aspects of the first black church in Providence, Rhode Island, established in 1819, as representing "both the older paternalism of the more enlightened master as well as early nineteenth century stirrings of black consciousness." Of the $2,200 needed to found the church, almost two-thirds came from whites, and during the early years white ministers conducted services in the church and taught the Sunday school.[84] The development of black churches in Boston was similar, and scholars have seen it as reflecting a response both to discrimination and to "the needs for self-expression which originated in the culture and experience of the black community."[85] By the late nineteenth century, and in many cases much earlier, the black church in both northern and southern cities had emerged as the most influential institution in the black community, far more independent from white control than the often weak secular institutions of that era.[86]

In exploring these and other aspects of the development of black urban life, there is a continuing need to focus on the role of black women. The

83. Albert Raboteau, *Slave Religion: The "Invisible Institution" in the Antebellum South* (New York, 1978); Rabinowitz, *Race Relations*, Chap. 9; Thornberry, "Development of Black Atlanta," Chap. 3.

84. Cottrol, *Afro-Yankees*, 57–59, 60.

85. Horton and Horton, *Black Bostonians*, 39; George Levesque, "Inherent Reformers—Inherited Orthodoxy: Black Baptists in Boston, 1800–1873," *Journal of Negro History*, LX (1975), 498–99.

86. There has been a tendency to focus on the larger mainstream churches (perhaps because more records are available) and to avoid the small storefront Baptist and Spiritualist churches that were to become so numerous during the Great Migration era. For a positive view of these latter institutions on the lives of migrants, see Kenneth Norman Miles, "Home at Last: Urbanization of Black Migrants in Detroit, 1916–1929" (Ph.D. dissertation, University of Michigan, 1978), Chap. 6.

pioneering scholarship of Gerda Lerner has brought to our attention the underestimated significance of black women's clubs to the history of black communities, especially in the social welfare area, and Adrienne Jones's recently completed dissertation on Jane Edna Hunter, the founder of the Phillis Wheatley Association in Cleveland, shows the importance of one black woman in a particular community. Janice Sumler-Lewis has described the remarkable women of the Forten-Purvis families of antebellum Philadelphia, who obviated the demands of traditional female roles to actively take part in the antislavery crusade and the early struggle for black equality.[87] But too often the role of women in black urban history is neglected, or restricted to a discussion of the black family. Particularly annoying is the continual failure of historians of particular black communities to analyze the history of black female occupations and to compare black women in this regard with their native-white and immigrant counterparts.

For too long the field of black urban studies was dominated by an almost exclusive concern for the effects of the external forces of racism and discrimination on black city dwellers. Sensing the biased and incomplete picture resulting from such an approach, historians recently have begun to stress the internal values, institutions, and organizations of the black community that have assisted it in surviving long decades of racial animosity. Certainly, as a research strategy, there is nothing wrong with focusing on a particular internal aspect of black urban life and excluding race relations from the analysis. But in searching for a comprehensive understanding, either of a single black community or of the Afro-American urban experience in general, the negative and delimiting effects of white racial attitudes and racial discrimination are too integral to the story to be omitted from the conceptual scheme. In two areas especially, the economic structure and the educational system, the impact of racial discrimination has been profound, with reverberations through many aspects of black urban life.[88] To

87. Gerda Lerner, "Early Community Work of Black Club Women," *Journal of Negro History,* LIX (1974), 158–67; Lerner (ed.), *Black Women in White America: A Documentary History* (New York, 1972); Adrienne Lash Jones, "Jane Edna Hunter: A Case Study of Black Leadership, 1910–1950" (Ph.D. dissertation, Case Western Reserve University, 1983); Janice Sumler-Lewis, "The Forten-Purvis Women of Philadelphia and the American Anti-Slavery Crusade," *Journal of Negro History,* LXIV (1981–82), 281–88.

88. Excellent case studies illustrating this point are Vincent P. Franklin, *The Educa-*

ignore the impact of racism, to pretend that black communities have always been self-sufficient, would create a romanticized stereotype of Afro-American urban life that would be as speciously optimistic as the early sociological theories of "disorder" were falsely pessimistic in their conclusions. Only by a thorough explication of all of the forces at work in the shaping of black urban society at different points in time—internal, external, and structural—can we hope to fashion a synthesis that will do justice to both the grandeur and the travail of that history.

---

tion of Black Philadelphia (Philadelphia, 1979), and Homel, *Down from Equality*. See also David B. Tyack, "Growing Up Black: Perspectives on the History of Education in Northern Ghettos," *History of Education Quarterly*, IX (1969), 287–97.

COMMENT

LAWRENCE W. LEVINE

I am not an urban historian and cannot comment on Kenneth Kusmer's paper from within that specialty. Indeed, as someone from outside of that enterprise, I found his paper especially useful in suggesting patterns and supplying bibliography. My comments come inevitably from my own areas of research and historical interest: that of folk history and what we call "popular culture."

In no part of my own research on the Afro-American oral and folk traditions have I experienced more difficulty in locating materials than in regards to urban black culture and life-styles. Only recently have scholars modified their tendency to regard folklore and the oral tradition as rural phenomena almost exclusively; for the most part they either confined their research and collecting activities to rural areas or were interested in collecting from urban blacks only those materials relating to their rural past.

Happily, we are no longer so completely the prisoners of these biases and can begin to understand the importance of the urban process and the urban oral tradition. One of the few points of disagreement I have with Kusmer comes from the fact that, just as we are beginning to understand the need to collect and analyze such materials in the urban setting, he warns us that "overemphasis on oral traditions in urban society may . . . lead historians to neglect the often important role that black newspapers have played in both shaping and reflecting values in black communities." Of course, the overemphasis on any source is distorting, but I find it ironic that Kusmer writes as if oral sources had dominated urban studies and overwhelmed newspaper sources, when the very opposite is true. The comprehension of how to locate and utilize oral and folk sources in the city is still in the embryonic stages, and it is premature to warn researchers against overemphasizing them. Indeed, aside from James Borchert's study of alley life in Washington, D.C., from 1850 to 1970, I know of no historical study of black urban life that utilizes these materials extensively. One can only agree with Kusmer that scholars must put greater emphasis upon the local impact of the black press and we must better understand the relationship of the black press to the entire black community. However, we must be aware of the danger that the continued overreliance upon printed newspaper sources could lead to the continued dominance of the black middle classes in our studies and the continued neglect of those groups whose history we are just beginning to recover. This is hardly the time to call for a deemphasis of Afro-American urban oral traditions. With this major exception, I agree with the agenda Kusmer seems to be suggesting for those who teach and write urban black history.

We must, as Kusmer argues definitively, drop the tendency to see black urbanization as a pathological process. In 1970, three Berkeley historians—Leon Litwack, Winthrop Jordan, and I—applied for a three-year federal grant to help us complete our studies of Afro-American culture. That the federal agency to which we had to apply in those days was the National Institute of Mental Health tells us a great deal about the prevailing conceptions of black culture.

We must, as Kusmer argues, focus upon as wide an array of urban communities as possible; we must focus upon the process of urbanization in the South as well as the North; we must understand that black urbanization antedated the Great Migration.

We must, as Kusmer argues, begin to synthesize the black urban experience, to weave the discrete histories of separate black communities into a larger mosaic.

We must, as Kusmer argues, make an effort to systematically understand those forces and elements that worked on black urbanites everywhere and helped shape their communities in similar ways in some instances and in quite distinctive ways in others.

I most definitely agree with Kusmer's willingness to understand that acculturation has not been an irreversibly progressive process, that it has not been a straight line that led unvaryingly in one inevitable direction. Human beings are much more complex than historians often allow and so is their culture. I recall that in my own work every time I found a point that I was certain indicated profound acculturation—the adoption of the solo individual voice in the blues or the adoption of a more clearly Western cosmology in gospel songs—I found other elements that indicated simultaneous revitalization of the traditional culture. As historians gradually discover this new physical and cultural law—that it *is* possible for cultures to move in two directions at the same time—they will also discover how very difficult it is to express such phenomena in uncomplicated words or theories. It is Kusmer's willingness to grasp the complexity of the urbanizing process that I applaud most of all.

In short, I find myself in substantial agreement with Kusmer's suggested agenda for Afro-American urban history. I would like in the remainder of my remarks to suggest a number of additions to or expansions of that agenda.

One likes to think we have come a certain distance in sophistication and knowledge since the time when Nathan Glazer and Daniel Moynihan, in *Beyond the Melting Pot*, their study of Afro-Americans, Jews, Irish, Italians, and Puerto Ricans in New York City, could list in their index after the word *slum* the injunction "see Negroes." Yet there are often atavisms in our thought and in our terminology that work to defeat our hard-won knowledge. Too frequently, historians perpetuate a term coined in a distant era to cover a specific situation and blindly and loosely apply it to a wide variety of situations and conditions in a much later age, so that a term that once helped to clarify now merely serves to confuse. Thus our analysis of American political history continues to be bedeviled by terms like *right* and *left*, created long ago to explain a very different political situation in France. Thus too our understanding of the Afro-American past continues to be confused by our use of the term *ghetto*, devised centuries ago to describe an urban area in which Italian Jews were forced to live.

It seems to me that high on the agenda of urban historians ought to be more careful analysis of the term *ghetto*. One obvious objection is that the term is too invariably other-oriented. It conjures up images of the powerful relentlessly and always successfully confining the unfortunate in designated areas regardless of the latter's wishes. The term invites us to see blacks always as passive victims and makes it difficult to ever perceive them as actors in their own right. The term helps to short-circuit our attempt to understand the urban process as, in part at least, the result of choice—an entire spectrum of choices made by the migrants rather than merely a predetermined scenario, always in control of the whites.

The term in its very unvaryingness also helps to defeat one of the things Kusmer wants: a sense of historical development, a subtle sense of change in time. This is certainly not promoted by applying a rigid, imprecise label to describe the widely varying circumstances prevailing in, let us say, the Harlem of the 1920s or the Harlem of the 1960s. The notion of ghetto blacks also constitutes a barrier against another of Kusmer's desired ends: a sense of the variety of peoples and life-styles in black urban communities. The term *ghetto*, as it has come to be applied, brings to mind only one segment of the diversity of groups that make up the Afro-American populace, blurs the distinctions between black northerners and southerners, migrants and old settlers, West Indians and native-born, and transforms a heterogeneous, dynamic group into a stereotyped monolithic mass.

This kind of historical reductionism prevents us from accomplishing what Armstead Robinson called for in his paper: the careful and critical comparison of black and immigrant communities in the cities. In 1983, when the new convention center was opened in Washington, D.C., a Washington *Post* reporter lamented its effect upon Chinatown and warned that continued development of the old downtown area would destroy Chinatown and thus Washington would lose the only part of the city that had even the semblance of a right to be called an ethnic neighborhood. Here we have the phenomenon of an otherwise sensitive observer who could see only a Chinese-American neighborhood in a city that is 75 percent black and is filled with the churches, stores, fraternal organizations, places of amusement, schools, formal and informal associations that go to make up innumerable black ethnic neighborhoods. One might venture to guess that he thought of these black neighborhoods as "ghettos."

Thus an urban concept, ghetto, too easily becomes a historiographical ghetto that prevents us from seeing the past in its full complexity, and prevents us from discerning distinctions—marked or subtle—or fully perceiving the dynamics of historical change. I am not suggesting that there were no important distinctions between Afro-American and Euro-American or Asian-American inhabitants of the city, only that we have not yet arrived at these distinctions through painstaking historical analysis. Nor am I suggesting that the term *ghetto* is never useful, only that we need to subject it to more careful, controlled scrutiny. Perhaps we need to devise a string of adjectives to be used along with the term to invest it with more meaning. Perhaps we need to create an entire new terminology. Whatever the solution, the problem is clear: we must free ourselves from the careless use of a concept that has come to mask more than it reveals and continues to bind us to the stereotypes of the past.

I would place high on the agenda for historians the investigation of the continued interaction between urban blacks and rural blacks—and I don't mean just the physical, spatial connections, which are crucial for us to comprehend better than we do, but also the cultural connections. Again, we have liked our history to be simple: rural/urban dichotomies are much easier to understand than rural/urban dialogues, but the latter are much closer to the truth. The fact is we are not dealing with migrants who made a final, inexorable move away from their geographical and cultural roots, but with men and women who continued to communicate with the relatives and friends they left behind, continued to visit them periodically, continued to send their children "down home" for vacations and visits, continued to maintain a deeply ambivalent relationship with a South that had been the place of both their confinement and their culture.

Ralph Ellison, who grew up in Oklahoma City during the 1920s, recalled that every fall a number of his classmates went with their parents back south to work in the cotton fields. Many parents tried to protect their children against the experience of the cotton patch—an aspect of the Old South they had come west to escape. But Ellison, who never shared the experience, only envied the children who made the annual migration: "The kids came back with such wonderful stories. . . . And it wasn't the hard work which they stressed, but the communion, the playing, the eating, the dancing, the singing. And they brought back jokes, *our* Negro jokes—not those told about Negroes by whites—and they always returned with Negro folk stories which I'd never heard before and which couldn't be found in any books I knew about. This was something to affirm and I felt there was a richness in it. . . . It seemed much more real than the Negro middle-class values, which were taught in school."

This cultural interaction Ellison speaks of was promoted not only by physical migration and remigration—patterns we need to learn much more about—but also by the new Afro-American popular culture that began to spring up in every black urban community. I would place an understanding of this new urban culture, which so often had its roots in the traditional folk cultures from which the migrants came, much higher on my agenda than Kusmer seems to. At one point in his paper, Professor Kusmer maintains that James Borchert "veers dangerously close to romanticizing the poor when he says that crap games and numbers were 'more of a recreational and communal activity than a way to win money.'" I would be less prone to dismiss Borchert's insight. Indeed, it is in line with Kusmer's own eloquent call away from seeing black urban life as primarily pathological for us to understand the multidimensional functions of such activities as numbers, the dozens, and the blues, which have been too easily dismissed either as manifestations of the oppressed condition of urban blacks or as "mere entertainment." Urban historians have not yet begun to exploit the wealth of suggestions in a work like Charles Keil's *Urban Blues*, which makes it clear that urban figures such as bluesmen played a number of roles in the community, from poets to priests, and that their music was integrated into the very life patterns and communal networks of their listeners.

A number of other items deserve to be high on the agenda as well. We have just begun to scratch the surface of the crucially important functions, memberships, and activities of the multiplicity of fraternal, social, and religious organizations that blacks belonged to and that provided them with so many outlets denied them in the larger society. Black America, no less than white America, was a society of joiners, and there can be no complete urban history that ignores the organizations they joined and the roles they played within those organizations.

We know equally little about the selective migratory process. Black migrants have been treated like leaves blown to northern cities by the winds of adversity. In reality, the process was far less deterministic. It is clear from such sources as oral testimony and the letters that migrants wrote to the Chicago *Defender* that migration was more often than not the result of careful choice, and we need to understand more about precisely who was making the choice and for what purposes.

Richard Wright has described a scene in a French café when he was relating to a white Frenchman and an African the various strategies used by black Americans to survive the American racial system. As he went into greater detail, the African began to kick him under the table. When Wright asked him why, the African replied, "Because you're giving away all of our secrets." "Secrets?" Wright countered. "We don't have any secrets!" "Now," the African thundered, "you've given away the biggest secret of them all!"

It's a good story with an interesting and provocative point, but we must not take it too literally. From the historian's point of view, there are still many secrets about the Afro-American past and Afro-American culture that remain inaccessible to us. Kusmer is absolutely right in urging us to see urban history as a primary key to unlocking the doors guarding those secrets and helping to provide answers for many of the questions that continue to plague the teachers and scholars of the Afro-American past.

COMMENT

JAMES OLIVER HORTON

Kenneth Kusmer's review of black urban history is impressive for its analytical organization. It begins by tracing the early sociological studies that concentrated on the rise of the urban ghetto as an outgrowth of the great migration of southern blacks northward after 1910. These studies were ahistorical in their approach and focused on the largest industrial cities of the North, where substantial numbers of black migrants settled during the first quarter of the twentieth century. Generalizing from their analysis of this environment, these sociologists emphasized negative aspects of the urban black life and the "pathological" character of black ghettos. There was disagreement among these scholars about the source of the perceived weakness and disorganization in black urban communities. Black and liberal white sociologists saw the "breakdown" of the black community as a direct result of class and racial discrimination, while conservative scholars attributed it to the "natural limitations" of race. Yet, almost all agreed that the black ghetto was injurious to effective community support and organization.

The theme of pathology in black urban life was picked up by historians as they turned their attention to the question of race relations in the twentieth-century urban North. Passed down from the early reform-oriented histories of the Progressive era, through the few state and local histories of race relations completed during the post–World War II years, urban black history was either ignored by historians or treated pejoratively by scholars with negative racial biases. With few exceptions, most notably Leon Litwack, revisionist historians of the period devoted their efforts to the study of slavery. Not until the early 1970s, Kusmer says, did recent historical study turn its attention to urban blacks. Spurred in large part by the Civil Rights Movement and the urban unrest of the 1960s, several historians focused their attention on the history of the conditions that festered in the memory of the ghetto and exploded in violence.

Although Kusmer does not say so, these historians who moved the study of urban blacks forward took direction from the "new social history." Many undertook their study influenced by the emerging prominence of the social science approach in historical research. This approach emphasized the case study as illustrated by the studies of eighteenth- and nineteenth-century communities that appeared during the late 1960s. During the next decade, scholars studying black communities in Detroit, Cleveland, Philadelphia, Boston, Washington, and other cities refined the history of the black city life and questioned the notion of the consuming pathology of black urban society.

Historians joined the growing scholarly criticism of Daniel Patrick Moynihan's Labor Department report, *The Negro Family: The Case for National Action*, and the federal social policies of the mid-1960s that resulted from that analysis. Their efforts provided a needed historical perspective and encouraged others skeptical of the "breakdown" theory. They mustered evidence to refute the thesis that community disorganization and a disproportionately high number of female-headed families was the historical norm among black people. A few even disputed the assumption that families headed by black women were necessarily less stable or less nurturing than those with two parents present. Thus, the black community studies of the last decade must be seen in an intellectual and political context not only of changing interests of historians of the Afro-American experience but of the burgeoning effort to write history from the bottom up and the social policy concerns of the period.

Kusmer's warning that urban black life must not become synonymous with black life in twentieth-century Chicago and New York is well founded. As he points out, there are important differences over time, by region, and in accordance with the size of the community in question. He correctly calls for comparative study of black communities that will consider these important differences. He suggests that comparisons be organized around the notions of external forces (the extent, manifestation, and impact of white racism on blacks), internal forces (the black response to such racism), and structural forces (the general social, economic, and political structures of the city that are often nonracial in character but which affect blacks in dramatic ways). These categories imply the need to broaden the study of black community in several important ways.

First, if we are to understand the most potent of external forces, white racism, studies like those of Winthrop Jordan, Joel Kovel, George Fredrickson, and others, which sought to investigate the disease among those afflicted, point the direction. Ronald Takaki and Edmund Morgan are two historians who explained the importance of racism as a window into the social, political, and economic organization of American society. Such study illustrates the constraints racism imposes on oppressed peoples of whatever race or class and its power in the hands of those who would use it to control the structure of society. Using Kusmer's formula, historians might link these external forces with the structural forces, which may differ regionally and over time.

The imaginative work of Henry Taylor, who is developing useful models for understanding the role of urban land-use policy in the formation of black community patterns and as a context for the growth of residential segregation, is especially relevant in this regard. Likewise, Spencer Crew's study of blacks in Elizabethtown and Camden, New Jersey, represents a legitimate concern that black community studies not be limited to larger urban centers but include secondary cities as well. Both Taylor and Crew suggest the need to view black community as a product of structural, external, and internal forces and in a comparative context. Organizing future research in this way opens exciting opportunities for the comparative study of racial-ethnic relations such as that currently under way in Philadelphia, Washington, and other cities. Most importantly, it serves to bring Afro-American history out of isolation, where it has been, not in reality, but in the minds of many.

In the move toward an integration of the Afro-American experience into the variety of other American experiences of oppressed people, care must be taken not to confuse race with ethnicity. Some historians have equated racism and the limitation it imposes on blacks with the limitations imposed on white immigrants by nativism and class or even religious prejudice. Intolerance and bigotry are deplorable in any form and can operate to

restrict the opportunity of any group, but to compare black social or economic mobility to that of specific ethnic groups without recognizing that
such comparison is complicated by the permanence of race as against ethnicity is misleading at best. The historical impact of slavery and the powerful role that race has played in American socialization handicap not only
black progress but also the attempts by historians to deal with the structural and external forces which help to shape Afro-American history.

The internal factors Kusmer suggests are most intriguing because of
the endless possibilities they imply for improving our understanding of the
complexity of Afro-American people and society. A few illustrations are
provided in the article. Kusmer is absolutely correct when he calls for
greater focus on the role of black women. Recent studies by Paula Giddings,
Dorothy Sterling, Jacqueline Jones, and Mamie Garvin Fields and Karen
Fields challenge historians to address the complicated issues confronting
women who must deal with the problems of gender even as they cope with
those of race. The important work of Sharon Harley on black women's
clubs in late-nineteenth-century Washington, D.C., that of Noralee Frankle
on black women in Reconstruction Mississippi, and the family history in
progress by Rosalyn Terborg-Penn are three further examples of the expanding attention this subject is receiving. I view my recent study of black
women in the antebellum North as a part of this ongoing work.

Yet this only touches the surface of the important work to be done. The
more general area of black community life to be investigated is that of class
structure. This topic is especially complex because of the interplay between limited occupational opportunity and wealth on the one hand and
social connections and shade of color on the other. The issue is further
complicated by the importance of the internal structure of black institutions, formal and informal, and the dynamic character of black activism
and leadership. It will not be possible to comprehend the meaning of class
structure among blacks until we establish some method for evaluating occupations and their relation to status in the black community. Clearly the
traditional approaches to class based on occupation must be modified
to have meaning for the limited job opportunities traditionally open to
blacks.

There is also a need for a greater appreciation of the importance of in-
tangible factors such as respectability and access to information that may
convey considerable status. Douglas Daniels, in his important study of

black San Francisco, suggested that some blacks, as a consequence of their work-related travel, could provide information about local or regional racial attitudes and could direct fellow blacks to reasonably comfortable and safe accommodations. The special status of those who possessed this "travelcraft" illustrates the kinds of noneconomic factors that, among poor people, vulnerable to prejudice and racial hostility, took on particular significance. To date we understand little of these important historical areas of black life.

A related interior issue among blacks is shade of color. Historians acknowledge the importance of the "mulatto question," but few go beyond such acknowledgment. In his fine study of free blacks in the South published in 1974, Ira Berlin provides useful statistical data on mulattoes and on their relative importance among southern free blacks. More recently studies by Joel Williamson, Laurence Glasco, the joint work of Theodore Hershberg and Henry Williams and that of James Roark and Michael Johnson have raised interesting questions of regional differences and changes over time on this important issue. My own comparative study of black society before the Civil War is highly suggestive on the question of regional differences in the role and status of mulattoes. It points to the importance of this status as a window into regional differences in black community organization and structure.

The direction and analysis outlined in Kusmer's article is one that is both suggestive for future study and a reaffirmation of current research in urban history, black history, and social history. The organizational categories provide a paradigm for community studies of various types and this model encourages the integration of Afro-American, ethnic, and women's history into the broad range of social history. At the same time it allows for tighter focus on the internal institutions and issues that remain imperfectly understood.

One further direction of study might be that which would acknowledge and investigate the active role blacks have played in the adoption and use of the rhetoric of the American ideal. In the eighteenth century, Massachusetts blacks pressed for the right to vote under the slogan "No taxation without representation." In the nineteenth century black reformers used the rhetorical message of the Declaration of Independence and the Bill of Rights to their advantage in civil rights and antislavery protests. By the time black activists of the 1960s held up the American ideal to the unflattering mirror of the American reality, the tactic had become traditional. It can be argued that blacks are the long-term guardians of the humanitarian principles celebrated in American rhetorical tradition. They have, through their continual protest, acted as constant reminders, pricking the national conscience, continually urging it toward its stated ideals. This effort has of course had varying degrees of success; yet without the continual action and vigilance of black protest, other oppressed class, ethnic, or gender groups may have been less successful in their drives for increased opportunity. When this story is told it will be one that casts Afro-Americans as major actors in the American drama.

V TEACHING, RESEARCHING, AND FUNDING

Trends and Needs in Afro-American Historiography

WILLIAM H. HARRIS

In December, 1974, August Meier went before the annual meeting of the American Historical Association to deliver a paper on the Afro-American historiography produced during the Civil Rights Movement.[1] In his long and thorough account, Meier discussed trends in black history, reviewed some of the literature, and proposed topics that historians still needed to study. In a sense, his presentation to the association marked the formal acceptance by the general historical profession of Afro-American history as a legitimate and respected field. The relationship between that time and the present is worth examining because it is through the legitimation of Afro-American history that continued funding support for research will be found.

American education in general, from kindergarten through graduate school, is in turmoil today. Just recently, a blue-ribbon committee appointed by the secretary of education issued a report that declared the future security of our nation at risk because of the inadequate level of education. What we are seeing as a result of this report is a mad rush everywhere to "do something" about education. The response to the committee's report is of extreme importance to those involved in Afro-American history. The concern is that many proponents of "doing something" are people

1. August Meier, "Afro-American History in the Age of the Civil Rights Movement" (Paper, American Historical Association Annual Meeting, Chicago, 1974).

who think that all the doing should take place in the sciences and mathematics. They are arguing for a back-to-basics approach to American education that overlooks much of what education ought to be.

The scholar's responsibility is to keep ever before the people of this country the importance of humanism if the nation and the world are to rise to a new level of human tolerance and understanding. No discipline is more important in passing on to succeeding generations a true sense of humanism than is the discipline of history. And no field in that discipline is more important than Afro-American history. I do so declare.

Thus, when I first began to consider this topic, I thought the most difficult matter that I would have to discuss would be how to go about funding additional research in Afro-American history. But as I thought further, the solution to that problem became clear. Without question, historians must continue to insist that the Congress of the United States appropriate adequate funds for agencies such as the National Endowment for the Humanities so as to provide support for research in history. Also, historians must continue to prepare proposals and make recommendations to private foundations and agencies such as the Lilly Endowment and the American Council of Learned Societies for such funding. But there is a fundamental fact about the history of the support of research in the United States that must be recognized. This fact is that the single greatest supporter of scholarly research in the United States has been the American university, and I suspect that universities will remain the greatest source of support for years to come. Therein lies the challenge to those who work in this field.

The difficulty for teachers and researchers comes from two directions. In the first place, the humanities in general are undergoing rough times as university administrators question what benefits students derive from studying history and other liberal arts courses. At the same time history departments, in their efforts to deal with budgets cut by deans, are more and more inclined to eliminate positions in Afro-American history. The real challenge to those in Afro-American history lies in this. They must be involved in helping everyone to understand the overall importance of history to any curriculum, and even more important, they must be involved in insisting that the history of black people in the American continents be understood as an essential part of the history of humanity. Indeed, I can think of no field that is more essential to the understanding of the history of the West than is Afro-American history. In short, it is as essential for a research history department to have an Afro-American historian as it is for that department to have a diplomatic historian or a military historian or a historian of Bismarckian Germany or any other of the fields into which the discipline is divided. This point must be made resolutely, giving no degree of comfort whatever to those who wish to suggest that Afro-American history is a fad-field that can somehow be done without or that its information can easily be patched into research or courses in some other field of American history. The most important publications of our time were produced by historians whose research was supported by faculty salaries while they taught reduced loads. Afro-American history must have the benefit of the same advantage.

I hasten to add that not all scholars of Afro-American history will find positions at research universities. There simply will not be enough places to go around. But no university should be permitted to be without an Afro-American historian in its department. Agencies such as the NEH and the private foundations do have a major role to play in helping to fund the research of scholars at small colleges at which the main mission is teaching and, consequently, the teaching load is heavy and leaves little time for research. Foundations, the Endowment, and major learning societies of our profession can help these scholars in other ways as well. One way is for agencies to sponsor conferences such as this, where colleagues heavily burdened with teaching (sometimes in fields other than that of their research) can fraternize with men and women who are on the cutting edge of research in the field. Such fraternization, I believe, will have the dual effect of removing from the minds of one group the inaccurate idea that those who have produced published work are extraordinarily brilliant and from the other group the idea that those who have not produced scholarly research have not done so because they are less brilliant. The result will be extended and mutual respect among colleagues working in Afro-American history but with different missions.

Scholarship on slavery has long been one of the richest veins of Afro-American history, and it remains so. In 1972, two new books came out that markedly affected our understanding of slavery and posed new questions that historians should ask.[2] Both books focused on the lives of the

2. John W. Blassingame, *The Slave Community* (New York, 1972), and George P. Rawick, *From Sunup to Sundown: The Making of the Slave Community* (Westport, Conn., 1972).

slaves themselves and provided additional evidence with which to refute the assumptions Stanley Elkins and others had made about the impact of slavery on the personalities of black people. Far from seeing plantation after plantation of sambos when they looked at the lives of slaves in the American South, both John Blassingame and George Rawick saw dynamic, structured communities in which black men and women maintained a sense of themselves as thinking individuals who understood the predicament in which they lived and who made decisions that affected their lives within that context. The essential point is that Blassingame and Rawick looked at slavery from the viewpoint of the slaves, whereas others had generally looked at the institution from the viewpoint of the masters. Their work was the beginning of a new historical perspective by which scholars first began to see slavery as a human institution.

At the time of the appearance of Blassingame's and Rawick's books, other historians had research under way that would result in major new studies of the American slave community. These studies, especially the works of Eugene D. Genovese and Herbert G. Gutman, published by Pantheon in 1974 and 1976 respectively, revealed even further the importance of studying the slaves themselves and produced exciting new interpretations.[3] Genovese roams broadly in *Roll, Jordan, Roll*, covering religion, the relationship between field hands and the black drivers, and the role of house servants, and giving his view of the similarity of slave experiences on all types of farm units and in all sections of the South. But the key to his discussion is the paternal relationship that he envisions as having existed between the slaves and the master class. It is a strange sort of paternalism that he describes, one in which both parties interpreted the arrangement differently so as to fit their own needs. The slaves never accepted slavery, and the master class never admitted that the slaves were in their own minds free. In this way the slaves were able to maintain their human dignity, and the whites could continue to demand of them their labor. If one can get beyond the seeming constraints that the concept of paternalism, with its conflicting connotations, imposes, it is clear that Genovese has made a major contribution in helping us to understand more clearly the crucial reality that, for all its pathos, brutality, and denial of basic human

3. Eugene D. Genovese, *Roll, Jordan, Roll: The World the Slaves Made* (New York, 1974), and Herbert G. Gutman, *The Black Family in Slavery and Freedom, 1750–1925* (New York, 1976).

rights, slavery was in the end a human institution in which thinking human beings, both black and white, interacted on a regular basis.

Herbert Gutman's *The Black Family* is truly an amazing book, one that shows again that Gutman is one of the most skillful historians working in the world today. Gutman finds no "tangle of pathology" among black families during slavery and Reconstruction, and convincingly refutes the notion that nineteenth-century black families were headed by females. He makes no effort to deny that family separations, both those that the master class forced and those in which spouses simply decided to go their separate ways, did in fact occur. But his major evidence shows that black families did stay together, that most of them were headed either by males or by both males and females, that black families operated on a set of principles determined by the slaves themselves, and that the families served as a source of strength that made it possible for black Americans to survive the rigors of slavery and Reconstruction. An important point that Gutman demonstrates through all this is that neither law (which did not recognize slave marriages) nor distance necessarily affected the sense of relationship that numerous blacks felt for each other. And he emphasizes as well the exogamous nature of black families, a factor that served to broaden black families and to increase the importance of extended family ties. But Gutman deals with more than just the structure of black families. He analyzes also the development of occupational structures among black people, particularly in the postwar years. Upon these findings rests the important contemporary relevance of his work: Poverty and the inability to find adequate employment, particularly among black males—and not the heritage of slavery—have caused what is now considered a breakdown in the black family structure.

Of all the books that have been published in Afro-American history during the past decade, none has been more ballyhooed, and then more roundly condemned, than William Fogel and Stanley Engerman's *Time on the Cross*.[4] Indeed, Herbert Gutman even interrupted his work on the black family to write a book-length critique.[5] Critics complained about

4. Robert William Fogel and Stanley Engerman, *Time on the Cross: The Economics of American Negro Slavery* (Boston, 1974), and *Time on the Cross: Evidence and Methods—A Supplement* (Boston, 1974).

5. Herbert G. Gutman, *Slavery and the Numbers Game: A Critique of "Time on the Cross"* (Urbana, 1975). It is important to keep in mind that this critique first appeared as a review in the *Journal of Negro History*. Another devastating analysis of Fogel and

both the methodology the authors employed in their work and the findings they produced, especially those for which they claimed notable originality. Readers were particularly struck by assertions such as "over the course of his lifetime, the typical field hand received about 90 percent of the income he produced," unaccompanied by any recognition of the idea that that field hand might have thought he was entitled to 100 percent of the rewards of his labor. Moreover, *Time on the Cross* raised serious questions in the minds of many about the utility of quantitative methods for historians if the evidence of counting could be treated in such a sterile way. For example, what purpose does it serve to point out, as Fogel and Engerman do, that the average hand received only 0.7 whippings per year, and not to stress that even one whipping was a convincing system of social control? Nor were many readers convinced that slaves, without being forced, identified with the interests of their masters, imbibed the work ethic, and strived to make the plantations profitable. Indeed, Fogel and Engerman would have us believe that Kenneth Stampp was only part right when he observed that Afro-Americans were simply white men with black skins. Fogel and Engerman's blacks even thought they were working for themselves, and enjoyed it all. Fogel and Engerman produced a mountain of evidence and demonstrated the wide range of sources that can be tapped through the use of computers and quantitative methodology. But their presentation of that evidence demonstrates clearly that counting alone is hardly enough to make one a historian.

Lawrence Levine's *Black Culture, Black Consciousness* is a much different kind of book than *Time on the Cross* and shows the tremendous insights that can be gained from the use of a wide range of nonquantifiable sources. Levine's work reveals in an unprecedented way the great richness of black culture during slavery and shows convincingly that many of the traditions, principles, and beliefs that blacks developed to sustain them during slavery survived into the period of freedom and remain a part of black culture. His book is required reading for all interested in gaining a fuller understanding of black culture and consciousness.[6]

In addition to the general studies of slave societies, several good books

Engerman's book is Paul A. David, Herbert G. Gutman, Richard Sutch, Peter Temin, and David Wright, *Reckoning with Slavery: A Critical Study in the Quantitative History of American Negro Slavery* (New York, 1976).

6. Lawrence W. Levine, *Black Culture, Black Consciousness: Afro-American Thought in Slavery and Freedom* (New York, 1978).

on various specific themes have been published in the past decade. Gerald Mullin and Leslie Howard Owen have both stressed the rebelliousness and desire for freedom among slaves.[7] And we have important new interpretations of urban and industrial slavery and of the role of black drivers in the supervision and management of slaves.[8] Moreover, the works of Peter Wood on South Carolina and of Edmund Morgan, T. H. Breen, and Stephen Innes on Virginia have extended considerably our understanding of race relations and slavery during the earliest years of North American settlement. Morgan has presented a novel and provocative thesis, arguing that the existence and spread of slavery in Virginia provided the basis on which social and economic stability among whites developed, thereby permitting the creation of the democratic ideas on which the Republic was founded. His is a strange thesis: The absolute unfreedom of some provided the basis of total freedom for others. And out of that came "freedom and liberty for all." A strange thesis, indeed. But it shows again the importance of black people to the development of the United States.[9]

The past decade has also witnessed an outpouring of scholarship on Reconstruction, but in the main no striking new interpretation of that period has been developed. What we have instead are fresh new insights on various aspects of the lives of blacks and whites as they intertwined during the first decades of "freedom" for blacks in the United States. Scholars continue to discuss the importance of land and education to the newly freed slaves, the careers of carpetbaggers and black politicians, the importance of black soldiers in the immediate postwar period, and, of course, the refusal of the federal and state governments to protect the rights of black men and women to land and jobs.[10] Of the many titles on this subject, Leon Litwack's Pulitzer Prize-winning book, *Been in the Storm So Long,*

7. Leslie Howard Owens, *This Species of Property: Slave Life and Culture in the Old South* (New York, 1976), and Gerald Mullin, *Flight and Rebellion: Slave Resistance in Eighteenth-Century Virginia* (New York, 1972).

8. Claudia Dale Goldin, *Urban Slavery in the American South, 1820–1860: A Quantitative History* (Chicago, 1976); Ronald L. Lewis, *Coal, Iron, and Slaves: Industrial Slavery in Maryland and Virginia, 1715–1865* (Westport, Conn., 1979).

9. Peter H. Wood, *Black Majority: Negroes in Colonial South Carolina from 1670 through the Stone Rebellion* (New York, 1974); T. H. Breen and Stephen Innes, *"Myne Owne Ground": Race and Freedom on Virginia's Eastern Shore, 1640–1676* (New York, 1980); and Edmund S. Morgan, *American Slavery—American Freedom: The Ordeal of Colonial Virginia* (New York, 1975). See also Duncan J. MacLeod, *Slavery, Race, and the American Revolution* (Cambridge, England, 1974).

10. For examples of work on these topics, see Eric Anderson, *Race and Politics in North Carolina, 1872–1901: The Black Second* (Baton Rouge, 1981); Mary Frances

stands out, not only for the clarity of the writing but for the significance he places on the importance to freed blacks of the survival systems they had developed during slavery. This big book, based on a wide range of rich sources, is a revealing portrait and analysis of the excitement black men, women, and children experienced as they shook off the chains of slavery and endeavored to fulfill their "intense desire for freedom."[11]

It is significant, of course, that scholars of the post–Civil War period have continued to pay considerable attention to efforts on the part of both blacks and whites to provide educational institutions to satisfy the freedmen's strong desire for education. Much of the discussion is still unnecessarily constrained by analyses of whether various institutions were for industrial training or liberal education, and thus the tremendous contribution made by all types of black schools is too often lost sight of. In this area of scholarly research historians must look beyond the gates of the institutions they are studying and see not only what happened in the institutions but what effect those activities had upon communities at large. Indeed, in many cities and towns throughout the South, especially during the period of formal segregation, the vast majority of teachers in black elementary and secondary schools received their education in black colleges and universities. Thus, these schools deeply affected the lives of large numbers of people who never attended them and, in many cases, never heard their names. Research now in progress on black educational institutions is

---

Berry, *Military Necessity and Civil Rights Policy: Black Citizenship and the Constitution, 1861–1868* (Port Washington, N.Y., 1977); James T. Currie, *Enclave: Vicksburg and Her Plantations, 1863–1870* (Jackson, Miss., 1980); Roger A. Fischer, *The Segregation Struggle in Louisiana, 1862–1877* (Urbana, 1974); William Gillett, *Retreat from Reconstruction, 1869–1879* (Baton Rouge, 1979); William C. Harris, *The Day of the Carpetbagger: Republican Reconstruction in Mississippi* (Baton Rouge, 1979); Jay R. Mandle, *The Roots of Black Poverty: The Southern Plantation Economy after the Civil War* (Durham, N.C., 1978); Donald G. Nieman, *To Set the Law in Motion: The Freedmen's Bureau and the Legal Rights of Blacks, 1865–1868* (Millwood, N.Y., 1979): Carl R. Osthaus, *Freedmen, Philanthropy, and Fraud: A History of the Freedmen's Savings Bank* (Urbana, 1976); Claude F. Oubre, *Forty Acres and a Mule: The Freedmen's Bureau and Black Land Ownership* (Baton Rouge, 1978); Lawrence N. Powell, *New Masters: Northern Planters During the Civil War and Reconstruction* (New Haven, 1980); Jerrell H. Shofner, *Nor Is It Over Yet: Florida in the Era of Reconstruction, 1863–1877* (Gainesville, 1974); and Charles Vincent, *Black Legislators in Louisiana During Reconstruction* (Baton Rouge, 1976).

11. Leon F. Litwack, *Been in the Storm So Long: The Aftermath of Slavery* (New York, 1979).

taking this broader view, and in fact many of the books published during the past decade are quite significant.[12]

During the past decade historians have devoted a good deal of attention to conditions and activities among nonrural southern blacks and the development of black communities in the North. These works have further refined our understanding of Jim Crow and of the origins of ghettos in northern cities. Three books in the University of Illinois Press's series "Blacks in the New World" are particularly helpful on this latter point, and John Dittmer's work on Georgia, also from the Illinois series, and that of Howard Rabinowitz are quite revealing for the South.[13]

It is significant that the decade of the 1970s, a relatively quiet time for protest activities among blacks, has seen the production of several good books on black nationalism and protest activities. Tony Martin's *Race First* is perhaps the most controversial and thought provoking of those that treat the question of black nationalism. His effort to rehabilitate Marcus Garvey gained him considerable criticism from some quarters, but his book nonetheless raises important questions in a fresh way.[14]

12. Ronald E. Butchart, *Northern Schools, Southern Blacks, and Reconstruction: Freedmen's Education, 1862–1875* (Westport, Conn., 1980); Elizabeth Jacoway, *Yankee Missionaries in the South: The Penn School Experiment* (Baton Rouge, 1980); Jacqueline Jones, *Soldiers of Light and Love: Northern Teachers and Georgia Blacks, 1865–1873* (Chapel Hill, 1980); Joe M. Richardson, *A History of Fisk University* (University, Ala., 1980); Robert G. Sherer, *Subordination or Liberation? The Development and Conflicting Theories of Black Education in Nineteenth-Century Alabama* (University, Ala., 1977); Donald Spivey, *Schooling for the New Slavery: Black Industrial Education, 1868–1915* (Westport, Conn., 1978). Those interested in the history of black education might do well to look also at four books for a slightly later period in the North. See Vincent P. Franklin, *The Education of Black Philadelphia: Social and Educational History of a Minority Community, 1900–1950* (Philadelphia, 1979); Caleton Mabee, *Black Education in New York State: From Colonial to Modern Times* (Syracuse, 1979); Judy Jolley Mohraz, *The Separate Problem: Case Studies of Black Education in the North, 1900–1930* (Westport, Conn., 1979); and Alfred A. Moss, Jr., *The American Negro Academy: Voice of the Talented Tenth* (Baton Rouge, 1981).

13. David Katzman, *Before the Ghetto: Black Detroit in the Nineteenth Century* (Urbana, 1973); Kenneth L. Kusmer, *A Ghetto Takes Shape: Black Cleveland, 1870–1930* (Urbana, 1976); David A. Gerber, *Black Ohio and the Color Line, 1860–1915* (Urbana, 1976); John Dittmer, *Black Georgia in the Progressive Era, 1900–1920* (Urbana, 1977); Howard N. Rabinowitz, *Race Relations in the Urban South* (New York, 1978). One can also profit from reading Arnold Taylor, *Travail and Triumph: Black Life and Culture in the South Since the Civil War* (Westport, Conn., 1976).

14. Tony Martin, *Race First: The Ideological and Organizational Struggles of Marcus Garvey and the Universal Negro Improvement Association* (Westport, Conn., 1976).

Among the numerous books on black protest, the angles on such activities differ widely. Some authors, such as James McPherson, James C. Harvey, and Harvard Sitkoff, have made broad examinations of the development of civil rights activities and, therefore, have written books that are as much about white people as central actors as they are about black people.[15] Others, such as Claybourne Carson and Robert L. Zangrando, have evaluated the activities and tactics of particular organizations. William H. Chafe, utilizing both traditional evidence and the resources of the Duke University Oral History Project, has produced a comprehensive study of the activities of an entire community as blacks—and liberal whites—took actions to end discrimination in Greensboro, North Carolina. His is the kind of history we need from cities and towns across the country if we are to be able to complete the picture of the countless men and women, most of whose names we will never know, through whom the Civil Rights Movement succeeded.[16]

In addition to discussions of the nonviolent protests of the twentieth century, scholars during the past decade have produced several books on the involvement of blacks in violent assaults against discrimination in America. Books by Robert Haynes and William Hair have concentrated on instances of racial violence during the early years of the century, and William Capeci, Jr.'s important study of the World War II riot in New York

For other books on black nationalism, see Willard B. Gatewood, Jr., *Black Americans and the White Man's Burden, 1898–1903* (Urbana, 1975); Floyd J. Miller, *The Search for Black Nationality: Black Immigration and Colonization, 1787–1863* (Urbana, 1975); Wilson Jeremiah Moses, *The Golden Age of Black Nationalism, 1850–1925* (Hamden, Conn., 1978); and Alphonso Pinkney, *Red, Black, and Green: Black Nationalism in the United States* (Cambridge, England, 1976).

15. James C. Harvey, *Black Civil Rights During the Johnson Administration* (Jackson, Miss., 1973); James M. McPherson, *The Abolitionist Legacy: From Reconstruction to the NAACP* (Princeton, 1975); Harvard Sitkoff, *A New Deal for Blacks: The Emergence of Civil Rights as a National Issue, The Depression Decade* (New York, 1978).

16. William H. Chafe, *Civilities and Civil Rights: Greensboro, North Carolina, and the Black Struggle for Freedom* (New York, 1980); Clayborne Carson, *In Struggle: SNCC and the Black Awakening of the 1960s* (Cambridge, Mass., 1981); and Robert L. Zangrando, *The NAACP Crusade Against Lynching, 1909–1950* (Philadelphia, 1980). For other studies on black protest, see Robert C. Dick, *Black Protest: Issues and Tactics* (Westport, Conn., 1974); Lee Finkel, *Forum for Protest: The Black Press During World War II* (Rutherford, N.J., 1975); David J. Garrow, *Protest at Selma: Martin Luther King, Jr., and the Voting Rights Act of 1965* (New Haven, 1978); and J. Harvie Wilkinson III, *From Brown to Bakke: The Supreme Court and School Integration, 1954–1978* (New York, 1979).

emphasizes that what happened there was much more a riot against vested interests than against individuals. When several studies now under way on the riots of the 1960s are completed, the same will undoubtedly be seen as having been the case for those as well. James Button has already suggested the lines of such discussions in his analysis of the political efficacy of the riots of the 1960s.[17]

A field in which considerably more work is needed is the study of the black working class. Philip Foner, in 1975, published an important study on the relationship between black workers within the United Automobile Workers of America, and Herbert Hill has written effectively about legal barriers facing black workers. Moreover, we now have a book on the Brotherhood of Sleeping Car Porters, the largest and most influential of the black unions.[18] But we need additional studies of the relationship between black workers and their unions and, more important, the relationship between housing discrimination and the availability of work for black people. This is a field rich with questions, and the newly available papers of federal agencies and the various organizations involved with workers provide ample new sources for such research. Moreover, this is an area of black historiography in which historians can make effective use of oral sources. Nell Painter's book on Hosea Hudson is a remarkable example of the kind of book that can be produced from these.[19]

No discussion of recent Afro-American historiography would be complete without mentioning George Fredrickson's important book on white supremacy. This superb analysis of the similarities between the develop-

17. James W. Button, *Black Violence: Political Impact of the 1960s Riots* (Princeton, 1978); Dominic J. Capeci, Jr., *The Harlem Riot of 1943* (Philadelphia, 1977); William Ivy Hair, *Carnival of Fury: Robert Charles and the New Orleans Race Riot of 1900* (Baton Rouge, 1976); Robert V. Haynes, *A Night of Violence: The Houston Riot of 1917* (Baton Rouge, 1976).

18. Philip S. Foner, *Organized Labor and the Black Worker, 1619–1973* (New York, 1974); James A. Geschwender, *Class, Race, and Worker Insurgency: The League of Revolutionary Black Workers* (Cambridge, England, 1977); William H. Harris, *Keeping the Faith: A. Philip Randolph, Milton P. Webster, and the Brotherhood of Sleeping Car Porters, 1925–1937* (Urbana, 1977); Herbert Hill, *Black Labor and the American Legal System*, Vol. I, *Race, Work, and the Law* (Washington, D.C., 1977); August Meier and Elliott Rudwick, *Black Detroit and the Rise of the UAW* (New York, 1979).

19. Nell Irving Painter, *The Narrative of Hosea Hudson: His Life as a Negro Communist in the South* (Cambridge, Mass., 1979). See William H. Harris, *The Harder We Run: Black Workers Since the Civil War* (New York: 1982), for a synthesis of black working class history.

ment of racial relations in the United States and South Africa is a convincing demonstration of the importance of race in American life. All Americans should be aware of his findings.[20]

Despite the richness of the historiography on Afro-Americans during the past decade, much remains to be done. Historians must give considerably more attention to the experiences of black women and to the permanent institutions that black people have established. What is needed now are not more studies of "the black church" or "the black schools" but histories of particular black organizations and institutions. I am aware that the major trend of historians now is away from institutional histories toward a concentration, through the new social history, on the population at large, but institutions that black men and women have built cannot be overlooked. We already have good institutional histories of white organizations. We must have the same for blacks, or the widely held view that black people have built nothing of permanence in this country will be perpetuated. The same can be said of histories of black leaders. Historians of the past have always emphasized the importance of charisma among black leaders. But overconcentration on charisma deflects our minds and makes it difficult for us to see that these leaders, despite their styles, were involved in the difficult work of creating institutions and organizations of permanence.

In addition to the scholarship that has been published in the past decade, important changes have been under way within the profession, the impact of which will be felt in the near future. At the time when Meier wrote his paper for the American Historical Association, he could tell the tale of the changes that had come about among historians of the black experience since Carter G. Woodson founded the Association for the Study of Negro Life and History in 1915 and almost single-handedly forced recognition of the history of black people as a fact and as a scholarly field. A long line of distinguished black scholars (A. A. Taylor, Lorenzo J. Greene, Benjamin Quarles, Charles Harris Wesley, and, of course, John Hope Franklin, to name a few) followed his lead. But at the time Meier spoke, most scholars in the field were white.

During the past decade, a growing number of young black historians have completed graduate work and are beginning the crucial work of training graduate students. This development will bring new perspectives

20. George M. Fredrickson, *White Supremacy: A Comparative Study in American and South African History* (New York, 1981).

to the study of the history of blacks as these graduate students begin to do their own research. Black historians of my generation generally were trained by white professors, and usually were encouraged to select research topics that were "main-line" or noncontroversial. In some cases the students brought backgrounds and perspectives to their research far different from those of their major professors and this produced manuscripts that were characterized by ambiguity. Work currently in progress shows that the graduate students in Afro-American history under the direction of black professors are being encouraged to ask penetrating questions about American society and the activities of black people.

The point of this discussion is not to imply that only black people can write worthwhile studies of Afro-Americans. If that were so, it would be meaningless to cite so much of the recent work on Afro-Americans. And, indeed, many of the younger scholars now in graduate school under black professors are white. It is clear that they will conduct their research with new perspectives as well. Nor should my comments about a new perspective be taken as a suggestion that history should be propagandized or that it should abandon the scientific methodology on which historians have always depended. Rather, what I have in mind is the development of a heightened sensitivity on the part of historians to the significance of black people in written histories. For example, it seems like a simple matter, I am sure, but the time has come for historians to change the practice of identifying Afro-Americans, even in books wholly about black people, as black, while the names of whites are simply written with no racial identification. The implication of such practice is that if an individual is important enough to be in a historical study, then he or she must be white unless otherwise described. In books about blacks, whites are the ones whose racial identity needs to be explained.

The quest for a change in perspective will improve overall the range of history and the level of our understanding of the numerous black experiences that have been lived in America. Tony Martin, for example, despite the criticisms that have been leveled at him for what some see as the exaggerated claims he makes for Marcus Garvey's place among black leaders, has contributed much to our understanding of both the man and his times. Indeed, regardless of what we might think about some of the details, we cannot help but see Garvey in a different light after reading Martin's book.[21]

21. Tony Martin, *Race First*.

Scholars have long lamented the "fact" that black people in America have been reluctant to become involved in radical activities. Such comments come from far too narrow a definition of what radical means. By and large, scholars have associated radicalism with the ideas of socialism and communism. But black people know quite well that it was a radical act for Frederick Douglass or Henry Highland Garnett to take the stands they did during the antebellum years. Indeed, in some parts of the American South, well into the twentieth century, the very act of attempting to go to the polls to vote was an act of radicalism. Even more so, the peaceful Civil Rights Movement of the 1950s and 1960s, with its modest aims of gaining equal justice for black people within the American system, was radical. It was radical because attainment of justice for blacks could be achieved only through major changes in the society. The deaths, beatings, burnings, and other sufferings that litter the road blacks have trod in their quest for justice seem sufficient evidence that blacks have made a radical assault on the system white Americans have constructed to deny them justice.[22]

Two recent books have taken us a long way toward seeing black people in this fuller light. Vincent Harding, in his study of the efforts of black people to survive during the years before the Civil War, and Mary Frances Berry and John Blassingame, in their overview of the history of Afro-Americans from the slave trade to the present, all emphasize the importance of permanence among the experiences of black people and stress the idea that black leaders were men and women of substance, not just individuals who had style. Although both books are filled with the pathos that has been part of the experience of black people in America, they both resound with examples of the determination with which Afro-Americans have endeavored to attain justice. Berry and Blassingame's title, *Long Memory*, emphasizes the collective wisdom and permanence of the black past, and Harding's *There Is a River*—a deep river indeed—is suggestive of the ever surging spirit among blacks to be free.[23]

In a review of those books, published in the *Journal of American History*, August Meier has lamented the pessimism these scholars show and

22. Vincent Harding, *There Is a River: The Black Struggle for Freedom in America* (New York, 1981), is helpful to understanding this meaning of radicalism in the activities of blacks in pre–Civil War America.

23. Mary Frances Berry and John W. Blassingame, *Long Memory: The Black Experience in America* (New York, 1982); Harding, *There Is a River.*

wonders "whither a black perspective" in regard to Afro-American historiography.[24] Professor Meier seems alarmed that these scholars are pessimistic. But it is a pessimism that is easily understood when one does perceive our time from the perspective of the black experience. It is a pessimism that I share as a historian and a sentiment I expressed in my most recent book. I wrote there, "Thus, contrary to my fondest hopes at the outset of this project, this is not an optimistic book," and I concluded in another place, in short, "This book is about the racism that has made it impossible for blacks to participate fully in American society."[25] Given the continually increasing gap between the earning power of blacks and whites while the unemployment rate of blacks already exceeds by more than two times that of whites, it is hardly time for optimism. Without question, pessimism is justified, and future work on the history of black people will have to take into account the interpretations of *There Is a River* and *Long Memory*.

Though much remains to be done, it is clear that the work of the past decade has contributed greatly to our understanding of black people and, necessarily, of the whole history of the United States. Work currently in progress, many of the preliminary findings of which have already appeared in articles and dissertations, suggests that the next decade will be equally as exciting. Scholars working in Afro-American history are on the cutting edge of the profession.

24. August Meier, "Whither the Black Perspective in Afro-American Historiography?" *Journal of American History*, LXX (June, 1983), 101–105.
25. William H. Harris, *The Harder We Run*.

VI INTEGRATING BLACK HISTORY

Integrating Afro-American History into American History

NATHAN I. HUGGINS

"Most people think American history is the story of white men, and that is why blacks want a history of their own." I began an essay in 1971 with that sentence. A blunt statement, but fair enough. American history seemed the story of white men and their institutions until the onrush of historical writing and reinterpretation that began in the late 1960s. Now that more than a decade has passed, it is a good time to rethink that statement. Until the mid-1960s it was impossible to describe what was then called Negro history as a legitimate field. Now one can hardly read a college catalog, a bibliography, or a publisher's list without a sense of remarkable change. Before the 1960s, those wanting to publish articles in Afro-American history were limited to the pages of the *Journal of Negro History*. Unless an article about blacks could pass as something on the Old South, Civil War, Reconstruction, or some such area, it would not likely find a place in the pages of "main-line" scholarly journals. The clamorous protests of the 1960s helped change things.

But this protest and agitation about race exclusion from American history was only part of the story. The triumph of the "new social history," the maturing of techniques of quantification (whereby previously mute and unsummoned witnesses could offer testimony), the ability of high-speed computers to make use of previously indigestible data, the vocal demands of women and others for acknowledgment in history, all contributed to a broad and deep change in American historiography. It was a collaborative and complementary (if not a cooperative) process; it was not just Afro-American history that marked the change. It is important to bear this in mind, because the revision has not been merely additive, that is to say just more about blacks included in historical writing and discourse. The character of the discourse has changed as historical problems have been freshly conceptualized, as the context has been enriched by a more heterogeneous history.

This is especially clear in fields like colonial history, where most of what has changed has been the work of historians not noted for their involvement in Afro-American history. Peter Wood, Edmund Morgan, Bernard Bailyn, and many others have, through their attention to ethnicity and race, changed profoundly how we think about the seventeenth and eighteenth centuries. It is certainly a far different social history from that of Carl Bridenbaugh.

Professor Bailyn, in his presidential address before the American Historical Association, described himself as having been a historian of the "Anglo-American experience," but went on to describe his present major project, which will include the peopling of America: people from the Congo as well as people from Northern Europe.[1] Similarly, we can see the great change in the history of slavery brought about by historians like John Blassingame, Leslie Owens, Herbert Gutman, George Rawick, Eugene Genovese, and others.

In Reconstruction, perhaps the liveliest American field at the moment, the works of Ransom and Sutch, Robert Higgs, Thomas Holt, Leon Litwack, and the forthcoming work of Eric Foner will transform our thinking about the period. Similarly, the works of Lawrence Levine, Sterling Stuckey, and Vincent Harding have changed the way we think about American culture in general.

Still, Afro-American history, like women's history, is a bit peculiar. These are not quite fields of history in the way that, say, social, economic, and intellectual history are. In such fields we are aware that history is being looked at through the prism of a specific discipline. Within either periods or fields, we assume that some centralizing principle or confluence of events offers special insight into a procession of events. The problem for Afro-American and women's history is that they are so essential to American

1. Bernard Bailyn, "The Challenge of Modern Historiography," *American Historical Review*, cxxxvii (February, 1982), 1–24.

history that it is perverse to think of it without them. A white American history and a male history ought to be, common sense tells us, unthinkable.

When I say that, I am also saying that we have read a lot—indeed, been brought up on—a lot of perverse history. But to pull these essential elements out for separate study does not, lacking a more realistic synthesis, produce a better history. Afro-American history as a subfield, therefore, is at once distinguishable, yet necessarily *within* the fabric. Much of what we do in the field is to bring a different angle of vision to well-known subjects and issues (*i.e.*, slavery and Reconstruction) or focus upon movements and their leaders (*e.g.*, Nell Painter's *The Exodusters* or her *Hosea Hudson*) or to bring attention through monographs to an important moment in time, an important issue in time, or a change that has occurred that makes a difference, that has consequence (*e.g.*, Darlene Hine's *Black Victory*). These should inform us and make us sensitive to the complexities and subtleties of the black experience.

That experience is illuminated, too, by biographies, which have increased greatly over the past decade. From Booker T. Washington to Langston Hughes, many black lives are now in published form, the obscure as well as the famous. Important collections of papers have been made accessible to scholars (*e.g.*, Herbert Aptheker's *Du Bois*, John Blassingame's *Douglass*, and Robert Hill's *Garvey*). In short, the work over the past decade has been to bring into view what has been latent in the warp and woof of American history.

As important as have been the accomplishments of the past two decades, we should not forget that the end of our study of history is the fabric itself. What we should expect in the end is no less than the reconstruction of American history. My metaphor of latent strands within fabric comports well with the rhetoric that was common in the 1960s, demanding history "from the bottom up." What we have witnessed is this latent matter being brought to the surface so that our view of the fabric is different. When we look at the whole, we ought to be seeing something different.

That American history is not what it once was is greeted by most of us with a great deal of satisfaction. The story of America I was told as a boy began with *our* pilgrim fathers and ended with my school days' present—the New Deal. That story, that continuum, that wholeness, that narrative is no longer available to us precisely because of changes brought about by the "new social" history, women's history, black history, etc. There has been a fragmenting and a faceting of the history so that the wholeness of the narrative no longer can contain all we now know to have been real, important, essential.

It has been a cause of complaint for a number of historians that the narrative is passé. While much of that complaint comes from conservative and reactionary impulses—the wish to hold to old values and clear away competing claims to historical significance—it is, nonetheless, important that we recognize that in an important way the *story* is what history is about. We all need to be calling for a new narrative, a new synthesis taking into account the new history. It is especially important for Afro-American historians, unless we are content merely to work in an eddy of the larger stream.

Afro-American history and American history are not only essential to one another. They share a common historical fate. Both the American nation and the Afro-American people are creations of the New World. Both were ruptured from tradition. History for both, therefore, has been problematic. Tradition is a legitimizing phenomenon. All peoples and all nations want to tie themselves to an ancient past (ideally, preliterate and mythic). The traditions are often related to place or to migration where antiquity alone would explain the *naturalness* and *rightness* of the present. Medieval political leaders liked to relate themselves (often as illicit offspring) to the myths of Homer and Virgil.[2] The modern state of Israel rests its territorial claims and its foreign policy on the Old Testament. Certainly, a nation born of revolution in a "New World" and a people snatched from the web of their tradition would face a similar problem of finding their legitimacy in history.[3]

The Founding Fathers were conscious that the actual history could not be the rationale on which their new nation could rest. They wanted to found their roots in a classical and honored past, while they were deliberately severing themselves from the one tradition that gave them place and

2. A number of still unpublished papers which were delivered at a conference at the Maison des Sciences de l'Homme in Paris, July 7–9, 1982, amplify this general idea. Susan Reynolds' "Medieval *Origines Gentium* and the Continuity of the Realm" is especially relevant. The conference addressed the general topic "Legitimation by Descent."

3. See my own paper at this conference: "The Afro-American and the Myth of American History."

reason. Afro-Americans, too, are new, a new people brought into being as a consequence of American history, a new people for whom after several generations in America it was impossible to trace back to any tradition beyond the American experience itself. This newness of people and nation has caused in both a problematic relationship with tradition.

Consider the generation of the so-called Founding Fathers. Here was a nation which they themselves had established, deliberately breaking from their immediate connections with the past. At the same time, nevertheless, they tried heroically to place themselves in a real, identifiable, classical tradition—one which could explain their present, more so than their past. America, the land and its native peoples, of course, had its own past, but it was not one the Anglo-American newcomers could honor (nor would that indigenous past honor them). America was not Britain or France or Italy or Greece, where the earth itself yielded up evidence that its contemporary generation belonged to something extending back beyond recorded time.

In America there were no ruins (except for Indian mounds) to be dug up, no statues as in Greece, the Holy Land, or Italy; no arches as in Rome; no Coliseum, none of that sort of thing. Yet, at the same time, this generation of new Americans went about identifying and naming their cities Rome and Troy and Athens and Syracuse and Ithaca and Utica and Alexandria and Augusta, names that clearly associated the present with an ancient past. And they did not simply choose place names, but they called on tradition to name the very institutions of their newly established polity. They might have called themselves a *commonwealth*, but they turned to the Roman *res publica* for *republic*. For their new leader, they thought of titles such as "His Mightiness," "His Highness," "Protector," "Regent," or "Serenity"; they chose "President" from *praesidens*. When they established themselves a legislature, it was not a "parliament," but a "congress," from *congressus*. Through it all, one sees this deliberate effort to establish a legitimacy with an ancient and glorious past.

As a further illustration, take the symbolism on the dollar bill. The great seal of the United States bears an eagle which, except for being an American bald eagle, suggests the eagle of the Roman legions. Both the olive branch and the sheaf of arrows it clasps—emblems of peace and war—have classical connotations and were not common symbols in this country before the Revolution. Then, the Latin phrase, *E pluribus unum*. On the obverse side, above the truncated pyramid, above the triangle in glory with the eye of God, one reads: *annuit coeptis*—he has favored our beginnings. Below the pyramid is *Novus ordo seclorum*—a new order of the ages. And at the base of the pyramid, in Roman numerals for greater dignity and authority, is MDCCLXXVI, which is when the new order of ages began. The Founding Fathers wanted to imbue 1776 with ancient virtue.[4]

In these pretenses the Founding Fathers were no different from Hugue Capet establishing a myth of descent from Aeneas, no different from all peoples who through myth and symbol attached themselves to a grand tradition from which they gain legitimacy and meaning. It was the rupture from their immediate and natural tradition (the final achievement of which was the American Revolution), the need to establish new birthright claims, that made their deliberate and self-conscious link with the classical past necessary.

Africans who were brought to America suffered a similar rupture from their immediate and natural tradition. They, too, were to become a new people, but it would not be easy to find a satisfactory linkage with any past known to them. The ancient European tradition was impossible, and the developing American myth of a providentially designed free society of democratic institutions did not accord with the black experience. For many, Christianity made possible the identification with the Children of Israel of the Old Testament.

But Afro-Americans lacked a specific and direct tie to Africa; we were alienated from, yet elemental to, the New World. Dissatisfied with our own history of slavery and oppression, we have desired to leap over the Afro-American experience altogether, to place ourselves in a tradition which is not immediately ours but certain to give us a sense of grandeur and legitimacy. Such mythologizing is not what we professional historians mean by historical study, but it is a deep human and social need which insinuates itself into our scholarship and criticism.

Even we professionals want history to give us legitimacy as a people or as a nation, and this is true whether we are Afro-Americans thinking of ourselves as a people or Americans thinking of ourselves as a nation. That is why the dominant Anglo-Saxon story of American history, that is to say the Bancroftian myth, persisted so long and with such strength in our his-

4. Howard Mumford Jones, *O Strange New World* (New York, 1963), 229.

toriography. The black and nonwhite experiences never comported well with the central myth—thus the tendency to deal with such groups as anomalous or egregious. That is why Afro-Americans have from the nineteenth century wanted to use the same history of America to demonstrate that we were here "before the Mayflower," that we were part of a developing nation and its history, and thus use American history to establish our birthright.

Consider the Sally Hemmings story, the power of it, its persistence. The evidence is circumstantial; we will never establish a *truth* all will accept. Certainly, we will never get Thomas Jefferson or Sally Hemmings to testify to the facts. There are those people, custodians of the Jefferson legacy, who have a clear stake in protecting not only his historical reputation but his progeny from the taint of race mixture. Similarly, there are those—I venture to say most black people—who *know* the rumors are essentially true despite gaps and problems with the evidence. Why is it so important? Sally Hemmings was certainly not the first or the only black woman so used. Why the fuss? It is not Sally Hemmings, but Thomas Jefferson who makes the difference. He was a Founding Father of the nation, and, the rumor had it, he sired children by a slave woman. In the overall effect of that story, it does not matter whether or not it was *actually* true. It is *symbolically* true. The story, like so many legitimizing myths, symbolically ties a people (through Sally Hemmings) to the founding of the nation. It is ironic, too, because of the illicit means of establishing legitimacy. That, too, is common in such birthright myths.

Alex Haley's *Roots*, to point to another example, for all of its many historical problems, captured the American imagination—white and black—like no recent work of history has. It accomplished two important things: (1) It evidenced the direct and specific connection between an Afro-American and a traditional Old World culture. It authenticated the Afro-American experience by means of an oral tradition, similar to the Old Testament and the *Iliad*. It authenticated an individual black man, a family, a family enlarged into the Afro-American people. (2) It integrated itself into the dominant Bancroftian myth of providential destiny of America, the American people and nation. The story ends with that onward, upward, progressive vision so characteristic of the American faith. Through *Roots*, black people could be mythically integrated into the American Dream. It does not matter whether or not Haley *actually* traced his family back to a

West African village. Whatever the truth, the story will continue to stand as emotionally and symbolically true.

In 1971, I was inclined to dismiss myth as not the proper work of historians. Although I still believe that professional historians have a responsibility not to pander to primal emotional needs and fantasies, I have come to appreciate better how the mythic can suggest itself into the most scholarly work. We blacks writing Afro-American history, no matter how much distance we like to maintain, are drawn to "tell the story of our people" in epic scale.

Vincent Harding's *There Is a River* and my own *Black Odyssey* are works driven by such need. There are many differences between these two works: differences in scale, in vision, in sense of history. Yet the similarities are noteworthy: their literary character, the use of literary devices to insinuate oneself and one's ideas into the experience of both the subject and the reader. Both attempt to include the reader into the *we* of the history. These are not *they* and *me* books. *We* and *our* are the dominant (though often implied) pronouns: we as reader, we as writer, we as Africans, we as Afro-Americans, we as slaves.

They are similar in another way: each has a dominant theme making the book cohere. That theme is explicit and relentless in Harding's work. In my own it is implicit, but nonetheless deliberate and obvious. Harding tells the history of black Americans as a story of resistance, with the "river" of resistance being the central metaphor. For my part, I make the slave experience one of transcendence of tyranny. The themes are not only narrative devices, they are instruments of historical selection and interpretation. The strokes are broad, antithesis muted or denied. In short, both works are attempts at epic.

In the attempt, however, both authors illustrate the problematic character of an Afro-American epic written in the late twentieth century. For, as one is asked to focus on the theme of resistance, the power of the oppressor necessarily remains dominant. As one is invited to celebrate the victory of the slave's humanity over the tyranny of his condition, one is drawn to the unmoved and immovable tyrant. It only reminds us (for those who need reminding) of the paradoxical character of the Afro-American experience. There is no way out of it. History "from the bottom up," as important as that is, will not turn the world upside down. Our reading of Harding or Huggins serves finally to convince us that the "river" and the "transcendence"—the oppression and tyranny that spawn them—have gone on, will continue to go on, far into the future. It is, perhaps, this problem that prompted August Meier to characterize *There Is a River* as "pessimistic."[5]

In a more general sense, these remarks suggest the central problem of the narrative (as well as the epic) for American history. One cannot imagine an updated George Bancroft persuading us. Contemporary Bancroftians like Carl Degler[6] bring our attention to the anomalies (blacks, at least) just as Harding and Huggins give silent authority to oppressors and tyrants. The modern American epic will have to discover the theme or metaphor that can bring all of the parts together in a common American story. Such a theme is latent in the American imagination. I think of the central idea in Martin Luther King, Jr.'s "I Have a Dream," as a force for unity, a river different from Harding's. It is surely more compelling and enduring than Booker T. Washington's metaphor of the hand and the fingers. As a practical matter, however, no such epic theme can work without the factual and experiential basis on which to make it credible. So far, such optimistic themes work better as dreams of future possibility and as America's unrealized calling than as history.[7]

Black Americans, like the American nation itself, will be forever searching into the past to provide a sense of legitimacy and historical purpose, forever bound and frustrated in the effort. I do not suggest this is something they ought not to do, but that it must be done again and again, never with satisfaction. In this regard, black Americans who work in this field are different from their white colleagues. It is *their* history, and in a deep, personal and emotional way they will never be able to escape their personal identification with it however much scholarly distance is achieved. That is fair enough and no different from other historians with what they consider *their* history.

I mean this to be neither a validating nor an invalidating idea regarding black or white historians working in the field. It is merely to state the ob-

---

5. August Meier, Review of Vincent Harding's *There Was a River* (New York, 1981).

6. Carl Degler, *Out of Our Past* (New York, 1959).

7. What George Bancroft, Alex Haley, Carl Degler, *et al.* have in common is the implicit sense of destiny moving toward some promise in the future, "The Dream." Such histories would seem to preempt the future, characterizing this "epic" story as American and unlike such classic epics as the *Iliad*.

vious. I hope we have moved beyond the view, pervasive within the profession before the 1960s, that a black historian's judgment about slavery, etc., had to be discounted as naturally biased, while whites had no ax to grind, and the equally foolish idea of the 1960s and 1970s that white historians could not write or comment on the black experience. I mean only to point to the dual character of history. We need to know how and why we use history: to serve both our needs of personal and group identity as well as for the more "scientific" and humanistic purposes of historical analysis. We should know the differences and not confound them.

Most of what we read as Afro-American history is really not so cosmic as all of this. Rather, it is quite limited, particular, and precise. Most do not address large, ideational issues. Most, I am forced to say, are rather parochial. It has been an "archaeological" work, digging and opening new ground. It brings to our attention particulars, data that is new to us. These shards, in themselves, are not startling discoveries, but they constitute a new history as far as Americans are concerned. We now have a number of monographs that have made genuine contributions.

So you get studies of blacks in Kentucky, blacks in Illinois, blacks in Indiana, or wherever. The history gets repeated again and again; we need the reiteration, each with its particular or special angle or twist. We need to know the sameness to discover in it what is unique. Sometimes the angle of vision is only slightly shifted: now it is "black men," now it is "black women." We take old, much-studied issues and institutions and reconsider them with blacks in mind. We look at individual lives, often by means of oral histories and interviews, to bring into our consciousness ranges of human experience previously remote or inaccessible to us. It is all extremely important work, and the production of the past decade has been impressive.

The danger, however, is that we see this work as the end and purpose of Afro-American history—creating a narrow specialty over which we establish a proprietary interest, squeezing our concerns to the point of historical insignificance. It is a danger because the American academic professions encourage such mindless territoriality, and because many are fearful to venture beyond their carefully cultivated certitudes.

We ought, rather, to see this work as the building blocks of a new synthesis, a new American history. Would that the work should raise such fundamental questions of American society as to provoke discourse among American historians to change the history they write. We are able now to say, as we were not fifteen years ago, that blacks (black leaders, the black experience, etc.) is *included* in the textbooks. That is not enough.

Recently, I was asked to review a manuscript for a college textbook in American history. It seemed all right; it omitted no notable group; it made no mistakes; it covered all the bases. It was, nevertheless, a poor history. The authors had a chapter on mid-nineteenth-century reform. William Lloyd Garrison and the abolitionists were there. Frederick Douglass was not. He was in another chapter, the one on blacks. Surely we must know that what actually happened in that historical moment was a consequence of the interaction between Douglass and Garrison. It cannot be told as a story of *black history* and *white history*. It must be told as one. While that idea is simple enough—a truism indeed—too few of us accept the radical implications of it. We do not put it into our thinking, our writing, our courses. That idea, nevertheless, is a key to any new, successful narrative of American history.

It may be that the Afro-American story remains too discordant with progressive assumptions to be comfortably incorporated into the American story, Alex Haley notwithstanding. Dominant, national narratives, after all, are *selected* from a matrix of historical experience. What is chosen, and how it is put together, tells us how a people would like to perceive themselves—their future as well as their past. As Americans, we have liked the succession of events to move in ever-ascending stages, each today better than all yesterdays. Surely there were problems, but there were reforms and resolutions. Things worked out. All national histories are not so optimistic and progressive as our own. Some are characteristically ironic, some cyclical, some fatalistic.[8]

Except for Alex Haley's *Roots*, I know of no treatment of the Afro-American story that shares the dominant optimism and faith in progress, certainly not one written in the late twentieth century. The Afro-American story has more been told in terms of failed hopes, frustrated and ambiguous victories, dreams deferred. In contrast to the dominant American story, it is most often characterized as tragic.[9] It may well be that the new American narrative, when it is written, will resonate to a more experienced, a wiser, nation. We might, then, see as if for the first time, the ele-

---

8. Hayden White, "Introduction," *Metahistory, the Historical Imagination in Nineteenth-Century Europe* (Baltimore, 1973).
9. *Ibid.*

mental truth in the black American experience; rather than being an anomaly, it is central to the story. That would result in a new American history, indeed.

We need not wait for such grand, synthetic efforts; there is much to be done. Old questions in American history demand new answers from the angle of vision of Afro-American history. Old topics seem different from that perspective: the city, economic development, citizenship, federalism, majority rule, and so on. On the scale of dissertation and monograph, with a new vision there is new history to be written if historians and teachers are willing to be genuinely challenging. Moreover, historians of the Afro-American experience must reach beyond ethnic history by choosing topics having historical significance beyond narrow bounds of race, by developing the implications of their work for the general history, and by raising through their work general questions, provoking discourse among historians and contributing to the new American history.

VII BLACK HISTORY COURSES

The Teaching of Afro-American History in Schools and Colleges

BETTYE J. GARDNER

It is particularly significant that the "state of the art" conference on the teaching of Afro-American history should be sponsored by the American Historical Association, for it was this organization's Committee of Seven which was given the charge in 1899 or assessing the "teaching of history and allied subjects in European as well as American schools."[1] The basic concern of the committee was the establishment of history as a school subject.[2] The eight decades that have passed since the report of the committee have been a time of tremendous turmoil and change. Two world wars, McCarthyism, the emergence of independent nations in the Third World, and the Civil Rights Movement of the 1960s were only a few of the historical events marking this century. Because Afro-Americans constitute the largest minority in this country, it is crucial that the nation not forget the question raised by W. E. B. Du Bois in the opening years of this century: "Would America have been America without her Negro people?"

As I reflected on that question, and on the need for a "state of the art" conference in 1983, it seemed somehow ironic that we must still justify the study and teaching of Afro-American history. Approximately fifty years ago Carter G. Woodson wrote his now classic study, *The Mis-Education of the Negro* (1933). His basic thesis dealt with the failure to present au-

1. Irving Morrisett (ed.), *Social Studies in the 1980s: A Report of Project Span* (N.p., n.d.), 2.
2. *Ibid.*

thentic black history in public schools. This neglect of Afro-American history and the distortion in many history books of the facts concerning blacks deprived black children and the whole race of a heritage and relegated them to nothingness.[3] Unfortunately, as we assess the status of Afro-American history in 1983, we seem to have come full circle, for Woodson's concerns are still viable today.

I focus here on the status of Afro-American history in selected colleges and universities, with some attention being given to the manner in which these courses are handled at the secondary school level. For most of this century, ours has been a nation made up of many races and cultures, yet it was Du Bois who, foreseeing a continuing problem between the white population and the people of African descent, wrote eloquently of the racial twoness felt by Afro-Americans.

> One ever feels his twoness—an American, a Negro; two souls, two thoughts, two unreconciled strivings; two warring ideals in one dark body. . . . The history of the American Negro is the history of the strife— this longing to attain self-conscious manhood, to merge his double self into a better and truer self. In this merging he wishes neither of the older selves to be lost. He would not Africanize America, for America has too much to teach the world and Africa. He would not bleach his Negro soul in a flood of white Americanism for he knows that Negro blood has a message for the world. He simply wishes to make it possible for a man to be both a Negro and an American without being cursed and spit upon by his fellows, without having the doors of Opportunity closed roughly in his face.[4]

It was this racial twoness that gave rise to the study and teaching of Afro-American history, with Carter G. Woodson and the Association for the Study of Negro Life and History providing most of the historical focus in the years between World Wars I and II. Unfortunately, as St. Clair Drake pointed out in a 1969 speech, "Negro history remained for a half century an extra curricular activity, important . . . within the black community and among a small group of scholars . . . but never able to overcome the lethargy and often hostile attitudes of school administrators, teachers and textbook publishers who resisted pleas for the curricular and textbook re-

---

3. Carter G. Woodson, *The Mis-Education of the Negro* (1937; rpt. Washington, D.C., 1969), *vi*.

4. W. E. B. Du Bois, *The Souls of Black Folk* (1903; rpt. New York, 1982), 45.

vision needed to set the record straight."[5] For a few brief years, between the late 1960s and the early 1970s, the interest in Afro-American history peaked; resources of every description were available, and interest was high among students, scholars, and lay persons. In 1983, however, we have pretty much returned to a pre-1960s status quo. At this point we need to take stock and perhaps chart a different course for the twenty-first century.

Building on an analysis of some syllabi that I reviewed two years ago for a curriculum project sponsored by the Institute of the Black World and a review of current syllabi shared by colleagues at Howard University, Ohio State University, the University of Maryland at Baltimore County, the University of Wisconsin, Morgan State University, and Purdue University, I have drawn certain conclusions concerning the teaching of Afro-American history. Although it is difficult to assess course content solely on the basis of course syllabi, one can determine approach, objectives, and the sources to be used. Many of the syllabi that I reviewed two years ago (these came from colleges across the nation) were clearly lacking in course objectives, goals, approaches, and familiarity with sources.[6] If Afro-American history courses do nothing more, they must provide students with a foundation for understanding and appreciating the black past. Without this foundation, students cannot develop a sense of place, of who they are and where they are in time. Moreover, Afro-American history, if properly taught, does not seek to replace old myths with new ones, but rather hopes to provide a perspective for understanding the black experience.

Course syllabi covering the antebellum period, for example, relied heavily on sources and class discussions relating to the institution of slavery, with little attention to the free black communities in Boston, New York, Philadelphia, Baltimore, New Orleans, and Charleston. The complexity of black life is missing if students do not understand that free blacks were much more than "slaves without masters." It is essential that students realize that in the cities mentioned, and in others, free blacks built enduring communities.

Another course, "American Women, Black and White, 1775–1968," reflected a certain unfamiliarity with sources relating to the experiences of

5. St. Clair Drake, "Black Studies: Toward an Intellectual Framework" (An address, Brooklyn College of the City University of New York City, 1969), 1.

6. Bettye J. Gardner, "Evaluation of Course Syllabi for Afro-American History Before 1865" (Unpublished paper, 1981).

black women. Michele Wallace's *Black Macho and the Myth of the Super-woman* (1979), one of the textbooks for this course, is not generally considered the best study of the historical experiences of black women. Although women's history, and black women's history specifically, is still handicapped by a sparsity of sources, there are a number of sound works available. Bert Loewenberg and Ruth Bogin's *Black Women in Nineteenth-Century American Life* (1976) is an excellent source which allows twenty-four black women to speak for themselves about their experiences. Several of the essays in Rosalyn Terborg-Penn and Sharon Harley's *The Afro-American Woman* (1978) would be relevant, as would Gerda Lerner's *The Majority Finds Its Past* (1979) and Darlene Clark Hine's recently completed *When the Truth Is Told* (1981). Although it is not clear from the syllabus, I would hope that such black women as Charlotte Forten, Frances Watkins Harper, Anna Julia Cooper, Ida Wells Barnett, Mary Church Terrell, and Mary McLeod Bethune, to mention only a few, find their way into the lectures and discussions of the course.[7]

It is also quite clear from the syllabi reviewed that few colleagues have begun to integrate the experiences of black women into Afro-American history courses. There are presently a number of black women working in the area of black women's history who can be contacted to serve as consultants and resource persons in regard to the teaching of black women's history as well as the integration of that history into Afro-American history courses.

Given the fact that publishers have little to offer in terms of textbooks in Afro-American history (most college teachers are using John Hope Franklin's *From Slavery to Freedom* [1948] or Benjamin Quarles' *The Negro in the Making of America* [1969]), greater use of primary sources would provide students with a different feel for the past. For example, from nineteenth-century city directories students can learn much about the ethnic makeup of neighborhoods and the occupations of free blacks. Wills, deeds, manumission records, permits, free papers, and church records can provide a feel for the nineteenth-century black experience that is not gotten from textbooks.

In teaching students about the experiences of blacks during slavery, the slave narratives should be assigned, both the collection of narratives by the

7. *Ibid.*, 4–6.

WPA and those written by individuals such as Frederick Douglass. Certainly plantation slavery dominated the Deep South, but what of the patterns of urban slavery? Comparisons and contrasts must be made if a balanced picture is to emerge and this requires searching out the information. *Crisis, Phylon,* and the *Journal of Negro History,* for example, are among the most important journals chronicling the black experience. Du Bois' editorials in *Crisis* are legendary, and some of the most scholarly research on Afro-American history is found within the pages of the *Journal.* Yet, there was little apparent usage of these sources.

The syllabi that colleagues have generously shared this year are outstanding for the manner in which they approach the teaching of Afro-American history. Although most of the syllabi are reflections of introductory courses, several are upper-level, specialized Afro-American history courses, such as the "History of Black Women in America," "American Law and the Afro-American Experience, 1619–1865," "Special Topics in Afro-American Studies," "Nineteenth-Century Black Nationalism," "The Seminar in Afro-American History" (a reading and research course), "Black Labor History from Colonial Times to the Present," and "Slavery in the American South."

In that these courses represent different approaches to teaching the Afro-American experience in America, I offer the following course descriptions as examples of what can be found at the college level.[8]

(1) The course, "Slavery in the American South," is designed to give students at the sophomore, junior, and senior levels a broad overview of the major components of the ante-bellum slave system as it operated on the southern plantation and in southern urban and industrial contexts. The class will also be exposed to several of the major controversies (involving historical interpretation and plantation realities) which should concern serious students of black American slavery.

In addition to viewing films on the "heritage of slavery" and on black resistance to bondage, class members will have an opportunity to study relevant topics which suit their own personal interests—later sharing their interests and findings with the rest of the class. These "sharing ses-

8. Syllabi cited from: (1) Professor William L. Van Deburg, Department of History, University of Wisconsin, Madison; (2) Professor Herbert Hill, Department of History, University of Wisconsin, Madison; (3) Professor Darlene Clark Hine, Department of History, Purdue University; (4) Professor Tom Shick, Department of History, University of Wisconsin.

sions" will be supplemented by commentary and hand-out materials from the professor as well as by group discussions of the required readings from the course texts.

During the semester, the course explores the controversy surrounding Fogel and Engerman's book *Time on the Cross* and its counter-essay, *Slavery and the Numbers Game*. Finally the course examines the nature and extent of Denmark Vesey's 1822 slave conspiracy and probes the "mind of the South" during the slave era in order to determine the attitudes of various segments of the population toward race and black bondage.

(2) The "Black Labor History" course examines the first slave laws based on race and the development of a dual racial labor system in America. A major theme of the course is the relationship between white and black workers in a racist society. The role of organized labor and its effect on the struggles of black workers is analyzed in successive periods with emphasis on the black response to white working class behavior. Major attention is given to the history of black labor organizations in the past and in the present. A comprehensive analysis is made of the effects of government policy and employer and labor union practices on the status of black workers. The consequences of automation and technological change for black labor in the contemporary period is studied as well as such issues as the changing judicial perception of employment discrimination, the role of federal contract compliance, and the effects of antipoverty programs among the urban black population. The social characteristics of the stable black working class that have been central to black protest and to community institutions for many generations are also studied. The history of the black worker is examined within the changing context of racial conflict in American society.

A course on the "History of Black Women in America" seeks to bring black women in America into sharper focus so that their roles, contributions, status, and lives may be thoroughly examined and evaluated. This course places special emphasis on the articulation and analysis of the historical and contemporary issues concerning black women as community leaders, wage earners, wives, mothers, professionals, and creative beings.

(3) This course seeks to enable students:

—to define and appreciate the contributions black women have made to America and to the survival of black people;

—to evaluate and understand the concept of "black matriarchy" and the diverse shapes and forms of the black family;

—to explain and critique both the psychological implications and sociological dynamics of being a black woman in white America;

—to destroy myths surrounding black women and their alleged social, political, economic, and educational advantages;

—to examine and place in its proper perspective the literature surrounding black men/black women relationships.

One of the best syllabi for an introductory Afro-American history course has the following course description:

(4) The purpose of this course is to analyze the historical experience of Afro-Americans in the United States from the turn of the century to the decade of the 1970s. This period in modern world history is remarkable for the rise and fall of European colonialism, the Russian revolution and its consequences, two world wars, and the emergence of non-Western nations as political forces in world affairs. This status at the start of the century as a predominantly rural, southern peasant population living under conditions of rigid racial proscription changed to that of an increasingly urbanized proletarian population that mobilized to challenge institutional racism in America. The goal in this course will be to identify and understand the historical forces (both within the Afro-American community itself and elsewhere) which shaped the Afro-American experience during the period.

While I am not suggesting that the approach taken in the previously mentioned syllabi is the only approach, I am suggesting that the teaching of Afro-American history is serious business. Our students must all come to understand and appreciate the rich experience of Afro-Americans throughout the history of this nation. And again we are reminded of Du Bois' question, "Would America have been America without her Negro people?"

Although many colleges and universities still offer Afro-American history courses, the same does not appear to be true at the secondary level. During my effort to gather data for this presentation, neither NEA nor the Council on the Social Studies could provide nationwide data reflective of the status of Afro-American history.

The Span Report on Social Studies in the 1980s cites as one of the six major problems facing the discipline "the fact that the traditional Social Studies curriculum gives little recognition to student developmental needs or societal issues. With few exceptions, attention to ethnic diversity has been of a temporary nature. Schools have included such topics, briefly replacing them after a trial period with traditional courses or gradually reducing the time devoted to them." The report further states that publishers tend to produce commercial materials that are of a traditional nature; hence teachers seeking alternatives must write their own materials.[9]

I would like to describe the approach being used in four large urban secondary school districts: Washington, Baltimore, Philadelphia, and Detroit. Washington and Baltimore have adopted the multi-cultural approach to the teaching of social studies, with Afro-American history making up one component. Detroit and Philadelphia still offer specific courses in Afro-American history. All four school districts have had to design most of their own materials.

The Washington secondary schools use "Pluralism in the U.S.A." as an overall theme. Social studies curriculum specialists wrote a curriculum resource bulletin for secondary schools in 1962 entitled "The Afro-American Experience in American History"; the guide was revised in 1972 and is still being used today. In 1974 a curriculum guide was also produced by social studies specialists on contemporary Africa. Both guides emphasize the fact that there is continuity between the African past and the experiences of black Americans and the resiliency of African culture. Teachers are encouraged to use these guides in all social studies courses. United States history and the history of the District of Columbia are required courses, with Afro-American history being offered as an elective.[10]

Social studies coordinators in the Baltimore city public schools, as in the Washington schools, have designed many of their own materials. The central thrust of the social studies curriculum in the Baltimore schools is also in the direction of multiethnicity and cultural pluralism. Dr. Samuel Banks, social science coordinator for the Baltimore city public schools, in an essay entitled "Blacks in a Multi-Ethnic Social Studies Curriculum," has pointed out that Afro-American or black history is not a separate history. The history of the black American is inextricably interwoven with the history of our nation. If black history is not taught and written within the perspective of our total history, then a distorted and inaccurate history will continue to prevail. The paramount goal, concludes Banks, "must be the

9. Morrissett (ed.), *Social Studies in the 1980s*, 85–86.

10. *The Afro-American Experience in American History: A Curriculum Resource Bulletin for Secondary Schools* (Washington, D.C., 1972), *Contemporary Africa*, 1974.

presentation of an authentic record which depicts the reality and truth of the role and contributions of black Americans to American history."[11]

The eleventh grade United States history text covers four themes, each of which examines the diverse roles of America's minorities. In Theme I, for example, entitled "People with Diverse Backgrounds Develop a Pluralistic Society," the experiences of black Americans—both slave and free—are examined. Students are expected to be able to identify and compare the experiences of free blacks during the slavery era, to examine the long and varied history of black nationalism, to recognize and identify the reasons for the formation of separate black churches, and to verify the nineteenth-century efforts of blacks toward self-help. For each of the four themes students are provided a list of additional sources and possible questions to be explored during class discussions.[12]

The division of social studies of the Philadelphia public schools takes very seriously its commitment to seeing that African and Afro-American studies are an intrinsic part of the curriculum. In its philosophy, the following considerations are especially important:

1. The traditional textbooks and the communication media perpetuated the myths and stereotypes which resulted in the shaping of national attitudes which were not only destructive but contradictory.

2. When the participation and contributions of Afro-Americans are studied from the perspective of national development, a new dimension is given to the history of the American people and the nation as a whole.

3. The struggles and aspirations of black people for freedom, justice, equality of opportunity, and a sense of dignity in American life are a constant reminder of the gap between democratic ideals and the social realities of today.[13]

Students at the twelfth grade level are introduced to Afro-American history as "an interdisciplinary approach within an historical framework."

11. Samuel Banks, "Blacks in a Multi-Ethnic Social Studies Curriculum," in *Inquiry Techniques in Teaching a Multi-Ethnic Social Studies Curriculum* (N.p., 1974), 29–30.

12. Baltimore City Public Schools, *United States History, Senior High School: A Guide for Teachers* (Baltimore, 1972), 57–59.

13. Office of Curricula and Instruction, the School District of Philadelphia, *African and Afro-American Studies, Major Concepts and Behavioral Objectives* (Philadelphia, n.d.), 1.

Among the "competencies and tasks" that students are expected to master are the following items:

Competency: Comparing and Contrasting
Task: Compare and contrast the migration trends of black Americans from the South to northern urban centers for the periods 1917–1920 and 1939–1943.

Competency: Research
Task: On the basis of the information provided by the inscription on his tombstone reproduced below, determine what values influenced Thaddeus Stevens to sell the burial plot he had owned in a segregated white cemetery and buy one in a black cemetery.

> "I repose in this quiet and secluded spot not from natural preference for solitude, but finding other cemeteries limited by charter rules as to race I have chosen this that I might illustrate in death the principles which I have advocated through a long life, Equality of man before his creator."

Competency: Recall
Task: Place the following important events in the order of their occurrence:

> Thurgood Marshall appointed to the U.S. Supreme Court
>
> Brown vs. Board of Education outlaws segregation in the public schools of the United States
>
> The Montgomery Boycott
>
> The March on Washington
>
> The Silent March down Fifth Avenue
>
> Plessy vs. Ferguson Supreme Court Decision [14]

The final school district to be discussed briefly is Detroit. Much like the program in Philadelphia, here there are a number of in-class activities and out-of-class experiences that Norman McRae, director of the Department of Social Studies, and his staff provide on Afro-American life and history. In addition to having a teacher's guide titled *The Negro in American His-*

14. Office of Curriculum and Development, School District of Philadelphia, *African and Afro-American Studies, Tasks, and Competencies* (Philadelphia, n.d.), 18–20; Conversation with Carolyn Holmes, assistant director, African and Afro-American Studies Program, October, 1983.

tory, which is very similar to the ones used by the other school districts, principals and teachers are continuously kept abreast of activities that are designed to broaden the educational experiences of their students. In a series of memoranda spanning a four-year period, Dr. McRae announced the availability of teaching guides for students and teachers on "Roots, the Next Generation," the Optimist Club's annual historical seminar, the Tuskegee airmen's program (designed to aid students in understanding the role of black airmen in World War II), teacher's guide for a 16mm film—"The Buffalo Soldier"—and the Detroit branch of the NAACP's black history quiz contest (quizzes were available for both elementary and secondary students).[15] It is clear from discussions with Dr. McRae and from his correspondence that every effort is made to make Afro-American history a living history. Among the many excellent sources available to teachers is *Blacks in Detroit* (1980), a reprint of articles which appeared in the *Detroit Free Press* during November and December, 1980.[16]

There are a number of ways in which students of all ages and faculties are being motivated to be aware of the Afro-American experience both in and outside the classroom. The National Education Association in cooperation with the Association for the Study of Afro-American Life and History (ASALH) sponsors the History Council Trenholm Memorial Writing Contest for high school students. The objectives of the contest are to encourage class and independent study of Afro-American life and history and to honor the life of Mr. Trenholm, who served as vice-president of the ASALH for twenty-five years and as executive secretary of the American Teachers' Association before its merger in 1966. The Maryland Commission on Afro-American History has recently published *A Guide to Afro-American History in Maryland, 1634–1978*. Although the guide is not definitive, it is meant to provoke discussion and further study. Accompanying the guide are a list of suggested questions and a bibliography intended to aid both teachers and students in studying the Afro-American experience in Maryland.[17]

15. Detroit Public Schools, *The Negro in American History: A Guide for Teachers* (Detroit, 1965); Conversation with Dr. Norman McRae, director of the Department of Social Studies, October, 1983; Memoranda—February 9, 1979, January 25, 1982, January 31, 1983, March 28, 1983.

16. Scott McGehee and Susan Watson (eds.), *Blacks in Detroit* (N.p., 1980).

17. National Education Association–Trenholm Memorial Writing Contest, *Guide to Afro-American History in Maryland, 1634–1978* (Maryland, n.d.).

More than 150 years ago John Russwurm wrote in the first issue of *Freedom's Journal* that for "too long have others spoken for us. Too long has the public been deceived by misrepresentations in things which concern us dearly."[18] Believing in this statement, the Consortium on Research Training, directed by Dr. George Breathett, was funded by the Office of Education in 1973 to support research in the humanities and social sciences. The consortium has as its mission "strengthening the research competencies of both students and faculties in several historically black colleges and universities." Dr. Breathett has commented that "where there is an absence of research, there is also an absence of quality teaching." Participants in the consortium were involved in a variety of topics relating to the black experience, several of which were later published.[19]

Realizing the need to see that the experience of Afro-Americans is shared across disciplines, the National Endowment for the Humanities has in recent years funded projects designed to enhance an appreciation of Afro-American life and history. Two such projects were the "Humanities Perspectives on the South" and "Southern Black Culture: The African Heritage and the American Experience," an NEH summer seminar for college teachers held at Spelman College in 1981. The "Humanities Perspectives" project, a pilot project, involved Jackson State University, the University of Arkansas, North Carolina A & T, and Southern University. Emphasizing the experiences of Afro-Americans in the South, each of these colleges designed humanities courses based on the regional and ethnic diversity within their particular areas. The humanities project at Spelman provided participants with the opportunity to develop interdisciplinary materials focusing on southern black culture. Each resultant syllabus was structured to contain some elements pertaining to Afro-American culture. Examples of syllabi developed were "Black Writers in American Literature," "Music Appreciation as a Study of African-American Musical Culture, 1619–1900," "Introduction to Literature: Perspectives on the African Diaspora," and "Afro-American History: A Study of Southern Black Culture."[20]

18. John W. Blassingame, "Black Studies and the Role of the Historian," in John W. Blassingame (ed.), *New Perspectives on Black Studies* (Champaign-Urbana, 1971), 220–21.

19. George Breathett, *Research in the Humanities and Social Sciences*, III (Greensboro, N.C., n.d.).

20. Humanities Perspectives on the South, a National Endowment for the Humani-

Teachers of history must be committed to providing students with a sense of the past, for, as Lerone Bennett concluded in a February, 1981, article in *Ebony Magazine*, "Each generation is dependent not only on the generations immediately preceding and following, but on all the generations that will run the race." It is the responsibility of historians and teachers working together to make sure that the dreams of the past can be fulfilled, that the slaves and the sharecroppers and the martyrs and victims did not bleed and dream and die in vain.[21]

---

ties Pilot Project. Conference, June, 1981, Savannah, Georgia; "Southern Black Culture . . . Syllabi for Undergraduate Courses in the Humanities," NEH Humanities Institute, June–July, 1981.

21. Lerone Bennett, *Ebony Magazine*, February, 1981, p. 42.

COMMENT

ROBERT C. HAYDEN

Bettye J. Gardner has given us a most telling account of the status of Afro-American history in contemporary education. The situation at the secondary level described by Gardner is accurate and more pervasive even than she suggested. Attention to ethnic/racial historical diversity in the social studies curriculum has been temporary and fleeting; even teacher-designed materials are not regularly used. Although guidelines issued by the American Historical Association for the certification of teachers of history at the secondary school level recommend *one course* that deals primarily with an American culture group other than the teacher's own, the guidelines do not specify any requirement in Afro-American history and culture. I believe that teachers must enter into discussion with the AHA and other similar groups for specific inclusion of Afro-American history in their official position papers on teacher certification. Afro-American history or courses on Africa are taught only if there happens to be a teacher who has established a course through personal interest, research, and study.

Of late, what James Banks at the University of Washington has called the "ethnic additive model" has been in use.[1] Banks conceptualizes ethnic studies as a process of curriculum reform that should lead from a total Anglo-American perspective on our history and culture (Model A), to

1. James A. Banks, *Multiethnic Education: Practices and Promises* (Bloomington, Ind., 1977).

multiethnic perspectives as additives to the major curriculum (Model B), and finally to a completely multiethnic curriculum in which every historical and social event is viewed from the perspectives of different ethnic/racial groups (Model C). In Model C the Anglo-American perspective is only one of several and is in no way superior or inferior to other ethnic perspectives. During the American Revolutionary War, for example, how did black people, free and slave, as well as the French, the Spanish, the Native Americans, and women view and participate in the struggle for freedom? Too often we learn only about the role of the British and the Minutemen.

According to Banks, many schools that have attempted ethnic modification of the curriculum have implemented Model B programs by adding courses on Afro-American history and culture. It is suggested here, however, that curriculum reform move *directly* from the total Anglo-American perspective of Model A to the complete multiethnic perspective of Model C. The schools that have Model B programs should also quickly move to Model C.

History should be the major discipline of the social studies, especially in grades six through ten. Briefly, my reasons for suggesting history as the organizing discipline in the public schools are as follows. History—properly conceived, organized, and taught—provides the best structure for giving students: (1) a unified sense of their own culture and an understanding of the possibilities of cultural difference; (2) an understanding of how ideas, politics, economics, technology, and other factors interact over short and long periods to constitute a relatively stable but still-changing civilization; (3) the experience of discussing and writing about significant events and ideas; and (4) a perspective on cultures and societies that can make more meaningful their courses in other areas of social studies.

I shall now describe an approach or teaching strategy to Afro-American history for the middle and high school levels of our public schools. I have directed projects using this approach in Philadelphia and Boston. I am concerned with not only what our students learn about their history but also how they learn it, and how what they learn can be used for black community development.

Learning the processes of history requires students to engage themselves in the activities of historians at a level of sophistication appropriate to their abilities. Note that I say students must engage themselves, not that teachers must engage students in these activities. Students have an inherent interest in the past, a curiosity about what has gone before them. Research is merely institutionalized inquiry, curiosity in action. It seeks in a systematic way to find the materials that will answer questions. The teacher's task is to help students frame the questions that can help them satisfy their curiosity and to channel the pursuit of answers toward productive ends.

Bettye Gardner cited in her paper the SPAN report on social studies, which said that traditional social studies curricula and textbooks give little recognition to student developmental needs. I want to address the developmental needs of young adolescents and teenagers. The method is to use the history of the local black community to teach Afro-American history in our middle and secondary schools. This approach utilizes the following six techniques: (1) family history studies; (2) oral history; (3) documentary research with primary and secondary source materials; (4) artifact collection, including archaeology above and below the ground; (5) historical photograph collection, study, and preservation; (6) historic building and landmark studies.

I propose that the following four basic questions can and should be answered by junior and senior high students and that these questions are especially important for black students: (1) How did Afro-American people in a given urban community live many years ago, from the 1800s through the early 1900s and up to 1960? (2) In what way does the present black urban community reflect what happened in the past? (3) Can we think about future urban communities using insights into and understandings about the past? (4) How do we provide a sense of community identity for the older and younger residents of an urban community?

Local urban communities provide rich opportunities for teachers to use tangible sorts of learning experiences in the middle-grade social studies curriculum. From physical contact with elements of their own community, young students can gain understandings that enhance their acquisition of abstract concepts and information processing skills. The community is the "laboratory" students can use to study data, draw conclusions, make decisions, and think about the future of their neighborhood, school, and city. While the learning sequence may not differ drastically from what would be utilized in the classroom using more traditional materials, the concreteness and the "real worldness" of past features of the local community are likely to stimulate a higher degree of personal commitment and enthusiasm for learning than can be anticipated when books, films, and other simulations of reality are used.

The "community laboratory" has unique features that give it more potential for providing learning than more familiar laboratories in the physical and biological sciences. Why do I say this? In the community laboratory, students are both participants and observers, not just observers alone. Generalizations and inferences developed from the community's historical setting assist students in understanding why they live as they do and how people working together can improve the quality of life in their community.

Learning in the community can have profound personal implications. For middle-grade and high school students, learning from the community can put to rest the myth that "learning" occurs only within the walls of the school building. By encouraging the view that learning occurs wherever learning opportunities are present, students can be led to see learning as a personally meaningful lifelong experience that can serve them long after their formal schooling has ended.

A successful community-focused history program for middle-grade students depends on two things: (a) a careful identification and categorization of stimulus experiences, the stimulus experiences being called historical residues, and (b) a clear explication of categories of anticipated student learning. These categories encompass the ability to make grounded generalizations, the ability to examine values, and the ability to make decisions.

What do I mean by historical residues as stimulus experiences? Historical residues are physical traces of a community's past. In a method drawing on techniques from the discipline of history, students might be encouraged to look at old buildings, family photographs, city records, diaries of early residents, old newspapers, and old maps. They could interview longtime residents or younger descendants of the early residents. Historical residues can serve as a mechanism for teaching students how to use the basic tools of historical investigation. Young students can learn how to make inferences from examinations of artifacts and other data and to write short historical accounts.

Anticipated pupil learnings—what are they? The art of making grounded generalizations is one. This involves students in cognitive processes requiring the organization of specific data from the local community. Through organizing data from historical residues, students can respond to questions such as: What has been left? What do these residues tell us about what life used to be like in the community? Why did you reach your conclusions? How might the accuracy of the conclusions be checked?

Examining values is another skill to be practiced. This is a two-part process. On one hand, students should look at the community to identify values underlying decisions that have shaped the community. On the other hand, they can test their own or their family's values for congruence against the wider values of the community. Suggested questions to elicit information regarding community values and personal values based on historical residues are: What values of people who lived in this community in the past are suggested by remaining residues? How do you feel about life in the past in this community as it is suggested by remaining residues?

Making decisions is a third category of student learning. Making decisions results from an interaction between available evidence and personal values. In the community setting, decision making by students parallels the policy decision process made by adults. Some examples of questions that students might ask about historical residues in decision making are: What do you think life in the community was really like in the past, and why did you reach that conclusion? What features of life derived from the community's past should continue to be emphasized, and why? Were there some things that happened in the past that set undesirable precedents for the present and for the future; what are they, and why?

I return to my four organizing questions: (1) How did Afro-American people in a given urban community live many years ago, from 1800 to 1960? (2) In what ways does the present urban black community reflect what happened in the past? (3) Can we think about future urban communities using insights into and understandings about the past? (4) How do we provide a sense of community identity for older and younger residents of the urban black community? These four questions were used to guide the approaches and activities of a class of eighth-grade Afro-American students and their teacher at the William L. Sayre Junior High School in West Philadelphia during 1979/80 and a mixed class of black, white, and Hispanic students at the Phillis Wheatley Middle School in Boston. The students, under the guidance of their teacher, had an intensive, year-long experience in researching and developing various aspects of the Afro-

American historic heritage of Philadelphia and Boston. The goals of the project were: (1) To develop a model at the middle/junior high school level for engaging students, teachers, parents, senior citizens, and other community residents in researching, documenting, interpreting, preserving, and disseminating the Afro-American historic heritage of their city. (2) To develop curricula for using the local historical/cultural background of the Afro-American community in the two cities. (3) To initiate a school-based permanent museum—resource center for the collection, study, interpretation, and preservation of local Afro-American history.

In exploring the local history of their West Philadelphia community, the students were involved in learning about people, places, and events. These were studied through the development of two major themes: the Afro-American experience of growing up in Philadelphia and the establishment and growth of the West Philadelphia black community. The six techniques mentioned earlier were used separately and in an integrated fashion by the students in their historical investigations. A publication, *Recovering the Afro-American Historic Heritage of Philadelphia: Oral History Accounts*, contains some of the oral histories collected by the students.

History can be thought of as a dialogue with the past. It should not be just the history of the few, but the history of the many. The great events in American history not only involved leaders but also had an enormous impact on the masses of nameless people. Historians must start to look at the people who could neither write nor read, in order to find out how they lived and how they responded to and contributed to American history. We need to understand those events of the past, local as well as national, as they were experienced by the wider segment of the population.

To identify people to be interviewed, the students made field trips to historic buildings and landmarks associated with Philadelphia's Afro-American history. To convey something of the nature of this project, let me mention the sites visited:

Mother Bethel African Methodist Episcopal Church at Sixth and Lombard Streets in South Philadelphia—the first African Methodist Episcopal church in America. Founded in 1787 by Richard Allen, this church has its own museum of historical artifacts and is the site of Richard Allen's tomb. The land that Mother Bethel occupies has been owned continuously by black people longer than any other land in the United States.

The Philadelphia *Tribune* offices on South 16th Street. The *Tribune* is the oldest continuing black newspaper in the country. It was founded by Christopher Perry, Sr., in 1884.

The Philadelphia Public Library. There on microfilm the students studied the *Tribune*'s coverage of the 1937 battle to abolish dual eligibility lists for black and white teachers and of the work of Floyd Logan's Educational Equality League.

The Stephen Smith Home at 4400 West Girard Avenue. This institution was founded in 1871 as a home for the aged and infirm by Stephen Smith, a wealthy black lumber merchant, fuel supplier, and real estate dealer. Students interviewed residents of the home.

Tindley Temple United Methodist Church at 762 South Broad Street. Founded in 1847 by former slave Charles Tindley, the Temple serves the poor and needy of all races.

Edwin M. Stanton Elementary School at 17th and Christian Streets in South Philadelphia. Over 110 years old today, this was a predominantly black elementary school that became a separate black school in 1920 through action of the Philadelphia Board of Public Education. It is a landmark in the struggle for early desegregation of the Philadelphia schools.

The 60th Street commercial district of West Philadelphia. Students identified businesses that were operating in the early 1950s along West Philadelphia's 60th Street by studying the advertisements in the 1952 Sayre Junior High School Yearbook. They then visited the addresses to see the transition of ownership and types of businesses now on 60th Street compared with thirty years ago.

The Scottish Rite Cathedral at 1514–20 Fitzwater. The students learned about the meaning and history of Free Black Masonry in the United States, founded by Prince Hall in Boston in 1787.

South Street/South Philadelphia neighborhood. As participant observers, the students walked the main and side streets of South Philly, the traditional site of the Afro-American community of Philadelphia and the center of Afro-American life in the city during the eighteenth, nineteenth, and early part of the twentieth centuries.

The field trips provided documentary materials for the students to study and discuss in their classroom. Individually, students identified neighbors and people in their churches to interview, using questionnaires developed in class. The recollections and stories gained through the interviews were useful in providing an understanding and feeling for the urban Afro-American experience in Philadelphia during the twentieth century. Again, to try to give a sense of this project and to show the connection between the sites and people interviewed, I cite some sketches of the people who gave oral history accounts:

Isaac C. Peyton, age 80, retired cook who migrated to Philadelphia from the South in 1923.

Leon Robinson, age 60, who was born and raised in Philadelphia and worked as a mailman for over thirty years.

Joseph B. Jones, age 46, who has lived all of his life in Philadelphia and has been a junior-high school social science teacher since 1964.

Robert A. Eaverly, age 53, born and raised in Philadelphia and formerly principal of Sayre Junior High School in Philadelphia.

Elizabeth Flora Stewart, age 57, a mother and grandmother who has raised her children and grandchildren in her native city of Philadelphia.

Sterling Bond Stewart, age 58, a chauffeur for twenty-eight years and formerly a construction worker who has lived all of his life in Philadelphia.

Alexander Chapman, age 44, born in South Philadelphia and a businessman—owner and operator of a hardware and bicycle repair shop on 60th Street in West Philadelphia.

Theodore Welsh, age 75, a barber whose father opened in 1907 the barber shop that he has been operating since 1934.

Raleigh H. Merritt, age 83, who studied at Tuskegee Institute in Alabama under George W. Carver and Booker T. Washington and who has had a real estate business in Philadelphia since 1932.

Eustace Gay, Sr., age 80, born in Barbados, West Indies, who served as a reporter-writer and managing editor of the *Philadelphia Tribune* for over fifty years and who was chairman emeritus of the *Tribune*. He resided at the Stephen Smith Home at the time of the interview.

I know that every urban center has the same kinds of people, places, and events that can become part of the curriculum of Afro-American teaching and learning in our public schools. Using this approach, students can gain and have reinforced the following concepts and skills:

Concepts	*Skills*
1. migration	1. data collecting
2. immigration	2. organizing data
3. power	3. interviewing

Concepts	Skills
4. identity	4. reading
5. community	5. reporting (written and oral)
6. protest	6. using census data
7. tradition	7. map reading
8. separatism	8. historical inquiry
9. prejudice	9. media technology
10. discrimination	10. questioning
11. leadership	11. drawing conclusions
12. survival	12. library research
13. family	13. critical thinking
14. citizenship	14. synthesizing of information
15. culture	15. values inquiry
16. history	16. decision making
17. neighborhood	17. creativity
18. minority	18. interpreting
19. heritage	

In summary, for grades six through twelve in the public schools the focus and development should be on the use of primary source materials in the teaching of Afro-American history. The curriculum should start with historical-social events—local, regional, and national. In the process teachers must be sure that they are teaching and reinforcing basic academic and intellectual skills. This is vital in order to avoid the miseducation that Carter G. Woodson talked about in *The Mis-Education of the Negro* (1933). If I can borrow a notion shared with me by Geneva Gay, we must be involved in a pedagogical politics that combines basic academic and intellectual skills with the learning of black history.

It is appropriate to remember that Carter G. Woodson, the "Father of Black History," found in 1937 that he could not neglect the students at the elementary and secondary levels, and so he began the *Negro History Bulletin* for public school teachers and students. These students found the materials inspirational and useful in their studies. Likewise, his books for young people showed a concern for the education of future leaders. In the same spirit of Carter G. Woodson, Vincent Franklin of Yale University came to Philadelphia several times to work directly with middle school teachers on course content. Since his book *The Education of Black Philadelphia, 1900–1950* had just been released, he was readily prepared to help with the identification and use of some of the primary sources cited earlier in describing the Philadelphia project. I urge the teachers and scholars in John Hope Franklin's fourth generation of black historians and those at the threshold of Thomas Holt's fifth generation to share their talents with those toiling at the public school level and help in creating appropriate and legitimate black history materials for the development of history and social studies courses.

VIII BLACK HISTORY AND THE COMMUNITY

History and the Black Community

JOHN E. FLEMING

My purpose is to place in perspective the importance of black history and its dissemination to the black community. Social history is the recorded collective experience of a group of people over a period of time. These experiences are not just randomly assembled facts about the past; from the perspective of the community, the history of a people is what they in the present find of value and of relevance to their lives and would like to pass on to future generations. Cultural values are intricately woven into a group's history, because it is these values that distinguish one group from another. Values are learned—they are learned through the socialization process by which one generation passes on to the next those things that are important to the group. Traditionally in America this has been done through various institutions: the family, the church, and the school.

To the degree that black institutions fail to transfer group values effectively, there is a need for alternative ways for black people to pass on from one generation to the next those values that they as a group feel are important and that have historically been significant for group identity. Even though the family and church are extremely important black institutions, what most deserves our attention at present are the educational institutions. Briefly, I want to illustrate how important these educational institutions have been historically; how we are losing control of these institutions as an important, if not the most important, means of educating our youth; and finally how we can use Afro-American museums as alternative institutions for transmitting cultural values.

To advocate the retention of black educational and cultural institutions is not to advocate racial segregation. Segregation of the races when enforced by law was and is morally wrong. There is no question that legally enforced racial segregation had to end. But in the aftermath of *Brown*, integration has come to mean that black institutions should be replaced by "superior" white institutions because, by their nature, black institutions have long been viewed as inherently inferior. This is the full implication of *Brown*, which few people understood in 1954 and not many more understand today.[1] While rejecting enforced segregation, we must also reject the notion that black institutions are inherently inferior.

If we accept the notion that institutions grow out of the exigencies of a people's life, then we cannot casually stand by and watch the destruction of black educational and cultural institutions. We must not forget that when Africans were first enslaved, whites attempted to develop institutions on the plantations that would indoctrinate Africans into accepting their condition of servitude. Slaveholders understood the necessity of controlling institutions that would make the African captives feel inferior and encourage them to accept an inferior status in the American social order. Southern apologists for slavery used theologians, philosophers, doctors, educators, lawyers, and historians to perpetuate the myth of the inferior black. The inferiority of the black race was a concept constantly reinforced throughout the day-to-day existence of the slaves.[2]

It was not enough for blacks to be legally enslaved; psychologically, whites had to believe that blacks deserved to be slaves because of their inferior nature. While there may have been a few slaves who internalized the Sambo personality traits, in reality slaves were smart enough to maintain a duplicity of roles: one in the presence of the master and the other within the slave quarters. Slaves were able to do this because they maintained

1. *Brown v. Board of Education of Topeka*, Supreme Court of the United States, 347 U.S. 483 (1954). In speaking for the Court, Chief Justice Earl Warren said: "We conclude that in the field of public education the doctrine of separate but equal has no place. Separate educational facilities are inherently unequal." See also Richard Kluger, *Simple Justice: The History of Brown v. Board of Education and Black America's Struggle for Equality* (New York, 1976), 748–78.

2. John W. Blassingame, *The Slave Community: Plantation Life in the Antebellum South* (New York, 1976), 15–40.

control of the socialization process within the slave quarters that allowed them to preserve their culture, their manhood, their womanhood.[3] We are just beginning to see and to understand through recent scholarship in Afro-American culture how the slaves established an elaborate socialization process and developed mechanisms for the internalization of those characteristics they deemed necessary for survival and for a positive self-image. A folktale about a black servant and her white mistress recounted in Lawrence Levine's *Black Culture and Black Consciousness* (1978) illustrates this attitude. Both women became pregnant and gave birth at the same time. One day the white woman ran into the kitchen crying in delightful amazement, "Oh, my baby said his first word today." Upon hearing this, the servant's baby, lying in his basket on the kitchen floor, looked up and asked, "He did, wha' 'id 'e say?"[4] Time and again we see through Afro-American folklore that slavery did not diminish black people's positive view of themselves, especially in relation to their view of whites, because, in spite of the system, they controlled the socialization process most critical to their own self-image.

By the time of the Civil War, free blacks understood the need for black institutions, but few black colleges had been established for higher education, and these were located north of the Mason-Dixon Line. In spite of legal and extralegal methods used by whites in an attempt to reenslave the freedman, blacks, assisted by white northern missionaries and philanthropists, established schools with a liberal arts emphasis to better enable blacks to protect their freedom and political and civil rights. In addition to establishment of free public education, a number of liberal arts colleges and universities were founded during this period. Although most offered little more than an elementary or secondary education, such names as Fisk University in Tennessee, Talladega College in Alabama, and Shaw University in North Carolina were indicative of the hopes and aspirations of the freedman. But such hopes and aspirations were short-lived.[5]

Through violent intimidation by southern whites, and the lack of en-

3. *Ibid.*, 98–103, 190–200.
4. Lawrence W. Levine, *Black Culture and Black Consciousness: Afro-American Folk Thought from Slavery to Freedom* (New York, 1977), 308–309.
5. John E. Fleming, *The Lengthening Shadow of Slavery: A Historical Justification for Affirmative Action for Blacks in Higher Education* (Washington, D.C., 1976), 30–31, 56.

forcement of the Reconstruction amendments and civil rights laws by the federal government, blacks were at the mercy of a hostile environment.[6] Following the *Plessy* decision of 1896, blacks were denied equal access to the very school system they helped to establish. What little money had been channeled into black schools was now diverted to white schools. Southern whites reasoned that blacks needed only enough training to enable them to perform the menial tasks assigned to them in what was rapidly developing into a caste society. It was during the early years of the age of Jim Crow that whites attempted to perpetuate the "slave mentality" in blacks by sidetracking their education from one of liberal arts to one that would make them suitable for their position at the bottom of society.[7]

Thus we come to understand that, as viewed by the larger society, the function of education within the black community was not only to socialize young blacks into the social order but also to reinforce and legitimize the preexisting economic disparities between the races. Even within this social and economic climate, blacks lost sight of neither the value of education nor the value of institutions controlled by black people. Consequently, black colleges grew out of the cultural exigencies of Afro-American life and not, as some have suggested, in response to the *Plessy* decision or a segregated, exclusionary society. These institutions were established by and grew out of a deep-seated desire on the part of blacks to learn. If we are to understand the importance of these institutions, we must view them first and foremost as institutions of higher education that serve the needs of black people.

W. E. B. Du Bois understood the significance of having institutions to educate teachers and leaders who would tackle the monumental task of eliminating illiteracy. Further, he viewed these institutions as preservers and promoters of Afro-American culture. Du Bois reasoned that if systematic discrimination and race prejudice were ever to be resolved it would be because these institutions provided the ammunition for the attack.[8]

The herculean task of educating blacks fell squarely on the shoulders of black colleges and universities, especially the private institutions. Often in the South not even elementary, not to mention secondary schools, were provided for blacks, which meant that these colleges had to provide elementary and secondary facilities for their students. The burden these in-

6. *Ibid.*, 37–38.
7. *Ibid.*, 52, 54–58.
8. *Ibid.*, 75–79.

stitutions carried was readily apparent when the United States Office of Education and the Phelps-Stokes Fund published their "Survey of Negro Education" in 1917. In spite of the dismal picture of black education that the survey painted, the study noted that "no type of education is so eagerly sought by colored people as college education."[9]

Although there is no doubt of the substantial job black colleges were accomplishing in providing the educational foundation, the fact remained that their resources were too limited to provide all of the higher educational needs of the black community. The glaring inequalities at the elementary and secondary levels continued to handicap the efforts of black colleges. As early as the 1930s, civil rights groups concluded that it was imperative that the attack upon the doctrine of separate but equal be made. The northern universities were not producing enough men and women with advanced degrees to meet the demands within the black community. Therefore the NAACP spearheaded the attack on the doctrine of separate-but-equal, first at the graduate level (*Missouri ex rel Gaines* v. *Canada* [1939]) and then in a direct assault on segregation in *Brown* v. *Board of Education of Topeka*. In a unanimous decision the Supreme Court ruled in *Brown* that school segregation violated the equal protection guaranties of the Fourteenth Amendment.[10] The legal battle was won, but the war was just beginning.

The Supreme Court added a caveat in its opinion destroying the doctrine of separate-but-equal: the Court found that black schools were inherently inferior. As if anticipating the reasoning in the *Brown* decision, Du Bois forewarned blacks in 1934 in writing in the *Crisis*:

> The thinking colored people of the U.S. must stop being stampeded by the word segregation. The opposition to racial segregation is not or should not be any distaste or unwillingness of colored people to work with each other, to cooperate with each other, or to live with each other. The opposition to segregation is an opposition to discrimination. But, the two things do not necessarily go together; there should never be an opposition to segregation pure and simple unless that segregation does involve discrimination.[11]

9. Dwight C. W. Holmes, *The Evaluation of the Negro College* (New York, 1969), 150.

10. Rayford W. Logan and Michael R. Winston, *The Negro in the United States*, Vol. II, *The Ordeal of Democracy* (New York, 1971), 13–15.

11. W. E. B. Du Bois, *The Crisis*, XLI (January, 1934), 20.

While none of us would advocate the reestablishment of legally enforced segregation, neither can we, as Du Bois did fifty years ago, accept the notion that majority black is "inherently inferior." We must understand fully what integration has cost black people as a group. Blacks were the ones to have their schools closed and teachers and principals fired or reduced in status. Blacks were the ones bused. Blacks were the ones who lost their football and basketball teams and opportunities for leadership. But, more importantly, they lost control of these institutions and therefore lost control over institutions that formally transmitted cultural values.

Prior to *Brown*, whites tried to enforce the belief of white superiority/black inferiority, but black teachers and principals instilled the opposite in the minds of black boys and girls. The development of racial stereotypes in the minds of children reinforces distorted social images. Black children grow up to feel inferior and white children grow up to feel superior. The system is geared to produce these results. American society provides an image of supermen and wonder women that leads white children to feel that there is no limit to how far they can excel, while black images, especially in the media, remain extremely stereotypical and, as a consequence, place severe limitations on the goals of black youths. Black people did not understand until their schools were closed that black teachers and principals insulated black children from cultural racism and reinterpreted societal indoctrination to fit the needs of the black community.[12]

Thus we conclude that black people as a group must no longer allow American society to view their every activity and trait in negative terms indicating inferiority even when they parallel precisely those of the majority. American scholars must no longer be permitted to view black actions and institutions as signs of pathological efforts to conform to other people's standards, other people's images, other people's goals.[13] The government should no longer be allowed to treat cultural differences as something to be cured or corrected rather than empathetically provided for.

With the disproportionate burden of integration that fell on the black community and with the closing of black schools, too often there were no role models or individuals to nurture black cultural values in youth. As a consequence, today's youth do not know of A. Philip Randolph, Mary

12. Unpublished interviews conducted by John Fleming of college students, faculty, and administrators who participated in the Institute for the Study of Educational Policy's Black College Project, 1979–1980, ISEP, Howard University, Washington, D.C.

13. Levine, *Black Culture and Black Consciousness*, 337–38.

McLeod Bethune, James Weldon Johnson, Sissieritta Jones, Ira Aldridge, Paul Cuffe, Denmark Vesey, and Mansa Musa. With the demise of and changes wrought in black educational institutions, the need for alternative and supportive institutions will become increasingly critical. These alternative institutions can and must be a valuable resource to supplement the education both black and white children receive in the public school system.

Afro-American museums offer alternative ways of teaching black history and culture. I am particularly biased in favor of museums because they offer a unique opportunity to be supportive of and creative in the education of youth. Not many black institutions of higher education have taken advantage of museums as a teaching facility. Among the few that have are Howard University, Hampton Institute, Tuskegee Institute, and South Carolina State. Of the museums associated with colleges, the most innovative is the proposed National Afro-American Museum and Cultural Center at Wilberforce, Ohio. Located on the eighty-eight-acre former campus of Wilberforce University, the center will be in close proximity to both Wilberforce and Central State University and will be able to offer students of these institutions unique educational opportunities.

For the student of history, the center will offer a holistic approach to the study of the Afro-American experience. In addition to traditional tools of the historical craft, the center will have oral and visual history programs and will emphasize folkloric, archaeological, and anthropological research. It will provide training in museum and archival studies. The museum through its various programs will research, collect, preserve, publish, and interpret cultural artifacts and displays for both public and educational purposes.[14] By re-creating the Afro-American environment as a background for black artifacts, we hope to create life as black Americans lived it in the past.

In addition to providing a greater understanding of Afro-American history and cultural values, the museum will help all Americans have a better understanding of themselves and the complexity of American social history. We owe this to our children and their children's children. We must strengthen our historical institutions and, where necessary, create new ones to assure our survival as a people.

14. John E. Fleming, *Introduction to the National Afro-American Museum and Cultural Center Project* (Columbus, Ohio, 1980).

From Slavery to Freedom: The View Through Film and TV Drama

ROBERT BRENT TOPLIN

Whether we like it or not, popular films and television programs significantly influence the way the public views history. As history teachers discover in classroom discussions, students state their understanding of the Russian Revolution in terms of the movie *Reds*, explain World War II by citing examples from the tv series *Winds of War*, and describe the Civil War with references to *Gone with the Wind*.

While commentators readily acknowledge that films and tv programs seriously affect views of the past, they give less attention to the reverse effect of the way in which media depictions *reflect* our perceptions of history. Over the years Hollywood and tv producers have eagerly tried to keep up with the changing fashions in historical interpretation. This phenomenon has little to do with the producers' commitment to an honest rendering of historical scholarship. It relates much more to the producers' conservative nature, to their desire not to go against the tide of currently popular attitudes. If these popular attitudes often correspond to trends in scholarship, it demonstrates, perhaps, how much our own professional thinking about the past is influenced by conditions of the present.

Media history often bears resemblance to interpretations favored by professional historians, but the presentations seen in film and tv are usually more sensational. Situations, events, and characters are enormously exaggerated for effect, and directors take great license in shaping the evidence, both visual and verbal, to ensure that the audience reaches the desired conclusion. Still, the connection between media history and scholarly history is evident.

The pattern is particularly noticeable in the way Hollywood and television have interpreted the black experience in America. Swings in the interpretive pendulum have been sharp in scholarship on black history, and they have been even more pronounced in the media versions. Historical writing traveled a long distance from the way U. B. Phillips and William A. Dunning and their followers viewed slavery and Reconstruction to the interpretations of Kenneth M. Stampp, John Hope Franklin, John Blassingame, and Nathan I. Huggins. The distance is even greater from the rampage of the KKK in *Birth of a Nation* to the exploits of Chicken George in *Roots*.

In the following brief discussion I would like to examine some of the main shifts in the way dramatic films and tv programs have treated slavery and the postemancipation experience of black Americans. The purpose of these comments is to explore the potential of studying film in the teaching of black history and American history. It seems a worthwhile endeavor for students to evaluate the way media images of the black experience have changed over the years. It can be helpful if we interpret the media's symbols and messages, weigh their impact, and consider what they tell us about the way Americans in earlier times viewed themselves and their history. As a classroom activity, this exercise need not be limited to viewing and discussing films. There is rich, accessible evidence in film reviews, promotion propaganda, scripts, and memoirs. Also, as Thomas Cripps has pointed out, it is often more useful to examine only segments of feature films to make a point than to spend valuable class time watching an entire film.[1]

Birth of a Nation (1915) represents almost everyone's favorite place to start an analysis of Hollywood's treatment of slavery, the Civil War, and emancipation. *Birth of a Nation* quickly became a classic, the first of the multireel extravaganzas with a cast of hundreds, a gilded budget, and extraordinary promotional fanfare. It was an astounding box-office success.

1. Thomas Cripps, "Films in the Classroom: The Afro-American Case," in Robert Brent Toplin (ed.), *American History Through Film* (Bloomington, Ind., 1983), 18. For an overview of recent films dealing with the black experience that provides information of use to the classroom instructor, see Charlotte R. Ashton, "The Changing Image of Blacks in American Film, 1944–1973" (Ph.D. dissertation, Princeton University, 1981).

Less than a year after it had opened in New York City, it had already played 6,200 times, to an audience estimated at three million.[2]

D. W. Griffith's film exaggerated fashionable historical interpretations of Reconstruction seen in the scholarship of Woodrow Wilson, William A. Dunning, James Ford Rhodes, and Walter Fleming. In various ways these historians had sounded the "Tragic Era" theme.[3] Their interpretive bias was close to that of the general society, which viewed Radical Reconstruction as a hopeless failure and considered the efforts to grant black suffrage a foolish mistake. In the 1920s America was moving toward sectional reunion after decades of bitterness over the Civil War. Southerners were proud to have Woodrow Wilson in the White House, the first president from their section since antebellum days. Indeed, Griffith cited books by Wilson for support when blacks criticized him for the implicit racism in *Birth of a Nation*. Griffith was pleased that Wilson gave the film a special showing in the White House and reviewed it favorably. "It is like writing history with lightning," said Wilson.[4] Of course, Griffith's inspiration for the story line came not from professional scholarship but from the popular novel by Thomas Dixon, *The Clansman* (1905).

Many film critics agreed with Griffith's claims that *Birth of a Nation* was true history put to drama. Dorothea Dix congratulated him for a fine job. The film was "history visualized," she said, urging everyone to "go see it, for it will make a better American of you."[5] Her idea of the film's purpose was close to one Griffith had in mind. As Lary May explains in *Screening Out the Past* (1980), Griffith thought he was operating in the Progressive spirit, and he intended his film to represent a moral statement for the reform of society.[6] A North Carolina writer also concluded that the film was good history. *Birth of a Nation*, he said, nicely showed "the fun

2. Edward D. C. Campbell, Jr., *The Celluloid South: Hollywood and the Southern Myth* (Knoxville, Tenn., 1981), 59.

3. Jack Temple Kirby, *Media-Made Dixie: The South in the American Imagination* (Baton Rouge, 1978), 6–7; Daniel Leab, *From Sambo to Superspade: The Black Experience in Motion Pictures* (Boston, 1975), 34–35.

4. Thomas Cripps, *Slow Fade to Black: The Negro in American Film, 1900–1942* (New York, 1977), 41–42.

5. Campbell, *The Celluloid South*, 58.

6. Lary May, *Screening Out the Past: The Birth of Mass Culture and the Motion Picture Industry* (New York, 1980), 60–93.

and frolic of plantation days as well as the heartache and pathos of the stricken South."[7]

Birth of a Nation deserves study in the classroom. It is difficult to find a better example of the way a film can tap the springs of prejudice. The film portrays slaves as generally happy while carrying out their duties in servitude. It shows Reconstruction bringing waste and corruption to the troubled South. Northern carpetbaggers are a venal lot, and black legislators are seen eating meat and chugging whiskey while trying to pass bills legalizing intermarriage. The most emotional moments involve the nightmare of rape. Especially unforgettable is the scene showing innocent young Flora pursued by Gus, the lustful mulatto. When reaching a precipice, Flora dives to her death rather than submit to Gus's passions.

Blacks were quick to show their disgust for *Birth of a Nation*, as Thomas Cripps has well demonstrated.[8] They hoped to apply local laws governing the young movie industry to ban the film or, at least, try to cut out some of the most offensive scenes. Their mobilization produced some small revisions in the Boston and New York City versions. Still, the controversy did not disturb the film's overall popularity. *Birth of a Nation* was enormously successful. As David M. Chalmers reminds us, it was also an important contributor to the revival of the KKK in the late 1910s and early 1920s.[9]

Blacks fared only slightly better in *Gone with the Wind*, another extravaganza dealing with the Civil War and Reconstruction period. The 1939 production gave glimpses of plantation life in antebellum times, then followed the troubled fortunes of its principal characters through the postwar years. It showed the masters treating slaves in a kindly, paternalistic manner, and portrayed the bondsmen as simple creatures who were dependably faithful. The most memorable negative portrait was presented by the whining Butterfly McQueen, who disintegrated into a state of panic when she was to deliver a baby.

Some observers have argued that *Gone with the Wind*, nevertheless, was

7. Campbell, *The Celluloid South*, 58, 61; Kirby, *Media-Made Dixie*, 2–9.
8. Cripps, *Slow Fade to Black*, 53–69; Thomas Cripps, *Black Film as Genre* (Bloomington, Ind., 1978), 15.
9. David Chalmers, *Hooded Americanism: The History of the Ku Klux Klan* (Chicago, 1965), 25–32.

a considerable improvement over *Birth of a Nation*. At least it portrayed blacks in a friendly role rather than as aggressors, notes Edward D. C. Campbell, Jr.[10] Perhaps the more blatant forms of racism evident in *Birth of a Nation* were less acceptable in the environment of 1939. The ideas of cultural anthropologists such as Franz Boas and Ruth Benedict were gaining favor, and, though race relations were far from benign, the "nadir" of the early twentieth century had been passed. Producer David Selznick seems to have been aware that expectations had changed, and he specifically tried to avoid the mistakes of D. W. Griffith.[11] Even some supposedly stereotypical roles in the film offered a degree of sophistication. Campbell points out that Hattie McDaniel showed considerable strength in the story as she played the familiar role of loyal servant. McDaniel represented the anchor of the family. She scolded Scarlett O'Hara when her behavior demeaned the family name. McDaniel insisted that the O'Hara family's sense of pride be maintained in all circumstances. Sad to say, though, *Gone with the Wind* did little for the individual black family's sense of pride.

Some blacks were unhappy with *Gone with the Wind*'s portrayals, but their protests were muted. Their anger was defused when McDaniel became the first black actress to win an Academy Award, and they found it more difficult to mobilize critical opinion, since the images of blacks in the film, though often unflattering, were not as transparently offensive as in *Birth of a Nation*.[12]

Other films of the 1930s and 1940s showed similar scenes of contented slaves and friendly, loyal free blacks. In this period most white audiences, and especially audiences in the southern theater markets, did not want to see blacks as assertive or competitive. These moviegoers preferred the styles of Bill Robinson and Hattie McDaniel—the dancing, cheerful darkie and the plump, loving maid. Many movie reviewers assumed the images were fact, as in the case of a Cleveland critic who said portrayals in the film *Hearts in Dixie* were "like the entire colored race, light-hearted, ready with its songs, dances and laughter."[13] Variations on the theme could be seen in films such as *The Little Colonel* (1935) and *Song of the*

10. Campbell, *The Celluloid South*, 128–129.
11. Kirby, *Media-Made Dixie*, 74.
12. Cripps, *Slow Fade to Black*, 360–65.
13. Leab, *From Sambo to Superspade*, 99–101; Campbell, *The Celluloid South*, 149–54.

South (1946). The latter, which featured James Baskett as "Uncle Remus," aroused protests from the NAACP for the way it idealized relationships. Yet some scholars see redeeming value in *Song of the South*, too, for the Uncle Remus stories may include subtle messages about the sophistication of its black characters. The interpretation of Lawrence Levine is relevant here. Levine shows that the trickery of Brer Rabbit and Brer Fox symbolized the cleverness of blacks in protecting their interests, and the stories carried a variety of subtle moral lessons.[14]

By the 1950s and 1960s black Americans were forcing down the walls of segregation and making significant efforts to penetrate the nation's economic and political life. Film and tv soon reflected the changes. Many factors contributed to these developments. The black soldier's involvement in World War II helped raise consciousness; prejudice came under assault after the fall of Nazi Germany; the Supreme Court challenged Jim Crow laws; the Johnson administration and Congress passed important civil rights bills; and, perhaps most important, black Americans organized to challenge discrimination.

Historiography went through a related revolution. Kenneth M. Stampp published *The Peculiar Institution* in 1954, demonstrating that life in slavery was no picnic. Later, John Blassingame showed the complexity of personality types on the plantation in *The Slave Community* (1972). In *Roll, Jordan, Roll* (1974), Eugene D. Genovese examined the way slaves built a spiritually meaningful life for themselves in difficult times, and Herbert Gutman identified the strength of family ties in *The Black Family in Slavery and Freedom* (1976). Studies of the postbellum years also struck down old assumptions. John Hope Franklin, Kenneth M. Stampp, and others challenged the "Tragic Era" concept of Reconstruction. They reviewed the achievements of the Radical state governments and traced the injustices done to blacks in the period, injustices that required a Second Reconstruction a century later to correct.

In this environment the perspectives of film and the new medium of television had to change. Clearly, scholarship was not the sole source of the revisions. The broader changes in society made a more direct impact on the writers, directors, and producers who worked with the mass media.

14. Lawrence Levine, *Black Culture and Black Consciousness: Afro-American Folk Thought from Slavery to Freedom* (New York, 1977), 81–83, 106–120.

Yet all of these alterations were interrelated—the transformations in popular attitudes, the shift in historical interpretations, and the rise of a new image of blacks in film and tv.

An early sign of the developing perspective appeared in *Band of Angels*, a 1957 release featuring Clark Gable, Sidney Poitier, and Yvonne DeCarlo. The story depicted DeCarlo as a beautiful debutante from a Kentucky plantation who learned upon her father's death that she was to be sold to the slave markets of New Orleans as part of her father's estate. Here was the old "tragic mulatto" theme that had excited white audiences since the days of *Uncle Tom's Cabin*. Poitier was Gable's talented but unhappy slave. He showed no love for servitude. Poitier represented the bright, independent, impressive black man that became his stock-in-trade in films such as *Guess Who's Coming to Dinner* and *In the Heat of the Night*. No longer was the Peculiar Institution viewed as generally acceptable for whites and blacks. Gable, the rakish ex-slavetrader felt remorse about his dishonorable profession, and Poitier, the ambitious bondsman, thirsted for freedom.

In the late 1960s and early 1970s the mood in many quarters turned more militant. America's tragedy in Vietnam contributed to the growth of anti-establishment attitudes and the New Left. Ghetto riots broke out in America's cities, and cries of "Black Power!" were heard frequently in the television news reports. Scholarship, too, took a more militant turn, as various writers related history in a strident voice.

Not surprisingly, the film industry responded with ultradramatic spin-offs of the new views. Some called the genre blaxsploitation films. The list included *Slaves* (1969), *Mandingo* (1975), *Drum* (1976), and *Passion Plantation* (1978). These films stressed the brutal aspects of slavery, portrayed blacks as seething rebels, focused on cases of slave breeding, and exposed sexual escapades involving blacks and whites. They easily achieved R and X ratings and titillated audiences with erotica as much as they excited them with violent action. These films drew big-city audiences to the theaters, but they fell short of tapping the huge general market of national interest in slavery. They also failed to show a believable black man, one beyond the one-dimensional stereotypes of lustpots or Nat Turners.

It remained for *Roots* to succeed in this competition and present *Gone with the Wind* from a black perspective. *Roots* broke the record for the tv medium's largest single program audience by garnering more than 80 million viewers for its last episode. *Roots* proved great theater, capitalizing on the public's love of multiepisode history in a soap opera format. Better than any previous dramatic film on slavery, it examined antebellum life through the eyes of the slaves. For once, a popular film showed the personality of blacks in depth, while all but a few of the whites were peripheral characters. We may excuse some of *Roots*'s historical slips (such as showing cotton culture in northern Virginia) in view of its larger accomplishments.

In the post-*Roots* years other dramatic programs attempted to follow up on the public's fascination with slavery, but none has even remotely replicated *Roots*'s success. Much of the difficulty was in the way those tv specials approached their subject matter. Treating slaves, masters, and poor whites in a stereotypical, one-dimensional manner, they easily bored audiences. The notable flops included *Freedom Road* (1979) and *Beulah Land* (1980).

Film depictions of postemancipation black life also reflected the changing mood in historiography and national sentiment. *Roots: The Next Generations* was more substantial than its predecessor in giving attention to historical detail. The second *Roots* nicely touched on some of the main currents of postemancipation black history: sharecropping, migration to northern cities, the growth of educational opportunities, the dispute between Booker T. Washington and W. E. B. Du Bois, the military experience, and the Civil Rights Movement. It was a stunning accomplishment. *The Autobiography of Miss Jane Pittman* (1974) was also noteworthy, for it scored high both with the critics and in the audience ratings. In a stellar performance, actress Cicely Tyson played a black woman who struggled through slavery and segregation and lived to see the civil rights revolution. The powerful, emotional conclusion of the story, when the old woman approaches the long-forbidden water fountain for a drink, beautifully drives home the meaning of discrimination.

Two other notable achievements in recent filmmaking deserve attention, because they reflect the coming of a more mature approach to studying black life on the screen. Both of them deal with twentieth-century subjects, yet their themes are relevant to the entire post–Civil War period. Both offer a positive view by stressing the strength of the family. The 1972 production *Sounder* told the inspiring story of a troubled black family in Louisiana during the Great Depression. The Morgans' pride and human dignity helped them to weather their difficulties. Jack Temple Kirby calls *Sounder* "probably the best film ever made about Southern black people."[15] Another positive picture of blacks during times of hardship emerges in *The Learning Tree*. Based on the autobiographical book by Gordon Parks, it shows the strength of black family life in Kansas amidst segregation and bigotry. Parks directed and produced the film and later went on to become a dean of black film directors.

In sum, media history of the black experience in America has been improving, but, as in the past, the form it takes on the screen is often a grossly exaggerated version of current trends in professional thought. It does not have to be this way. In the last twenty years scholarship on the black experience has mushroomed. Its level of sophistication has also risen, and several books about slavery, emancipation, and segregation have captured the Pulitzer Prize, the National Book Award, the Bancroft Prize, and other awards. We should hope that, somehow, Hollywood and tv producers will try to capitalize on this outpouring of exciting scholarship and use it as the basis for new programming. The opportunity exists for media history that is both authentic and highly entertaining. The history of the black experience is so abundantly rich in human drama that it can be told without the wild excesses of interpretation that have frequently characterized Hollywood and tv history.

15. Kirby, *Media-Made Dixie*, 147.

The Power of History: Interpreting Black Material Culture

CAROLE MERRITT

The power of history is its ability to tell us who we are and where we came from. That the study and teaching of American history has largely neglected the African-American experience distorts for all Americans their sense of self. For black Americans, of course, the neglect has been more damaging. Lacking knowledge of how they have shared in the American tradition, many blacks are not fully aware of their claim to this country. To know that one's people were present when the nation first developed and that their work and culture have been distinctive, yet integral, elements of American life is to be able to assert one's rights with dignity and force. Black identity, therefore, has political relevance, shaping the community's self-image and collective action. For this reason, the study and teaching of history transcend scholarship in the narrow sense and pose a public mission to correct popular misconceptions of the American experience. One of the challenges of this mission is to engage the black community in a reassessment of its past.

Contrary to common belief, the record of black life in this country is abundant and rich. Various documents capture many aspects of the black community and how it developed within the broad patterns of American history. Admittedly, the record is very incomplete. Specific references to the daily course of black life are scattered; personal accounts of ordinary people are scarce; and too often our information is limited to the legal and economic systems. But a huge body of census data, tax records, court proceedings, family papers, and personal narratives holds evidence of the form and substance of heretofore neglected areas of the black experience. None of these sources is new, but their use in the systematic analysis of social structure is a fairly recent approach in historical research. Access to the black past is hampered not so much by a dearth of evidence as by the tedious task of compiling and analyzing large quantities of data.

Material culture is another kind of historical evidence that has been little used to research the past. It is not as accessible as public and private records, but it is no less rich for the study of black history. Material culture consists of the physical objects made by people to sustain and enrich their lives, including, for the most part, buildings, household and personal items, and other three-dimensional products of work, leisure, science, and art. Such articles surviving from the past have an immediacy that goes beyond even the best of verbal accounts. Uncompromised by memory or interpretation, they are history's direct presence. Historical evidence that is visual and tangible may more effectively capture the attention and imagination of a people who have been alienated from their past. Moreover, when historical scholarship recognizes the significance of everyday artifacts, it endorses a people's common heritage. This paper cites a few examples of material culture and discusses their significance for the understanding and appreciation of the black experience.

Some of the material culture of black life consists of archaeological finds from black communities that developed in this country in the eighteenth and nineteenth centuries. Excavations of slave dwellings in Georgia and South Carolina, for example, have unearthed building materials, food remains, buttons, beads, and fragments of iron, glass, and ceramics that help in the reconstruction of slave conditions. Such evidence provides the detail of life that is often lacking in written accounts. It documents the distinctive content of African-American ways of life that are beyond memory and, in the traditional sense, unrecorded.

In 1979 an archaeological project excavated slave occupation sites in the interior coastal plain in Berkeley County, South Carolina.[1] The investigation found evidence of distinctive African-American ceramics and architecture. The sites under study were the late-eighteenth-century slave

1. Soil Systems, Inc. of Marietta, Georgia, under contract with Interagency Archaeological Services, conducted the excavations as mitigation of the adverse impact of a federal canal project.

settlements of the Yaughan and Curiboo plantations along the Santee River, where rice and indigo were cultivated. These slave communities were at an early stage of development in the second half of the eighteenth century, when slave importation to this country was at its peak and when the black population in the area outnumbered whites eleven to one. These factors explain in part the development of a distinctive and perhaps dominant African-American tradition that is reflected in the slave material culture. The project's ceramic collection consisted largely of colonoware—fragments of earthen bowls and jars that had been made by hand and used for cooking and serving one-pot meals. Distinctive from the colono made by Native Americans, these slave vessels are similar in form to twentieth-century Nigerian pottery and were fired by a comparable technique.[2] They demonstrate the promise of material culture for rediscovery of a past that has been slighted in the written record. The study of slave housing at Yaughan and Curiboo found that much of it was probably of mud-wall construction. Posts were closely set in trenches; clay mixed with water to a mortarlike consistency filled the spaces between. Such building techniques are common throughout Africa.[3] The findings of the South Carolina excavations are instructive not only to scholars but also to the public, who have an opportunity to visualize some aspects of slave life nearly two hundred years ago and better appreciate its African origin.

Fortunately, African-American colono, which disappeared nearly two hundred years ago, is of a durable material that was preserved below ground. Of the many artifacts of early black American life that are more perishable, some have survived through continued manufacture and use. One such item is a fanner, a shallow coiled basket made of coarse grass and palmetto, that was used for the winnowing of rice in this country from the seventeenth to the early twentieth century. To separate the grain from the chaff, threshed rice was placed in the basket and repeatedly tossed in the air so that the wind could carry off the husks. These baskets are virtually identical to the fanners used by Senegambian people for the last two hundred years. They belong to the African tradition of rice culture

2. Patrick H. Garrow, "Investigations of Yaughan and Curiboo Plantations," paper presented at the Southeastern Archaeological Conference, New Orleans, November, 1980.

3. Thomas R. Wheaton, Jr., "Architecture at Curiboo and Yaughan Plantations," paper presented at the Southeastern Archaeological Conference, New Orleans, November, 1980.

that dates from the first century A.D. Slaves imported to work the rice plantations of coastal Georgia and South Carolina were skilled in the cultivation of this crop. Coiled baskets like the fanners they used are still made for tourists by women of Mount Pleasant, South Carolina.[4]

These artifacts of rice culture represent opportunities for meaningful research and teaching of American history. Fragments of colono, the remains of mud-wall houses, and fanner baskets suggest the need for further scholarship on continuity and change in African-American culture. The specific African origin of Santee River colono needs to be determined. That the mud-wall houses investigated did not have interior fireplaces poses questions about early slave household life. Fanner baskets will probably continue to stimulate study of the social context of their craft in this country. These items of material culture also facilitate the community's understanding of the black experience. They direct attention to the significance of slave culture and introduce students and the out-of-school public to the rich detail of ordinary life. Moreover, they generate innovative ideas for curriculum development, special school projects, interpretive exhibits, and other public programs for a broad audience.

The inaccessibility of archaeological resources limits their use in the study of black history. Although a wealth of information lies buried in the ground, it is costly to investigate. The collections of museums and other repositories are more available, but are generally weak in African-American artifacts. However, a significant body of black material culture exists outside traditional institutions. Many black families, for example, have preserved household and personal articles of nineteenth- and twentieth-century black life, including clothing, furniture, food utensils, tools, and decorative objects. Although these items are, for the most part, unknown to scholars and the general public, they have great potential for increasing the community's understanding and appreciation of its heritage.

People are often unaware of the historical and cultural significance of ordinary objects in their possession. One of the most common domestic items of black material culture in this country is the strip quilt. Composed of rectangular pieces of cloth, usually cotton or wool, these quilts were at one time present in many black households in the southern United States.

4. John Michael Vlach, *The Afro-American Tradition in Decorative Arts* (Cleveland, 1978), 7–19.

Although they are still made, few persons are aware of the possibility that they derive from design concepts prevalent in West Africa, where men weave strips of cloth on small looms with narrow warps. The asymmetry in pattern and use of color distinguish African-American quilting from the rigid formality of European-American quilting. The strip quilt, like African-American music, has an improvisational quality that is uncharacteristic of other traditions of folk art in this country.[5] The utility of quilts probably helped to ensure the survival of distinctive African-American textile design. Quilting alone or in groups, women had ample opportunities to transmit and elaborate on the strip pattern.

The systematic location and documentation of black material culture in private hands is a major research task. For the last several years, community-oriented associations have taken the lead in this effort. Often in cooperation with museums, historical societies, and other traditional educational institutions, these associations have initiated exhibitions and other public programs to increase the awareness of black history and culture.[6] Many of their activities have evolved from innovative research of black life. Working through local leaders, churches, community centers, and other organizations, field researchers have identified a number of significant objects, many of which are common items like strip quilts. Some, however, are unusual pieces that recall a past for which the physical evidence has largely disappeared.

A recent exhibit project on black family history located a stick doll that a woman over ninety years old had saved from her childhood in Keysville, Georgia, near Augusta. The doll is made from a stick about a foot long, which after years of handling has a rich patina. The tapered end forms the head; a nub represents an arm. Clothed in a plaid dress, the doll is apparently like those that slave girls fashioned from forked sticks. It is also similar in form to the African dolls that do not bear strict resemblance to the human body. Whether the African and American dolls share a common

5. *Ibid.*, 55–67.
6. One notable example is the Cleveland chapter of The Links, Inc., a national women's service organization that spearheaded with the Cleveland Museum of Art an exhibition, "The Afro-American Tradition in Decorative Arts," in 1978 and 1979. Another example is the African-American Family History Association, which from 1980 to 1984 conducted a project of three family history exhibits in Atlanta in cooperation with the Atlanta Public Library, the Georgia Department of Archives and History, and the Atlanta University Center Woodruff Library.

tradition will require further research, but the Keysville doll is a rare material reference to the history of African-American childhood.[7]

One of the most extraordinary collections of black material culture in this country is the house and furnishings of the Alonzo Herndon family in Atlanta, Georgia. The 1910 Beaux Arts mansion and its contents reflect the taste of upper-class America, but more importantly they symbolize the achievements of a black man, who rose from slavery to wealth and power as founder and president of the Atlanta Life Insurance Company, one of the nation's largest black financial institutions. The life and work of the two generations of Herndons who lived in the home represent some of the broad patterns of economic and social development that shaped the black community for over a century. Designed by the Herndons and built by black craftsmen, the home offers an opportunity to study and interpret several aspects of African-American history.[8] Like much of black material culture, the Herndon home's historical and cultural significance is primarily its association with black life. The house and its furnishings are, for the most part, European-American in style. However, at least one item in the family's collection is as distinctively African-American in form as colonoware, fanner baskets, and strip quilts. A headkerchief that belonged to one of the family's earliest known ancestors has been preserved for five generations. It is a brown and white checked cloth of homespun cotton that belonged to a woman who spent most of her life in slavery. The headkerchief is a characteristically African-American style of headdress. Systematic research is needed to document this article of clothing more fully. However, scattered literary references suggest that the color of a headkerchief and the way it was tied had special significance. For example, in the 1860s a young woman observed in the process of religious conversion was wearing a white headkerchief knotted in an unusual fashion.[9] The Herndon headkerchief beautifully demonstrates the power of black material culture. This tangible evidence brings us face to face with a family's

7. Carole Merritt, *Homecoming: African-American Family History in Georgia* (Atlanta, 1982), 42, 43, 111.

8. The Herndon Home is a house museum which is owned and operated by the Alonzo F. and Norris B. Herndon Foundation.

9. Melville J. Herskovits, *The Myth of the Negro Past* (New York, 1941), 149; Thomas Wentworth Higginson, *Army Life in a Black Regiment* (New York, 1900), 195, 196.

African-American origins, and reminds us of its heroic struggle to overcome slavery. Such artifacts instruct all Americans on the distinctiveness of the black cultural heritage, providing a critical perspective on the present. The nineteenth-century headkerchief places the Herndons and their twentieth-century mansion in historical context, representing the cultural source that nurtured their accomplishments. That the family preserved such an item reflects the high value they placed on their history and suggests a direct relationship between appreciation of one's past and command of one's present.

The immediacy of material culture can effectively pull us into history, bridging the gap of time and heightening our sense of place. As the black community reassesses its past, material culture has the special promise of providing new information, posing new questions, and suggesting new interpretations of the African-American experience. It offers the opportunity of linking scholarship with the community's information needs. Archaeological research, for example, can further the mission of reeducating the public about its past. Since material culture consists largely of the artifacts of ordinary life, it is of particular value in the study and teaching of the history of African-Americans, who have felt alienated from their humble beginnings. To know the significance of common history is to appreciate its dignity. Such knowledge can revitalize a community. It informs a people's sense of self, endorses its heritage, and, indeed, empowers it.

IX BLACK WOMEN

Lifting the Veil, Shattering the Silence: Black Women's History in Slavery and Freedom

DARLENE CLARK HINE

Present and future investigations of Afro-American women's past should increase our understanding of the complex interrelationships of gender, class, and race. For three and a half centuries Afro-American women have carried special burdens. They have responded in dichotomous ways: by protesting racial and sexual discrimination or by somehow avoiding it; by rationalizing the psychological impact of racism and sexism or by transcending their victimization. These multiple dichotomies are most graphically revealed through an examination of black women's institutional and organizational lives and their work, and also in their cultural contributions and aesthetic expressions. Black women's history is just beginning to emerge as a vital area within women's and Afro-American history, and much work remains to be done. In this essay I will trace the contours of the field and assess its prospects by synthesizing much of the current literature. Specifically, I will examine the following themes: sex roles and female networks, the black family, work, religion, social reform, and creative expressions.

Before the Civil War the vast majority of black women were slaves. Emancipation required finding ways to give meaning to freedom within a society devoted to circumscribing all attempts of black people to, in fact, be free. Subsequently, industrialization and urbanization not only altered the location but influenced the transformation of the lives and work experiences of the majority of black women. Even more profound were the social upheavals and proliferation of racial and sexual stereotypes of the late nineteenth and the early twentieth centuries which affected how black women defined themselves in relationship to each other and to the larger society. Whether slave or free, black women occupied key familial roles as mothers, daughters, wives, and sisters. Although recent works in Afro-American history have devoted a great deal of attention to the structure, function, and stability of black families under slavery, with few exceptions these works, in attempting to establish the vital importance of the male figure, have tended to deemphasize the role of black women within the family.[1] It is, of course, important and necessary to provide a more balanced portrayal of the actual male/female roles in the black family in slavery and freedom in order to obliterate the myth of the ubiquitous black matriarch. Nevertheless, it is critical that the black woman remain visible in the family. Scholarly revisions must not obscure the indisputable fact that the black woman bore primary responsibility for reproducing the slave labor force and for ensuring the continuation of the black race during and after the demise of the Peculiar Institution.

As wives and mothers, black women nurtured the sick, performed all of the domestic chores, provided primary socialization of slave children, wet nursed white children, fulfilled the conjugal needs of their men, and all too often endured the forced passion of slave masters and the vengeful brutality of plantation mistresses. Perhaps the most challenging task confronting black women under slavery was how to maintain a relatively healthy opinion of themselves as sexual beings. To the slave masters they were remunerative slave breeders and vulnerable sexual objects. Although instances abound in the literature about black male slaves who fought and died, the men were, on the whole, unable to offer much protection for the sexual integrity of their wives, daughters, and sisters. Indeed, the abused

1. Herbert G. Gutman, *The Black Family in Slavery and Freedom, 1750–1925* (New York, 1976); John W. Blassingame, *The Slave Community: Plantation Life in the Antebellum South* (New York, 1972); Eugene D. Genovese, *Roll, Jordan, Roll: The World the Slaves Made* (New York, 1974); Robert William Fogel and Stanley Engerman, *Time on the Cross: The Economics of American Negro Slavery* (Boston, 1974); Suzanne Lebsock, "Free Black Women and the Question of Matriarchy: Petersburg, Virginia, 1784–1820," *Feminist Studies*, VIII (Summer, 1982), 271–92; Suzanne Lebsock, *The Free Women of Petersburg: Status and Culture in a Southern Town, 1784–1860* (New York, 1984); Shepard Krech III, "Black Family Organizations in the Nineteenth Century: An Ethnological Perspective," *Journal of Interdisciplinary History*, XIX (1982), 429–52.

black woman often had to convince her mate that the test of his masculinity was self-restraint, not some action that would deprive her of a husband or her children of a father. White plantation mistresses were equally powerless and often displayed considerable hostility toward the abused slave woman. In fact, they frequently blamed the victim for the sexual transgressions of their husbands and sons. As a result, black women, beginning in slavery, were compelled to construct a sexual self, based on the foundation of self-reliance.[2] Given the fact that many slave marriages possessed virtually no legal sanction and were seldom recognized in the larger society, future scholars would do well to explore how black women, in fact, viewed marriage. How did their view of marriage differ from or resemble those views held by men and white women?

Gender relationships between black slaves were problematic even without the sexual intrusions of white men. Although scholars have devoted scant attention to the social relationship between husband and wife, some writers have suggested that black women shared a greater degree of equality with black male slaves than was the case between white men and women. If such was the case, this equality of status certainly derived, in part, from the fact that black women performed many of the same tasks on slave plantations as did the men. They engaged in hard physical labor, chopped and picked cotton, felled trees, mended fences, cared for livestock, and cultivated food crops. Yet it must be pointed out that similar economic or employment responsibilities do not necessarily reflect equal social relations. There was still a sexual division of labor on the plantations. Black women also had to perform socially and biologically determined sex-role stereotyped work. In reality, then, the division of labor on most plantations was decidedly unequal. While all slaves worked hard, the black women slaves were burdened with extra jobs performed only by members of their sex. In the absence of further research, one can only

2. Rennie Simson, "The Afro-American Female: The Historical Context of the Construction of Sexual Identity," in Ann Snitow, Sharon Thompson, and Christine Stausall (eds.), *The Powers of Desire: The Politics of Sexuality* (New York, 1983), 229–35; Harriet Jacobs, *Incidents in the Life of a Slave Girl* (Boston, 1861); Elizabeth Keckley, *Behind the Scenes: Thirty Years a Slave and Four Years in the White House* (1868; rpt. New York, 1968); Genovese, *Roll, Jordan, Roll*, 485, 501; Gerda Lerner (ed.), *Black Women in White America: A Documentary History* (New York, 1973); Catherine Clinton, *The Plantation Mistress: Woman's World in the Old South* (New York, 1982), 188.

speculate about the tensions this inequitable distribution of work assignments must have engendered in many of the slave cabins.[3]

Performing sex-differentiated work did, however, afford black women the opportunity to develop a separate world of informal female networks that reinforced intrasexual reliance. These networks usually evolved through organized group activities such as spinning, weaving, quilting, cooking, and attending each other in childbirth and providing health care. These female slave networks allowed the women to forge a common consciousness concerning their oppression as women while devising strategies for survival. Through their women networks they were able to communicate their feelings, share experiences and world views, and assist each other in the development of positive self-images and self-esteem in spite of the slave-owning society's best efforts to define them to the contrary.[4] Consequently, their interactions engendered an even stronger sense of community among slaves.

In addition to midwifing, doctoring, and other domestic chores, group activities such as quilting facilitated woman bonding and cooperation between female slaves and contained significantly larger social implications. Black women, as slaves and freedwomen, converted quilt making into a social and community affair. Former slave Mary Wright, of Kentucky, reminiscing about quilting offered, "Den wemns [women] quilt awhile, den a big dinner war spread out, den after dinner we'd quilt in de evening, den supper and a big dance dat night, wid de banjie a humming 'n us niggers a dancing."[5] Deserving added emphasis is the fact that the quilt, thus

3. Angela Davis, "Reflections on the Black Woman's Role in the Community of Slaves," Black Scholar, III (1971), 2–15; Deborah G. White, "Ain't I a Woman? Female Slaves, Sex Roles, and Status in the Antebellum Plantation South" (Ph.D. dissertation, University of Illinois, Chicago, 1979; Jacqueline Jones, "'My Mother Was Much of a Woman': Black Women, Work, and Family Under Slavery, 1830–1860," Feminist Studies, VIII (Summer, 1982), 235–69; Jacqueline Jones, Labor of Love, Labor of Sorrow: Black Women, Work, and the Family from Slavery to the Present (New York, 1985); Debra Newman, "Black Women in the Era of the American Revolution in Pennsylvania," Journal of Negro History, LXI (July, 1976), 276–89.

4. Deborah G. White, "Female Slaves: Sex Roles and Status in the Antebellum Plantation South," Journal of Family History, VIII (Fall, 1983), 248–61; Darlene Clark Hine and Kate Wittenstein, "Female Slave Resistance: The Economics of Sex," Western Journal of Black Studies, III (Summer, 1979), 123–27; Jessie Parkhurst, "The Role of the Black Mammy in the Plantation Household," Journal of Negro History, XXIII (July, 1938), 349–69.

5. Quoted in Irene V. Jackson, "Black Women and Music: From Africa to the New

created, represented the individual and collective expression of the voice, vision, structure, and substance of the creators' personal and spiritual lives. One of the most famous black women quilters was former slave Harriet Powers (1837–1911) of Athens, Georgia. One of her two "Bible Quilts" (1898) now adorns the walls of the Smithsonian Institution in Washington, D.C. The quilt is divided into rectangular panels, each devoted to a particular biblical scene. The panels are filled with appliquéd silhouettes of human figures, geometric motifs, and other design combinations that resemble the styles found among the people of ancient Dahomey in West Africa.[6] In much the same way that we can examine the quilts, scholars of the black female experience must analyze other cultural contributions and expressions including hymns, spirituals, blues, lullabyes, poems, novels, sermons, household implements, toys, folktales, and slave narratives.[7]

To be sure, families and female networks were important institutions shaping black women's lives and experiences. Yet, any discussion of the institutional history of black women would be seriously flawed without a simultaneous examination of their involvement in and relationship to the black church and black religion. By the first half of the nineteenth century, religion had become the center of the spiritual and community lives of most women, and of black women in particular. Women, regardless of race and status, played a prominent role within the congregations, organizing voluntary missionary societies, teaching Sunday schools, and raising funds. Representative black women such as Sarah Woodson Early, born on November 15, 1825, in Chillicothe, Ohio, offer illuminating testimony of their

World," in Filomina Chioma Steady (ed.), *The Black Woman Cross-Culturally* (Cambridge, Mass., 1981), 393.

6. John Michael Vlach, *The Afro-American Tradition in Decorative Design* (Cleveland, 1978), 67; Gladys-Marie Fry, "Harriet Powers: Portrait of a Black Quilter," in *Missing Pieces: Georgia Folk Art, 1770–1976* (Atlanta, 1976), 16–23; Robert Farris Thompson, "African Influence on the Art of the United States," *Journal of African Civilization*, III (November, 1978), 44; Gladys-Marie Fry, "Slave Quilting on Ante-Bellum Plantations," in *Something to Keep You Warm* (Roland Freeman Collection of Black American Quilts from the Mississippi Heartland Exhibit Catalog), 4–5.

7. Gloria T. Hull, "Black Women Poets from Wheatley to Walker," in Roseann P. Bell, Bettye J. Parker, and Beverly Guy-Sheftall (eds.), *Sturdy Black Bridges: Visions of Black Women in Literature* (New York, 1979); Arna Alexander Bontemps (ed.), *Forever Free: Art by African American Women, 1862–1980* (Alexandria, Va., 1980); Eileen Southern, *The Music of Black Americans: A History* (New York, 1971); Lawrence W. Levine, *Black Culture and Black Consciousness: Afro-American Folk Thought from Slavery to Freedom* (New York, 1977).

work in the church. Woodson married A.M.E. minister Jordon Winston Early in 1868 and shared with him the tasks of religious leadership. She described her work and that of other black church women: "We assisted in superintending the Sabbath-schools when near enough to reach them; always attending and often leading in prayer meetings; and [we] took an active part in visiting the sick and administering to the wants of the poor and needy, and in raising money to defray the expenses of the Church and served most heartily in its educational work."[8]

At some fundamental level all black churches espoused a theology of liberation, self-determination, and black autonomy. Northern black churches were especially active in and supportive of the abolition movement. The promises embodied in Christian scriptures permeated all of Afro-American culture and possessed special meaning for black women's psychic survival and transcendence. The black church became the training arena that enabled free black women prior to the Civil War to acquire leadership and organizing skills and an increased commitment to winning freedom for the slaves and more control over their own lives. For black slave women religious faith nourished hope for release from their earthly oppression and degradation. The body could be tortured and abused while the soul remained pure and untouched. In the latter decades of the nineteenth century black women enlarged their already considerable influence within the church and extended its sacred horizons to encompass pressing secular concerns. In short, the black church ultimately served as an institutional base giving moral sanction to black women's quest for freedom and the advancement of the race.

One important aspect of black religious life remained unchanged after the Civil War. The hierarchy, ministers, and theologians of most religions and congregations remained male. Not all black women were satisfied with their significant but nevertheless subordinate and relatively invisible roles within black churches. Denied official positions of leadership, a few extraordinary free black women found religious audiences of their own. One such woman was Jarena Lee, born free at Cape May, New Jersey, in

8. Ellen N. Lawson, "Sarah Woodson Early: Nineteenth-Century Black Nationalist 'Sister,'" *Umoja: A Scholarly Journal of Black Studies*, V (Summer, 1981), 21; Jacquleyn Grant, "Black Women and the Church," in Gloria T. Hull, Patricia Bell Scott, and Barbara Smith (eds.), *But Some of Us Are Brave: Black Women's Studies* (New York, 1982), 141–52.

1783. She was a protégée of the Reverend Richard Allen, founder and leader of the African Methodist Episcopal Church. Allen was not averse to Lee's leading prayer meetings, but he at first drew the conservative theological line against female preaching. Later, Allen relented and endorsed her desire to preach. In the single year 1827 Lee traveled 2,325 miles, alone, and delivered 178 sermons, a remarkable feat for any woman during this period in American history. In her autobiography, Lee defended her right to preach: "O how careful ought we to be, lest through our by-laws of church government and discipline, we bring into disrepute even the word of life. For as unseemingly as it may appear now-a-days for a woman to preach, it should be remembered that nothing is impossible with God. And why should it be thought impossible, heterodox, or improper for a woman to preach? Seeing the Savior died for the woman as well as for the man." [9]

Perhaps the best-known itinerant preacher in the antebellum period was the legendary Sojourner Truth, who combined her mission of serving her people and espousing the right of women with a mission to spread the news of a God of love. For Sojourner Truth the abolitionist and women's rights movements were but the secular counterparts of spiritual salvation. At one gathering she declared, "Then that little man in black there, he says women can't have as much rights as men, because Christ wasn't a woman! Where did your Christ come from? From God and a woman! Man had nothing to do with Him." [10]

Like Lee and Truth, Rebecca Cox Jackson was also an itinerant preacher and religious visionary. Born a free black in 1795 near Philadelphia, Jackson experienced a profound spiritual awakening at age thirty-five and felt compelled to preach. Unable to overcome the strong opposition of her family and friends, Jackson severed relations with the Bethel A.M.E. Church in Philadelphia and joined the Watervliet Shaker Community near Albany.

9. "The Life and Religious Experiences of Jarena Lee: A Colored Lady Giving an Account of Her Call to Preach the Gospel," in Dorothy Porter (ed.), *Early Negro Writings, 1760–1837* (Boston, 1971), 494–514; Bert James Loewenberg and Ruth Bogin (eds.), *Black Women in Nineteenth-Century American Life: Their Words, Their Thoughts, Their Feelings* (University Park, 1976), 135.

10. Loewenberg and Bogin, *Black Women in Nineteenth-Century American Life*, 236; See also Arthur Huff Fauset, *Sojourner Truth: God's Faithful Pilgrim* (Durham, 1938); Olivia Gilbert, *Narrative of Sojourner Truth, a Northern Slave* (1850; rpt. Boston, 1884); Hertha Pauli, *Her Name Was Sojourner Truth* (New York, 1962).

Four years later, in 1857, she left the community and was granted the right to found a predominantly black Shaker sisterhood in Philadelphia. In 1878 eight black women, three black children, and three white women lived in the Shaker commune, members of Jackson's spiritual family. She died in 1881.[11]

Amanda Berry Smith, born at Long Gree, Maryland, in 1837, like her A.M.E. predecessors, grew disillusioned by the restrictions on women and ventured forth to become an itinerant preacher (without ordination) and a missionary. She traveled extensively in foreign lands: England in 1878, India in 1880–1881, and Liberia for eight years. Throughout her traveling Smith observed and commented on the common universal exploitation and oppression of women.[12]

Religion, though significant, was not the sole outlet for the talented, intelligent, and spirited free black woman. Many free black women played instrumental and catalytic roles in the reform and humanitarian movements of the early nineteenth century. They were active in founding mutual aid societies and antislavery, suffrage, and temperance organizations. As we shall see, black women were the ones to raise the question of women's rights within the black organizations and issues of racism within white women's organizations. Maria Stewart, born free in 1803 and raised in Hartford, Connecticut, is heralded as the first woman to break with convention and speak in public to a mixed audience of men and women on behalf of black rights and advancement. In an 1832 address before the newly formed Afric-American Female Intelligence Society in Boston, she declared: "Me thinks I heard a spiritual interrogation—'Who shall go forward, and take off the reproach that is cast upon the people of color? Shall it be a woman?' And my heart made this reply—'If it is thy will, be it even so, Lord Jesus!'" Stewart cursed the institution of slavery and urged black women to "awake, arise: no longer sleep nor slumber, but distinguish yourselves."[13]

11. Jean McMahon Humez, *The Gifts of Power: The Writings of Rebecca Jackson, Black Visionary, Shaker Eldress* (Boston, 1981). Also see "Gifts of Power: The Writings of Rebecca Jackson," in Alice Walker's *In Search of Our Mothers' Gardens* (New York, 1983), 71–82.

12. Amanda Berry Smith, "An Autobiography of Mrs. Amanda Smith, the Colored Evangelist," in Loewenberg and Bogin (eds.), *Black Women in Nineteenth-Century American Life*, 171; Marshall W. Taylor, *Amanda Smith, or the Life and Mission of a Slave Girl* (Cincinnati, 1886).

13. Maria Stewart's speech included in Loewenberg and Bogin (eds.), *Black Women*

For free black women the line between involvement in religious institutions and in the women's suffrage movement was a permeable one. Because their religious orientation was toward spiritual liberation and personal autonomy, suffrage for black women became the political expression of their persistent yearnings to be free. Prominent antebellum free black women such as Sarah Mapps Douglass, a teacher in the Institute for Colored Youth, and the three Forten sisters of Philadelphia—Sarah, Margaretta, and Harriet—attended, in 1833, the opening meetings of the Female Anti-Slavery Society of Philadelphia. Margaretta Forten later became the recording secretary of the society. Likewise, Susan Paul was present at the organizational meeting of the Boston Female Anti-Slavery Society and later served as one of its vice-presidents and as treasurer.[14] Here as in other aspects of their lives, black antislavery activists contributed to the abolitionist cause in spite of the racial discrimination and prejudice of their white female colleagues.

The experiences of Sarah Mapps Douglass are a revealing commentary on the racism that existed among white women in the antislavery movement. When Douglass attempted to attend the national meeting of the Female Anti-Slavery Convention in New York City in 1837, she learned that "colored members were unwelcome." An astonished white activist from South Carolina, Angelina Grimké, noted that, in the New York society, "no colored sister has ever been on the Board and they have hardly any colored members even and will not admit any to the working S[ociety]." Only the timely intercession and persuasive powers of Grimké reversed the bar against black women delegates' attending the convention. When Douglass at one point wavered in her resolve to attend the convention, Grimké implored her to reconsider:

in Nineteenth-Century American Life, 192; Maria W. Stewart, Meditations from the Pen of Mrs. Maria W. Stewart, Negro (Washington, D.C., 1879); Maria W. Stewart, "What If I Am a Woman," in Lerner (ed.), Black Women in White America, 562–66. Also see Rosalyn Cleagle, "The Colored Temperance Movement: 1830–1860" (M.A. thesis, Howard University, Washington, D.C., 1969).

14. Ira V. Brown, "Cradle of Feminism: The Philadelphia Female Anti-Slavery Society, 1833–1840," in Pennsylvania Magazine of History and Biography, CII (April, 1978), 143–66; Janice Sumler-Lewis, "The Forten-Purvis Women of Philadelphia and the American Anti-Slavery Crusade," Journal of Negro History, LXVI (Winter, 1981–1982), 281–88. Also see Sumler-Lewis, "The Fortens of Philadelphia: An Afro-American Family and Nineteenth-Century Reform" (Ph.D. dissertation, Georgetown University, Washington, D.C., 1976); Willie Mae Coleman, "Keeping the Faith and Dis-

You my dear Sisters have a work to do in rooting out this wicked feeling as well as we. You must be willing to come in among us tho' it may be your feelings may be wounded by "the putting forth of the finger," the avoidance of a seat by you, or the glancing of the eye. . . . I earnestly desire that you may be willing to bear these mortifications. . . . They will tend to your growth in grace, and will help your sisters more than anything else to overcome their own sinful feelings. Come, then, I would say, for we need your help.[15]

At Grimké's insistence Sarah Douglass and Sarah Forten attended the meeting. Across the ocean another black woman abolitionist, Sarah Parker Remond, appealed to English women to fight against the enslavement of darker members of their sex. When lecturing in London in 1859, Remond focused on the exploitation of black women slaves. She declared, "If English women and English wives knew the unspeakable horrors to which their sex were exposed on southern plantations, they would freight every westward gale with the voices of moral indignation and demand for the black woman the protection and rights enjoyed by the white."[16]

From the 1830s to the turn of the century black women encountered similar white hostility when endeavoring to attend suffrage and women's rights meetings. Even Sojourner Truth, that ardent defender of blacks' and women's rights, was subjected to repeated indignities when attending early women's rights conventions. One male heckler, at the 1851 Woman's Rights Convention in Akron, Ohio, challenged her to prove that she was a woman and some white women activists objected to her being allowed to speak, fearing that too close an association "with abolition and niggers" would damage their cause. It was amidst this climate of racial and sexual hostility that Truth delivered her often repeated, "Ain't I a Woman" speech:

Well, children, war dar is so much racket dar must be someting out o'kilter. I think dat 'twixt de niggers of de Souf and de women at the Norf all a talkin 'bout rights de white men will be in a fix pretty soon. But

turbing the Peace, Black Women: From Anti-slavery to Women's Suffrage" (Ph.D. dissertation, University of California, Irvine, 1982).

15. Katharine DuPre Lumpkin, *The Emancipation of Angelina Grimké* (Chapel Hill, 1974), 104–105.

16. Ruth Bogin, "Sarah Parker Remond: Black Abolitionist from Salem," *Essex Institute Historical Collections*, C (April, 1974), 120–50; Dorothy Porter, "Sarah Parker Remond, Abolitionist and Physician," *Journal of Negro History*, XX (July, 1935), 287–293; Coleman, "Keeping the Faith," 15–16.

what's all diss here talkin' bout? Dat man ober dar say dat women needs to be helped into carriages, and lifted ober ditches and to have da best places . . . and ain't I a woman? Look at me! Look at my arm! . . . I have plowed, and planted and gathered into barns, and no man could head me—and ain't I a woman? I could eat as much as any man (when I could get it), and bear de lash as well—and ain't I a woman? I have borne five children and I seen 'em mos all sold off into slavery, and when I cried out with a mother's grief, none but Jesus hear—and ain't I a woman?[17]

Sojourner Truth was a paradigm to women's rights advocates because her personal experiences proved that women could raise children, do heavy labor, survive persecution, endure physical and sexual abuse, and still emerge triumphant and transcendent. At an 1867 Equal Rights Association convention the indomitable Sojourner Truth warned, "There is a great stir about colored men getting their rights, but not a word about the colored women; and if colored men get their rights, and not colored women theirs, you see the colored men will be masters over the women, and it will be just as bad as it was before."[18]

In the wake of the death of slavery, black women continued their struggle for race advancement and sexual elevation. Blacks, for the most part, entered freedom with little more than the rags on their backs. Merely staying alive became a struggle. Witnessing the suffering and deprivation, black women like Elizabeth Keckley, a personal servant of Mary Todd Lincoln, swung into action. In 1862 Keckley organized the Contraband Relief Association, composed of approximately forty members. The association collected money, clothing, and food to distribute to the thousands of freedmen and freedwomen who flocked to the nation's capital.[19]

17. Pauli, *Her Name Was Sojourner Truth*, 176–77; Loewenberg and Bogin, *Black Women in Nineteenth-Century American Life*, 235; Bell Hooks, *Ain't I a Woman: Black Women and Feminism* (Boston, 1981), 160; Rosalyn Terborg-Penn, "Discrimination Against Afro-American Women in the Woman's Movement, 1830–1920," in Rosalyn Terborg-Penn and Sharon Harley (eds.) *The Afro-American Woman: Struggles and Images* (New York, 1978), 17–27. Also see Terborg-Penn, "Afro-Americans in the Struggle for Woman Suffrage" (Ph.D. dissertation, Howard University, Washington, D.C., 1976), and her "Discontented Black Feminists: Prelude and Postscript to the Passage of the 19th Amendment," in Lois Schraf and Joan M. Jensen (eds.), *Decades of Discontent: The Woman's Movement, 1920–1940* (Westport, Conn., 1983), 261–78; Adele Logan Alexander, "How I Discovered My Grandmother . . . and the Truth About Black Women and the Suffrage Movement," *MS* (November, 1983), 29–37.

18. Lerner, *Black Women in White America*, 569–70.

19. Keckley, *Behind the Scenes*, 113–16; Coleman, "Keeping the Faith," 59–61.

The tradition of slave female networks and the free black woman's improvement associations and their work in antislavery organizations and voluntary associations provided the foundation upon which black women forged powerful national organizations. Characterized by a special brand of black female militancy, national women's networks flourished in the late 1890s and the early twentieth century. In 1892 Fannie Barrier Williams, a prominent member of Chicago's black elite, lamented that "Afro-American women of the United States have never had the benefit of a discriminating judgment concerning their worth as women." Williams, a native of Brockport, New York, attended the New England Conservatory of Music in Boston and the School of Fine Arts in Washington, D.C., and taught school in the South before moving to Chicago. During the 1890s Williams gained international fame for her outspoken defense of black women. Responding to repeated allegations of the immorality of black women and the inferiority of the black race, the embattled Williams declared, "I think it but just to say that we must look at American slavery as the source of every imperfection that mars the character of the colored American."[20]

In the late nineteenth century, America moved inexorably toward a society best characterized as "biracial dualism." While white Americans, north and south, accepted black subordination as representing the Darwinian natural order, black leaders of the race focused almost completely on winning educational, political, and economic rights. Black women, on the other hand, focused on eradicating negative images of their sexuality. Thus, by the late 1890s there developed a major division of emphasis within the black protest tradition. Black men attacked racial discrimination as it operated in the public corridors of power. Black women, whose center of influence had always existed primarily in the family, in the church, and in their female associations, believed that part of the overall struggle for true racial advancement depended upon the extent to which they obliterated all negative sexual images of themselves. In an 1893 speech Williams proclaimed, "This moral regeneration of a whole race of women is no idle sentiment—it is a serious business; and everywhere there is witnessed a feverish anxiety to be free from the mean suspicions that have so long underestimated the character strength of our women."[21] His-

---

20. "Fannie Barrier Williams," in Loewenberg and Bogin, *Black Women in Nineteenth-Century American Life*, 236–79; "A Northern Negro's Autobiography," in Lerner, *Black Women in White America*, 164–66.

21. Loewenberg and Bogin, *Black Women in Nineteenth-Century American Life*,

torian Linda Perkins has perceptively observed that "throughout the nineteenth century, the threads that held together the organizational as well as the individual pursuits of black women were those of 'duty' and 'obligation' to the race. The concept of racial obligation was intimately linked with the concept of racial 'uplift' and 'elevation.'"[22]

Black women leaders such as Josephine St. Pierre Ruffin of Boston, Mary Church Terrell of Washington, D.C., and Mary Margaret Washington of Tuskegee, Alabama, heeding Williams' exhortations, launched, in the mid-1890s, a movement to mobilize black women from all walks of life and to engage them in the battle for racial and sexual equality. Ruffin, born in Boston in 1842 and educated in Salem's public schools, founded, in 1894, the Woman's Era Club and edited its newspaper, the *Woman's Era*. She was a founder of the Association for the Promotion of Child Training in the South and the League of Women for Community Service. Mary Church Terrell was the third black woman college graduate in the country (Oberlin College, 1884) and the first black woman appointed to the board of education in the District of Columbia. Mary Margaret Washington, an 1889 graduate of Fisk University in Nashville, Tennessee, served as director of girls' industries and dean of women at Tuskegee Institute.[23]

In 1895 this national mobilization movement of black women received increased impetus from an unexpected source when James W. Jack, then president of the Missouri Press Association, wrote a letter to Florence Belgarnie, secretary of the Anti-Slavery Society in England, declaring that "the Negroes of this country are wholly devoid of morality" and that "the women were prostitutes and all were natural thieves and liars." Ruffin, upon learning of the comment, immediately transformed it into a weapon to persuade black women of the critical need for organization. She wrote to hundreds of black women insisting that "the letter of Mr. Jack's . . . is

263–79. Also see Anna J. Cooper, *A Voice from the South by a Black Woman of the South* (Xenia, Ohio, 1892).

22. Linda Perkins, "Black Women and Racial 'Uplift' Prior to Emancipation," in Steady (ed.), *The Black Woman Cross-Culturally*, 317–34; Sylvia Lyons Render, "Afro-American Women: The Outstanding and the Obscure," *Quarterly Journal of the Library of Congress*, XXXII (October, 1975), 306–21.

23. Bettye C. Thomas, *Twenty Nineteenth-Century Black Women* (Washington, D.C., 1979), 31; Hallie Quinn Brown, *Homespun Heroines and Other Women in Distinction* (Xenia, Ohio, 1926); Sadie Iola Daniel, *Women Builders* (Washington, D.C., 1970); Sylvania G. L. Dannett, *Profiles of Negro Womanhood*, Vol. 1, 1619–1900 (Chicago, 1964); Mary Church Terrell, *A Colored Woman in a White World* (New York, 1940).

only used to show how pressing is the need of our banning together if only for our protection." Ruffin, in subsequent correspondence, stressed the broad ramifications of negative sexual images. Even white southern women, she pointed out, objected to the formation of interracial women's organizations because of the alleged immorality of black women. She declared, "Too long have we been silent under unjust and unholy charges." Ruffin aroused black women and informed them that it was their "'bounded duty' to stand forth and declare ourselves and principles [and] to teach an ignorant and suspicious world that our aims and interests are identical with those of all good aspiring women."[24]

Ruffin and the black women whom she contacted had just cause to be alarmed by Jack's characterization of all black women as prostitutes. Arrest statistics of black women on charges of illegal solicitation in Nashville and Atlanta underscore the broader social ramifications of this stereotype. In a typical one-year period in Nashville ending October, 1881, there were 136 arrests of white females on charges of streetwalking as compared with 791 arrests of black women. In 1890 Atlanta listed 380 females among its 5,601 arrested whites as compared with 1,715 of the 7,236 arrested blacks. Clearly, the actions of law enforcement officials reflected a shared belief in the stereotype that depicted all black women as natural prostitutes. It is highly unlikely that women became prostitutes because they were immoral. Certainly more work on this matter is needed, especially on economic factors.[25]

By 1896 black women leaders had mobilized sufficiently to create the National Association of Colored Women (NACW). The NACW merged the resources and energies of scores of local and regional clubs into one strong organization in order to attack the prevailing negative image of black womanhood. Throughout the following decades the NACW grew at a phenomenal rate. By 1914 it had a membership of 50,000 and had become the strong, unwavering voice championing the defense of black women in a society that viewed them with contempt. Terrell was elected

24. Josephine St. Pierre Ruffin's speech is included in Elizabeth Lindsay Davis, *Lifting as They Climb* (Washington, D.C., 1933), 13–15. Also see Gerda Lerner, "From Benevolent Societies to National Club Movements," in Lerner, *Black Women in White America*, 435–36.

25. Howard Rabinowitz, *Race Relations in the Urban South, 1865–1890* (Urbana, 1980), 46; Bettina Aptheker, *Woman's Legacy: Essays on Race, Sex, and Class in American History* (Amherst, 1982), 62–63.

first president of the NACW and occupied the position until 1901. In her initial presidential address she declared that there were objectives of the black women's struggle that could only be accomplished "by the mothers, wives, daughters, and sisters of this race." She proclaimed, "We wish to set in motion influences that shall stop the ravages made by practices that sap our strength, and preclude the possibility of advancement." Elaborating, Terrell noted that while blacks, in general, and women, in particular, were subordinate in this society, neither the efforts of the black males nor the concerns of white women would lead them to address the twin ills of racism and sexism endured solely by black women. Terrell then went to the heart of the black woman's dilemma. Like Williams and Ruffin before her, she spoke out of a Victorian world view that insisted on measuring a race's progress by the status of its women. She boldly announced, "We proclaim to the world that the women of our race have become partners in the great firm of progress and reform. . . . We refer to the fact that this is an association of colored women, because our peculiar status in this country . . . seems to demand that we stand by ourselves."[26] Her speech again underscored the importance of black women's self-reliance. Under slavery they had to protect their own sexual being and during freedom they had to defend their sexual image.

Although considerable scholarly attention has been devoted to the club women's movement, there still remains a great deal to be done in the area of black women's involvement in voluntary and self-help associations. In virtually every city and rural community in twentieth-century America

26. Mary Church Terrell, "First Presidential Address to the National Association of Colored Women," Nashville, Tennessee, September 15, 1897, in Mary Church Terrell Papers, Box 102-5, Folder 127, Library of Congress; Gloria M. White, "The Early Mary Church Terrell, 1863–1910," in *Integrateducation*, XII (November–December, 1975), 40ff; Dorothy Sterling, *Black Foremothers: Three Lives* (Old Westbury, N.Y., 1979), 118–58; Beverly Jones, "Mary Church Terrell and the National Association of Colored Women, 1896–1901," *Journal of Negro History*, LXVII (Spring, 1982), 20–33. Also see Ruby M. Kendrick, "They Also Serve: The National Association of Colored Women, Inc., 1895–1954," *Negro History Bulletin*, XVII (March, 1954), 171–75; Gerda Lerner, "Early Community of Black Club Women," *Journal of Negro History*, LIX (April, 1974), 158–67; Cynthia Neverdon-Morton, "The Black Woman's Struggle for Equality in the South," in Terborg-Penn and Harley (eds.), *The Afro-American Woman*, 43–57; Lawrence B. de Graff, "Race, Sex, and Region: Black Women in the American West, 1850–1920," in *Pacific Historical Review*, XLIX (May, 1980), 285–313; Linda Faye Dickson, "The Early Club Movement Among Black Women in Denver, 1890–1925" (Ph.D. dissertation, University of Colorado, Boulder, 1982).

there existed an organized grouping of black women, often led by a cadre of elite educated black middle-class matrons. These clubs and organizations gradually added to their primary concern of upgrading sexual images a concern for women's suffrage and progressive social reform. Almost every black women's club, regardless of who founded it or the ostensible reason for its establishment, focused to some extent on alleviating one or more of the many social problems afflicting an increasingly urban, impoverished, politically powerless, and segregated black population. Before the emergence of the modern welfare state, blacks had to rely on their own initiative in order to provide adequate educational institutions, suitable health care programs, and settlement houses. They slowly and unrelentingly erected a nationwide network of institutions and organizations welding together the entire black population. Ida Wells Barnett of Chicago, Jane Edna Hunter of Cleveland, and Sallie Wyatt Stewart of Evansville, Indiana, are but three examples of midwestern black women who established black settlement or community houses during the era of progressive reform. Moreover, throughout the twenties black women mobilized support for the establishment of black branches of the Young Women's Christian Association, and their institution-building activities reflect the same spirit of volunteerism seen among white women in American society during the Progressive era.

No accurate social or cultural history of black America is possible without a detailed examination of the institutions crafted by still unrecognized local black women. The creation of educational, health care, and recreational institutions spearheaded by diverse black women's clubs and voluntary associations followed no standard pattern. Rather, women launched new projects or worked to transform existing institutions into structures more adequately designed to address the needs of their respective constituencies. Recurring concerns were for education for the young, food, shelter, and clothing for the aged, medical and nursing care for the sick. While considerably more work needs to be done in the area, two examples will illustrate this all too frequently ignored dimension of black institution building and internal cultural development. In the South, the black women of New Orleans organized and founded in 1896 the Phillis Wheatley Sanitarium and Nursing Training School, which eventually became, in the 1930s, the Flint-Goodridge Hospital and School of Nursing of Dillard University. Counterparts in the midwest, the black women in Indianapolis,

Indiana, founded in the 1870s and continue to the present to support the Alpha Home for Colored Aged.[27]

The pressing need of blacks, and black women in particular, for education motivated several black women, most notably Mary McLeod Bethune, to launch new institutions for their sex. Bethune, born on July 10, 1875, in Mayesville, South Carolina, graduated from Scotia Seminary in 1894 and entered the Mission Training School of the Moody Bible Institute of Chicago. After teaching in a number of mission schools, she settled in Daytona, Florida, where she founded the Daytona Literary and Industrial School for Training Negro Girls. Reflecting on her work years later, Bethune recalled, "The school expanded fast. In less than two years I had 250 pupils. . . . I concentrated more and more on girls, as I felt that they especially were hampered by lack of educational opportunities." Eventually, however, she agreed to merge with Cookman Institute, an educational facility for Negro boys under the auspices of the Methodist Church. Thus, in 1923 the now co-ed institution was renamed the Bethune-Cookman College. Bethune was an active participant in the black women's club movement, serving as president of the National Association of Colored Women (1926–1928). She helped to create the women's section of the Commission on Interracial Cooperation. Most importantly, in 1935 she founded the National Council of Negro Women. Throughout her later years she played a major role in the nation's political affairs, becoming the first black woman to hold a federal post as administrator of the Office of Minority Affairs within the National Youth Administration during Franklin Delano Roosevelt's presidency.

Bethune is a pivotal figure in twentieth-century black women's history. Her life and work is inarguably one of the major links connecting the social reform efforts of post-Reconstruction black women to the political protest activities of the generation emerging after World War II. All of the various strands of black women's struggle for education, political rights, racial pride, sexual autonomy, and liberation are united in the writings,

27. For a case study in one state, see Darlene Clark Hine, *When the Truth Is Told: A History of Black Women's Culture and Community in Indiana, 1875–1950* (Indianapolis, 1981); Coleman, "Keeping the Faith," 77–88; Thomas C. Holt, "The Lonely Warrior: Ida B. Wells-Barnett and the Struggle for Black Leadership," in John Hope Franklin and August Meier (eds.), *Black Leaders of the Twentieth Century* (Urbana, 1982), 39–62; Alfreda M. Duster (ed.), *Crusade for Justice: The Autobiography of Ida B. Wells* (Chicago, 1970); Sterling, *Black Foremothers*, 60–117.

speeches, and organizational work of Bethune. A good biography of this vital figure is sorely needed.[28]

The turn of the century witnessed many black women engaged in creating educational and social welfare institutions within their communities. Yet, as involved as these women were in the work of institution building, they never lost sight of the major problem confronting black men in America. Indeed, for the young Ida B. Wells (1862–1931) overcoming racism and halting the violent murder of black men remained a central mission among her wide-ranging struggles for justice and human dignity. As a young woman, Wells co-founded in 1891 the militant newspaper *Free Speech* in Memphis, Tennessee. Her scathing editorials denouncing local whites for the lynching of black men on the pretext of protecting the sanctity of white womanhood provoked a mob to burn her press and threaten death should she show her face again in the city.[29]

Exiled north, Wells, without pause, launched a veritable one-woman international crusade against lynching. When the National Association for the Advancement of Colored People (NAACP) was formed in 1910, Wells insisted that the leadership take an unwavering stand against lynching.

28. B. Joyce Ross, "Mary McLeod Bethune and the National Youth Administration: A Case Study of Power Relationships in the Black Cabinet of Franklin D. Roosevelt," in Franklin and Meier (eds.), *Black Leaders of the Twentieth Century*, 191–219; Florence Johnson Hicks (ed.), *Mary McLeod Bethune: Her Own Words of Inspiration* (Washington, D.C., 1975); Mary McLeod Bethune, "Faith That Moved a Dump Heap," *Who, the Magazine About People* (June, 1941), 31–35, 54; John B. Kirby, *Black Americans in the Roosevelt Era: Liberalism and Race* (Knoxville, 1980), 111–21. For a good discussion of other black women educators, see: Daniels, *Women Builders*, 137–67; Charlotte H. Brown, *The Correct Thing to Do* (Boston, 1940); Lessie Lois Fowle, "Willa A. Strong: An Historical Study of Black Education in Southeastern Oklahoma" (Ph.D. dissertation, University of Oklahoma, Norman, 1982); Evelyn Brooks Barnett, "Nannie Burroughs and the Education of Black Women," in Terborg-Penn and Harley (eds.), *The Afro-American Women*, 97–108. Burroughs founded the National Training School for Women and Girls in Washington, D.C., on October 19, 1909. Linda M. Perkins, "The Black Female American Missionary Association Teacher in the South, 1861–1870," in Jeffrey J. Crow and Flora J. Hatley (eds.), *Black Americans in North Carolina and the South* (Chapel Hill, 1984), 122–36.

29. Paula Giddings, *When and Where I Enter: The Impact of Black Women on Race and Sex in America* (New York, 1984), 19–31; Thomas C. Holt, "The Lonely Warrior: Ida B. Wells-Barnett and the Struggle for Black Leadership," in Franklin and Meier (eds.), *Black Leaders of the Twentieth Century* 39–62; Alfreda M. Duster, *Crusade for Justice: The Autobiography of Ida B. Wells* (Chicago, 1970); David M. Tucker, "Miss Ida B. Wells and Memphis Lynching," *Phylon*, XXXII (Summer, 1971), 112–22.

Years later Wells withdrew from the NAACP when the organization's leaders failed to adopt the more militant race-conscious posture she advocated. Wells proved equally unsuccessful in persuading leaders in the women's suffrage movement to speak out against racism and to denounce the atrocity of lynching. The young white leaders of the National American Women's Suffrage Association early declared that the organization had only one objective—woman suffrage. These women, especially southern members, feared that too close an association with black issues would jeopardize their cause. It would not be until 1930, the year before Wells's death, that black and white women joined forces to launch the Association of Southern Women for the Prevention of Lynching.[30]

Neither the Great Migration to southern and northern cities nor the ratification of the Nineteenth Amendment to the United States Constitution granting women the right to vote altered the political status and material conditions of the lives of the majority of black women. Like their male counterparts, hundreds of thousands of black women had quit the rural South before and during the World War I years and ventured to northern cities in search of the "promised land." Many single young black women trekked to cities seeking better jobs, decent housing, equal education, freedom from terrorism, adventure, and intellectual stimulation. They left behind, or so they dreamed, racial discrimination, grueling poverty, second-class citizenship, and sexual exploitation. While the war raged and the economy boomed, jobs in industries and factories appeared both abundant and accessible. When the war ended black women and men fortunate enough to have secured employment were quickly dismissed, as employers preferred to give their jobs to returning white veterans. For black women the migration experience only confirmed that the promised land was littered with all but identical racial and sexual ills as had plagued their southern odyssey.[31]

30. Rosalyn Terborg-Penn, "Discontented Black Feminists: Prelude and Postscript to the Passage of the Nineteenth Amendment," in Schraf and Jensen (eds.), *Decades of Discontent*, 272–73.

31. Alice Kessler-Harris, *Out to Work: A History of Wage-Earning Women in the United States* (New York, 1982), 237; William H. Harris, *The Harder We Run: Black Workers Since the Civil War* (New York, 1982), 51–76. Also see Florette Henri, *Black Migration: Movement North, 1900–1920* (New York, 1976); Delores Elizabeth Janiewski, "From Field to Factory: Race, Class, Sex, and the Woman Worker in Durham, 1880–1940" (Ph.D. dissertation, Duke University, 1979); Sharon Harley, "Black

Black women's work experiences were repeated during the Second World War. Traditionally, wartime crises led to improvement in the status of women, as many scholars have argued. The male labor shortage encouraged employers to seek women to work on assembly lines in defense plants and in other occupations that are normally closed to their sex when a full contingent of male workers is available. For black women, however, the status of being the last hired and the first fired remained true throughout the World War II years and after. As historian Karen Tucker Anderson has demonstrated, "both during and after the war, black women entered the urban female labor force in large numbers only to occupy its lowest rungs. Largely excluded from clerical and sales work, the growth sectors of the female work force, black women found work primarily in service jobs outside the household and in unskilled blue-collar categories." As late as 1950, 40 percent of the black female labor force remained mired in domestic service. The remaining numbers were involved in unskilled blue-collar labor and in agriculture. Only a small percentage of black women belonged to the white collar professions, concentrating in teaching, nursing, and social work. By 1974 women made up 46 percent of the total black professionals, yet they constituted only 7 percent of the engineers, 14 percent of the lawyers, 24 percent of the physicians and dentists, and 25 percent of the life and physical scientists. On the other hand, black women represented 97 percent of the black librarians, 97 percent of black nurses, and 78 percent of the noncollege black teachers. There is little evidence to suggest that these percentages have changed significantly in the past decade.[32] Again, more work needs to be done comparing the economic development of black women with that of their white female counterparts.

In the face of continuing economic subordination, some black women

Women in a Southern City, 1890–1920," in Joanne V. Hawks and Sheila L. Skemp (eds.), *Sex, Race, and the Role of Women in the South: Essays*, (Jackson, Miss., 1983), 59–74.

32. Karen Tucker Anderson, "Last Hired, First Fired: Black Women Workers During World War II," *Journal of American History*, LXIX (June, 1982), 96–97; Lois Rita Helmbold, "Making Choices, Making Do: Black and White Working Class Women's Lives During the Great Depression" (Ph.D. dissertation, Stanford University, 1982); Claudia Golden, "Female Labor Force Participation: The Origins of Black and White Differences," *Journal of Economic History*, XXXVII (March, 1977), 87–112. Also see Phyllis A. Wallace, *Black Women in the Labor Force* (Cambridge, Mass., 1980).

sought relief and escape, as well as symbolic empowerment, through involvement in radical protest movements. During the 1920s black women had formed a woman's arm of Marcus Garvey's Universal Negro Improvement Association (UNIA). Amy Jacques Garvey headed the division and edited the women's department of the UNIA's official organ, *Negro World*. In numerous speeches and essays Amy Garvey reminded Afro-American women that they were the "burden bearers of their race" and as such had the responsibility to assume leadership in the struggle for black liberation both at home and abroad.[33] Here, too, is an area in need of much work, for the role black women played in the UNIA has received scant scholarly attention.

Black women supported A. Philip Randolph's March on Washington Movement, which was initiated in 1941 to end discrimination in defense industries with government contracts. They remained steadfast in their support of the NAACP and the National Urban League, the more traditional black civil rights organizations. During the course of the war black women did achieve one victory. From 1942 to the end of the war black women rallied behind the leadership of nurses Estelle Massey Riddle and Mabel K. Staupers and the National Association of Colored Graduate Nurses (NACGN) to win integration of black nurses into the United States Armed Forces Nurses Corps.[34]

In addition to cooperating with male leaders of protest and black rights groups and supporting the efforts of women's professional societies in the ongoing quest for integration and first-class citizenship, black women created their own national political organization. In 1935, Mary Church Terrell joined Mary McLeod Bethune in signing the charter of the first council of organizations in the history of organized black womanhood—the National Council of Negro Women (NCNW). The local leadership of

33. Terborg-Penn, "Discontented Black Feminist," in Schraf and Jensen (eds.), *Decades of Discontent*, 269; Mark D. Matthews, "'Our Women and What They Think' Amy Jacques Garvey and *The Negro World*," *Black Scholar*, X (May–June, 1979), 2–13.

34. Susan M. Hartman, "Women's Organizations During World War II: The Interaction of Class, Race, and Feminism," in Mary Kelley (ed.), *Woman's Being, Woman's Place: Female Identity and Vocation in American History* (Boston, 1979), 317; Darlene Clark Hine, "Mabel K. Staupers and the Integration of Black Nurses into the Armed Forces Nurses Corps," in Franklin and Meier (eds.), *Black Leaders in the Twentieth Century*, 241–57.

the NCNW represented a cross section of black women from all walks of life, though the national officers were all well-educated, middle-class professional women. The unity of women engaged in the struggle is demonstrated by the cooperation whereby Estelle Massey Riddle, president of the NACGN, was elected second vice-president of the NCNW, while Terrell served as first vice-president and Bethune became the president.[35]

The NCNW declared as its purpose the collecting, interpreting, and disseminating of information concerning the activities of black women. Moreover, the NCNW leaders desired "to develop competent and courageous leadership among Negro women and effect their integration and that of all Negro people into the political, economic, educational, cultural and social life of their communities and the nation." To achieve these and other objectives, NCNW leaders founded an official organ, *The Aframerican Woman's Journal*, and dedicated it to achieving "the outlawing of the Poll Tax, the development of a Public Health Program, an Anti-lynching Bill, the end of discrimination in the Armed Forces, Defense Plants, Government Housing Plants and finally that Negro History be taught in the Public Schools of the country."[36]

This increased organizing activity evidenced during the Great Depression and World War II era reflected black women's growing determination to overthrow a tripartite system of racial and sexual oppression, economic exploitation, and political powerlessness. Undoubtedly, millions of black women had acquired deeper understanding of their entrapment in the prison of white supremacy through membership in such clubs and organizations. Club membership and associations encouraged in black women the forging of a certain mental attitude and a readiness to work and die, if need be, for the liberation of their people. These organized and aware black women became one of the major, albeit invisible and unrecognized, foundations upon which was based the modern Civil Rights Movement of the 1950s and 1960s. The as yet undiminished proliferation of studies of the Civil Rights Movement will remain incomplete as long as scant attention is paid the roles played by black women such as Rosa Parks, Ella

35. "Purposes of NCNW—1935," Press Release, November 11, 1948, The Papers of Mary Church Terrell, Container 23, Library of Congress, Washington, D.C. Also see Mary Church Terrell, *A Colored Woman in a White World* (Washington, 1940).

36. "Purpose of NCNW—1935," Press Release, November 11, 1948, in Terrell Papers.

Baker, and Fannie Lou Hamer. What is now required is a full-scale, detailed treatment and scholarly analysis of the Civil Rights Movement written from the perspective of black women participants. Biographies and autobiographies of key female leaders and activists in the movement, similar to Anne Moody's *Coming of Age in Mississippi* (1967) or Daisy Bates' *The Long Shadow of Little Rock: A Memoir* (1962), will shed new light on the origins and evolution of the largest mass movement of black Americans for social change in the country's history.[37] Even a brief examination of the lives of Rosa Parks and Ella Baker suggests new directions to be taken in future scholarship. The recent work of sociologist Aldon D. Morris is a welcome contribution to civil rights studies in that the author takes pains to elaborate and interpret the roles of black women in the struggle.[38]

Traditional accounts of the history of the Civil Rights Movement portray Rosa Parks as a quiet, dignified older lady who spontaneously refused to yield her bus seat to a white man because she was tired, her feet hurt, and she quite simply had had enough. Actually, Parks, a long-time member of black women's organizations and of the NAACP, was deeply rooted in the black protest tradition and had refused several times previously, as far back as the 1940s, to comply with segregation rules on buses. Morris has astutely observed that Parks's arrest triggered the Civil Rights Movement because "she was an integral member of those organizational forces capable of mobilizing a social movement." It is equally as important to note that Parks was firmly anchored in the church community in Montgomery, where she served as a stewardess in the St. Paul A.M.E. Church.[39]

The difference between Parks's previous protests and arrests and the December 1, 1955, incident was that members of the Women's Political Council, organized by professional black women of Montgomery in 1949 for the purpose of registering black women to vote, swung into action. Since its inception, the WPC had been a major political force within Montgomery. The members consistently challenged the segregation practices and laws before meetings of the city commission. They had demanded the hiring of

37. Anne Moody, *Coming of Age in Mississippi* (New York, 1968). Also see Sara Evans, *Personal Politics: The Roots of Women's Liberation in the Civil Rights Movement and New Left* (New York, 1980).

38. Aldon D. Morris, *Origins of the Civil Rights Movement* (New York, 1985).

39. *Ibid.*, 51, 52, 53.

black policemen and protested the inadequacies of parks and playgrounds in the black community. Some of their demands were met, others ignored. The morning after Parks's arrest, however, leader Jo Ann Robinson, an English teacher at Alabama State College, announced to students and colleagues that the WPC would launch a bus boycott to end segregation forever. She wrote the leaflet describing the Parks incident and rallied the community for action.[40] The women of the WPC were not alone. Similar groups and individuals across the South were ready and eager to heed the call for social action. Black women had been organizing for over a hundred years and their infrastructure of secular clubs and sacred associations was already firmly in place.

Of the many black women participants in the Civil Rights Movement, Ella Baker deserves special recognition and study. Baker was the central figure in the Southern Christian Leadership Conference's (SCLC) Atlanta office during the 1950s. Her determined opposition to assigning black women subservient roles in the hierarchical structure of social-change movements aroused the ire of her male colleagues. Baker was born in 1903, in Virginia, and raised in North Carolina. In 1927 she quit the South and migrated to New York, where she eventually worked in developing the Young Negro Cooperative League. From 1941 to 1942 Baker served as the national field secretary for the NAACP, a position requiring her to travel throughout the South conducting membership campaigns and developing NAACP branches. Baker, when promoted director of branches for the NAACP, attended 157 meetings and traveled 10,244 miles, all within a twelve-month period.[41]

By the time Baker joined SCLC as its first associate director, she had accumulated considerable organizational experience and had cultivated an invaluable network of community contacts throughout the South. Initially Baker performed the routine chores in the central office, her interpersonal and organizational skills ignored and untapped by the male ministerial leadership. Soon there was considerable friction within SCLC, occasioned in part because of Baker's belief in women's equality and her refusal automatically to defer to men. Moreover, Baker insisted that the effectiveness of a people's movement depended upon the careful cultivation of local leadership among the masses. In particular, she objected that the Civil Rights Movement was structured around Martin Luther King, Jr., to such

40. *Ibid.*
41. *Ibid.*, 102–104, 114.

a degree as to block the development of skills among women, young people, and other members of the black community. She advocated a "group-centered leadership" approach which would allow the movement to become more democratic and would minimize internal struggle for personal advantage. Baker and the older male leaders clashed over the types of organizational structure that should be established at SCLC headquarters. She emphasized that SCLC should have clearly defined personnel assignments and obligations. Not surprisingly, Baker's recommendations were seldom taken seriously and rarely implemented by the SCLC leadership. In his study on the origins of the Civil Rights Movement Morris concludes that "it appears that sexism and Baker's non-clergy status minimized her impact on the SCLC" in the late 1950s. Yet, of all the early civil rights leaders Baker was the one to grasp the significance of the student sit-ins begun in Greensboro, North Carolina, on February 1, 1960. She persuaded the SCLC to underwrite the conference, pulling together more than three hundred students from across the South. Out of this meeting emerged the Student Nonviolent Coordinating Committee (SNCC).[42]

Another heroine of the Civil Rights Movement was Fannie Lou Hamer (1917–1977). Born in Montgomery County, Mississippi, Hamer spent most of her adult life working as a sharecropper and time keeper on a plantation four miles east of Ruleville, Mississippi. In 1962, she was fired for attempting to vote. Thereafter threats on her life and severe physical abuse plagued her existence. Undaunted, Hamer became involved in SNCC and from 1963 to 1967 served in the capacity of field secretary. On April 26, 1964, when the Democratic party refused to permit blacks to participate, Hamer and others founded the Mississippi Freedom Democratic Party (MFDP). She became vice-chairman. Later in the summer of 1964 Hamer led a delegation of Mississippi citizens to the Democratic National Convention in Atlantic City. There the MFDP challenged the seats of the regular Mississippi delegation. The result of the challenge was an unprecedented pledge from the national Democratic party not to seat delegations that excluded Negroes at the 1968 national convention. A full-scale scholarly biography of Fannie Lou Hamer is long overdue.[43]

The voice and moral vision of black women in the Civil Rights Movement and later in the Women's Liberation Movement may have been muted and unheeded, but the silence was irrevocably shattered during the dec-

---

42. *Ibid.*
43. Giddings, *When and Where I Enter*, 287–90, 293–94.

ades of the 1970s and 1980s. A new black woman emerged in the wake of the Civil Rights Movement. She was unveiled to the American public through the creative expression of over a dozen outstanding black women novelists, poets, artists, and musicians. Even today American society— black and white, male and female—knows not what to make of this new black woman so forcefully unleashed by a galaxy of creators, or indeed, what she portends for the future. Some would contend that the black woman holds the key to the country's future. Actually, the new black woman is not all that new. What is new is the fact that we are beginning to listen and to see her on her own terms and in her own right.

In 1859 Harriet Wilson, a domestic servant, wrote the first black novel, the semiautobiographical *Our Nig*. Frances Ellen Harper later in the century published her novel, *Iola Leroy*, in which she chronicled the struggle of a black woman to maintain her pride, dignity, and racial commitment during the years of slavery and Reconstruction. The 1920s witnessed the birth of the Harlem Renaissance. It was an era rich in black creativity. Although numerous black women writers, artists, musicians, and performers participated in and enhanced the cultural richness and ethos of the period, their work, until quite recently, remained neglected and unexamined.[44] Only since the recent appearance and critical acclaim accorded Alice Walker's *The Color Purple* (1983), Toni Morrison's *Tar Baby* (1982), and Gloria Naylor's *The Women of Brewster Place* (1982), among others, have Americans begun to recognize the literary achievements and contributions of black women.

Although twentieth-century black women's writing in its great diversity defies easy characterization, there are common threads. Harlem Renaissance novelists Jessie Redmond Fauset, Nella Larson, and Zora Neale Hurston and the post–World War II writers Margaret Walker, Ann Petry,

---

44. Barbara Christian, *Black Women Novelists: The Development of a Tradition, 1892–1976* (Westport, Conn., 1980), 41–54; Carol Watson, "The Novels of Afro-American Women: Concerns and Themes, 1891–1965" (Ph.D. dissertation, George Washington University; Washington, D.C., 1978); David Levering Lewis, *When Harlem Was in Vogue* (New York, 1982), 120–25, 140ff; Erlene Stetson (ed.), *Black Sisters: Poetry by Black American Women, 1746–1980* (Bloomington, 1981); Roseann P. Bell, Bettye J. Parker, and Beverly Guy-Sheftall (eds.), *Sturdy Black Bridges: Visions of Black Women in Literature*; Deborah E. McDowell, "The Neglected Dimension of Jessie Redmond Fauset," *Afro-Americans in New York Life and History*, V (July, 1981), 33–49.

Gwendolyn Brooks, Alice Childress, and Lorraine Hansberry, along with the more contemporary recent authors Gayle Jones, Toni Cade Bambara, Maya Angelou, Ntozake Shange, and Paule Marshall, all reveal a strong sense of race and class consciousness and political engagement. There are important generational differences, to be sure. The more contemporary authors write increasingly and boldly of the sexual conflict between black women and men. Their tone is distinctively more feminist, or "womanist" as Alice Walker would describe it, and their works are much more stylistically unconventional. They stress women's oppression as well as black oppression under capitalism and often offer radical visions of family, sexual, and community relations in ways that repudiate repressive white cultural norms.[45] While recently published biographies of Zora Neale Hurston, blues singer Ma Rainey, and the diaries and letters of Alice Dunbar Nelson are a step in the right direction, we need similar studies of such cultural luminaries as blues singer Billie Holiday, playwright and pan-Africanist Lorraine Hansberry, painter Elizabeth Catlett, and gospel singer Mahalia Jackson.[46]

No complete study and understanding of black women's history is possible without a simultaneous examination of the shape and contours of their creative outpourings. Scholars, historians, and literary critics have only recently begun to scale the rocky and complex terrain of the minds and works of creative black women. When the story of black women is told in all its complexity, pain, and beauty, then and only then will we be in a position to comprehend fully the meaning of black lives at the end of the rainbow and by extension the entire American experience. There is much work ahead of us.

45. Darlene Clark Hine, "To Be Gifted, Female, and Black," *Southwest Review* LXVII (Autumn, 1982), 357–69.

46. Sandra R. Lieb, *Mother of the Blues: A Story of Ma Rainey* (Amherst, 1981); Robert Hemenway, *Zora Neale Hurston: A Literary Biography* (Urbana, 1978). The Elizabeth Catlett Papers are available at the Amistad Research Center in New Orleans, Louisiana. Gloria T. Hull (ed.), *Give Us Each Day: The Diary of Alice Dunbar-Nelson* (New York, 1984); Mamie Garvin Fields with Karen Fields, *Lemon Swamp and Other Places: A Carolina Memoir* (New York, 1983).

Secondary School History Textbooks and the Treatment of Black History

JAMES D. ANDERSON

The purpose of this essay is to review and analyze the portrayal of the Afro-American experience in secondary school history textbooks. Although we are never certain as to what messages students internalize from the materials they read, the question What do history textbooks tell their readers about black Americans? has been asked repeatedly over the past several decades. At the heart of this question is an honest concern that students be told the full truth about the formation and development of the American nation and the fear that we still suffer the effects of decades of omissions, distortions, and untruths perpetrated by both conscious and unconscious efforts to expose generations of American students to a politically usable past that rationalizes and reinforces the historical domination of white Americans over black Americans. Hence, this analysis starts with a review of the long-standing efforts by many scholars and concerned groups to make authors and publishing houses fully aware of the fact that the historical development of blacks and other minority groups in America has been neglected or, in many instances, distorted in United States history textbooks. This neglect and distortion have led not only to a misunderstanding of the black experience in America but to a one-sided and therefore superficial understanding of the evolution and meaning of the overall American experience.

The other major focus of this essay is a comparison of selected secondary school history textbooks copyrighted between 1977 and 1981. Six well-known and widely used textbooks were chosen for careful examination. Others were reviewed more casually to determine the extent of conformity. The focus on recent textbooks is designed to reveal the impact on these of scholarly and political movements during the 1960s and early 1970s. This period witnessed a dramatic reawakening of scholarly interest in the black experience, which resulted in an outpouring of high-quality articles and books. To be sure, many black historians during the first half of this century produced the historical scholarship sufficient for a balanced and sensitive treatment of the black presence in American history. But it was not until the Civil Rights and Black Power movements of the 1960s that white historians, government and school officials, and the media responded to the misrepresentation of the black experience in United States history. Hence, as the new historiography provided a broader scholarly foundation for correcting the traditional neglect and distortion of the black experience, changes in civil rights law and public opinion provided a firmer social basis for ending the deep-seated discrimination against minorities in schools, classrooms, and the history textbooks. Did these changes lead to more accurate and sensitively written secondary school history textbooks? The second half of the essay attempts to answer this question. But let us first examine the history of this problem, which is instructive in its own right.

Textbook Criticism, 1933–1982

Among scholars who have investigated the treatment of minorities in history textbooks there is substantial agreement that writers and publishing companies have for centuries either consciously or unconsciously produced a racist historiography that generally ignores, distorts, or falsifies the history of Afro-American life and culture. Significantly, this is not a recent discovery. Lawrence D. Reddick's 1933 Master's thesis, "Racial Attitudes in the South's American History Textbooks," was one of the first studies to examine the unfair and inaccurate presentation of the black experience in school history textbooks. In 1935, W. E. B. Du Bois ended his study *Black Reconstruction* with a chapter ("The Propaganda of History") criticizing texts in widespread use at the time that distorted the black presence in America. Charles E. Russell, before the Twenty-ninth

Annual Conference of the NAACP in 1938, documented and attacked the racism prevalent in textbooks. This critique was continued as evidenced in an NAACP pamphlet entitled "Anti-Negro Propaganda in School Textbooks" published in 1939. Moreover, during the same period the Association for the Study of Negro Life and History, founded in 1916 by Carter G. Woodson, not only led a relentless assault on racism in history textbooks but sought to replace the superficial and distorted history with more scholarly accounts in the *Journal of Negro History*. However, white writers and publishing companies, generally rejecting or ignoring the research and findings of black historians, continued to produce grossly biased history textbooks as though there were no substantial body of scholarship at variance with their faulty judgments on the role of blacks in American history.[1]

During World War II, Germany's fascism and America's racism provided a catalyst for the emergence of numerous other efforts aimed at combating racism in textbooks. Dissatisfaction with racist textbooks in the 1940s was notable in two dissertations written by black female doctorates. Edna M. Colson's "An Analysis of the Specific Reference to Negroes in Selected Curricula for the Education of Teachers" and Marie E. Carpenter's "The Treatment of the Negro in American History School Textbooks" documented once more the neglect and mistreatment of blacks in the writing of American history. In 1949, a major study of secondary school textbooks and their treatment of minorities in American history was conducted by Howard E. Wilson. The Committee on the Study of Teaching Materials, a ten-person staff headed by Wilson, analyzed 315 textbooks and related materials over a five-year period. This study, entitled *Intergroup Relations in Teaching Materials*, was published by the American Council on Education. It found history textbooks to be lacking in a balanced and comprehensive treatment of minorities, resulting in distortions, racial stereotyping, and general historical miseducation.[2]

1. Lawrence D. Reddick, "Racial Attitudes in the South's American History Textbooks" (M.A. thesis, Fisk University, 1933); W. E. B. Du Bois, *Black Reconstruction in America: An Essay Toward a History of the Part Which Black Folk Played in the Attempt to Reconstruct Democracy in America, 1860–1880* (New York, 1935); Zachary L. Cooper, "Blacks in American History Textbooks: An Analysis of Two Middle School Textbooks" (Ph.D. dissertation, University of Wisconsin–Madison, 1979), 10.

2. Marie E. Carpenter, "The Treatment of the Negro in American History School Textbooks: A Comparison of Changing Textbook Content, 1826 to 1939, with Develop-

By the end of the 1940s there were already more than enough studies revealing the neglect and mistreatment of Afro-Americans in textbooks. For instance, Marie E. Carpenter's dissertation, which was published as a book in 1941, was critical of textbooks in use from 1826 to 1939. In 1944, the United States Office of Education, as part of its opposition to fascism, issued a mimeographed circular entitled "Sources of Instructional Material on Negroes" prepared by Ambrose Caliver. This report was revised by Theresa B. Wilkins and published in January, 1946, by the National Education Association. The results of this study, as with all the others, left little doubt that major revisions were needed in order to eliminate racism from school textbooks and to present a balanced and integrated view of the American experience.[3]

Thus, the continued failure in the 1950s to interweave Afro-American life and culture into American history textbooks was ironic as well as tragic. If the historical viewpoints of the pre-1950s had been conditioned by racist social values and ways of thought and a tradition of racist historiography, it was no longer necessary for textbook historians to be imprisoned by certain historical sources and social attitudes. On the one hand, there was a solid tradition of antiracist scholarship, dating back to the early 1930s, that was specifically critical of the textbook treatment of minorities. On the other hand, there were excellent historical sources that had been developed by such outstanding historians as W. E. B. Du Bois, Carter G. Woodson, Horace Mann Bond, Lorenzo Greene, Lawrence D. Reddick, Charles Wesley, John Hope Franklin, A. A. Taylor, and Rayford Logan, to name only a few of them. To persist in writing and producing racist and misleading history, authors and publishing companies had to close themselves to criticism and ignore the excellent scholarship of generations of nonracist historians. Textbook writers did not respond to evidence, logic, or reason as they continued to neglect and mistreat minorities in American history textbooks. Instead, their behavior contributed to

---

ing Scholarship in the History of the Negro in the United States" (Ph.D. dissertation, Columbia University, 1941); Edna M. Colson, "An Analysis of the Specific References to Negroes in Selected Curricula for the Education of Teachers" (Ph.D. dissertation, Columbia University, 1940); Committee on the Study of Teaching Materials in Intergroup Relations, *Intergroup Relations in Teaching Materials* (Washington, D.C., 1949).

3. Cooper, "Blacks in American History Textbooks," 11.

the continued destruction of reason and the misrepresentation of blacks in the American experience.[4]

It has been claimed that the shoddy treatment of minorities in history textbooks prior to the 1970s was due in significant part to the heavy emphasis on political and military history. As one writer put it, "It was not until social and cultural history appeared in the textbooks that any significant attention was given to the black experience." While there may be some truth in this assertion, we should not overlook the long-standing efforts to provide a balanced and integrated presentation of blacks in American military history. W. E. B. Du Bois' unpublished manuscript "The Black Man and the Wounded World," a history of Afro-Americans in World War I, represents an early effort to demonstrate blacks' rightful place in American military history. Emmett J. Scott's *The American Negro in the World War* was also a part of that effort.[5]

In 1942, for instance, the Army Institute at the University of Wisconsin initiated plans to offer American soldiers a correspondence course entitled "The Negro in Africa and America." Horace Mann Bond, a member of the subcommittee on education of the Joint Army and Navy Committee on Welfare and Recreation, was chosen to write the textbook for the proposed correspondence course. In 1943, Bond completed a manuscript which included such chapters as "The Recent Military History of Africa," "The French New World—Haiti and the Great Black Soldier, Toussaint L'Ouverture," and "The Negro in the United States—Military History: The War of the Revolution and the War of 1812." The manuscript also contained chapters on Afro-Americans in the first and second world wars. By the time Bond completed a draft of his textbook, the Army Institute rescinded its decision to offer a correspondence course on Afro-American military history and decided instead to merely adopt for use in camp libraries some books about black Americans. Today Du Bois' and Bond's unpublished manuscripts are deposited in the Fisk University Archives.[6]

4. John Hope Franklin, "The New Negro History," *Journal of Negro History*, XLII (April, 1957), 89–97.

5. W. E. B. Du Bois, "The Black Man and the Wounded World" (MS in Special Collections, Boxes 54, 55, 56, and 57, Fisk University Archives, Nashville, Tennessee).

6. Horace Mann Bond's unpublished manuscript is in Special Collections, Box 327, Fisk University Archives; see also Bond to F. G. Wale, June 3, 1942, and Bond to Edwin R. Embree, January 7, 1943, Box 327, folder 4, Fisk University Archives.

But the efforts to include Afro-Americans in American military history continued as evidenced by Benjamin Quarles's *The Negro in the Civil War* (1953) and *The Negro in the American Revolution* (1961). Thus, the claim that insignificant attention was given to the black experience in history textbooks written prior to the 1970s because political and military history dominated the pages is at best a half-truth. Indeed, it seems that earlier attempts to integrate the black presence in American military history fared no better than the attempts to include blacks in American social and cultural history. The essential and persistent theme is one of omission and distortion irrespective of whether textbook writers have focused on social and cultural or political and military history.

It is clear that the pre-1960s studies of textbook racism, although scholarly and instructive, had little or no impact on actual textbook compositions. This fact is well demonstrated in doctoral dissertations written by Zachary Cooper and Mark Hilgendorf. In 1961, the Brooklyn branch of the Association for the Study of Negro Life and History and the Emma Lazarus Federation held a joint conference to determine how the textbooks used in Brooklyn dealt with Afro-American and Jewish people. The results of a study authorized by the joint conference found the textbooks "woefully bad in both instances and atrociously so with Negroes." Also, in 1961, Lloyd Marcus conducted the Anti-Defamation League's study to assess the progress in the treatment of minorities in American history textbooks. The study found that of forty-eight leading secondary school history and social studies textbooks a majority presented a largely white, Protestant, Anglo-Saxon view of history and the then current social scene. The complex nature and problems of American minority groups were largely neglected or, in a number of cases, distorted. Marcus' study, *The Treatment of Minorities in Secondary School Textbooks*, echoed the findings of earlier studies.[7]

During the decade of the 1960s the question of adequate representation of minorities in history textbooks received a wider range of attention. The decade saw the beginning of institutional attention by state departments of education. In 1962, the New York City Board of Education issued a state-

7. Cooper, "Blacks in American History Textbooks," 11–12; Lloyd Marcus, *The Treatment of Minorities in Secondary School Textbooks* (New York, 1961); Mark Steven Hilgendorf, "Revisionist Interpretations of Slavery in Senior High School American History Textbooks" (Ph.D. dissertation, Duke University, 1982), 8.

ment entitled "Policy Statement of the Treatment of Minorities in the Public School Textbooks." This statement informed publishers that the city board of education would not recommend "any social studies textbooks or other instructional materials which do not adequately treat the roles of various minority groups in American culture." Two years later, 1964, the California State Department of Education reported the findings of six American historians from the University of California who reviewed seven history textbooks widely used in the state. The six historians, Kenneth Stampp, Winthrop D. Jordan, Lawrence Levine, Robert Middlekauff, George G. Sellers, and George W. Stockings, Jr., surveyed (1) *Trail Blazers of American History*, (2) *The Story of American Freedom*, (3) *America Is My Country: The Heritage of a Free People*, (4) *The Growth of America*, and (5) *The Story of America*. The report of the panel found very little variation in the textbooks' treatment of the Afro-American past. The historians found that generally the texts reflected views rejected or drastically modified by good current historical scholarship and that many of the views reinforced ideas of white superiority and black inferiority. The greatest failing of these books was their virtual omission of the Afro-American experience.[8]

In 1965, the Michigan State Department of Education, as part of its responsibilities under the social studies textbook act of 1965, created a committee that analyzed and evaluated six widely used junior and senior high school textbooks. The committee noted errors of both omission and commission—an avoidance of nearly everything controversial and a reliance on outdated historical research. As one committee member put it, the textbook treatment of blacks "exemplified everything that must infuriate the Negro." Like the New York and California studies, the Michigan study criticized textbooks for consistently ignoring or stereotyping the Afro-American's role in American history.[9]

Much of the criticisms of textbook racism before the 1960s came from minority organizations (*i.e.*, NAACP and the Association for the Study of Negro Life and History) and minority scholars such as Lawrence D. Reddick, W. E. B. Du Bois, Marie E. Carpenter, and Edna M. Colson. Minority scholars and organizations continued to lead the assault on text-

8. Hilgendorf, "Revisionist Interpretations of Slavery in Senior High School American History Textbooks," 9–12.
9. *Ibid.*, 11.

book racism during the sixties and seventies. However, during this era many nonminority scholars began criticizing the inadequate representation of minorities in history textbooks. Louis R. Harlan's *The Negro in American History* and Irving Sloan's *The Negro in Modern American History Textbooks* represent those efforts. Many others contributed to the attack on textbook deficiencies. Consequently, concrete measures were proposed to upgrade textbook content and to establish criteria for textbook choice that would encourage an integrated and balanced treatment of minority populations. State departments of education, and a few large city boards of education, were the instruments through which textbook change passed from a predominantly internal academic consideration to a legislative and policy priority. These events together with the Civil Rights Movement and the growing euphoria over black history promised significant changes in the textbook treatment of minorities.[10]

The decade of the 1970s, however, opened with the same observations of earlier decades. The practical impact of textbook criticism, advanced historical scholarship, and antiracist political movements upon the authors and publishers of history textbooks was decidedly limited. In 1970, Michael Kane published a study entitled *Minorities in Textbooks: A Study of Their Treatment in Social Studies Textbooks*. In the preface, referring to the earlier 1949 Anti-Defamation League study, Kane wrote: "It is not unreasonable to expect that, over twenty-one years, the readily admitted shortcomings of social studies textbooks in their treatment of racial, religious and ethnic groups would have been corrected. But they have not." After analyzing forty-five leading history textbooks, copyrighted from 1967 to 1970, Kane concluded that "a significant number of texts published today continue to present a principally white, Protestant, Anglo-Saxon view of America, with the nature and problems of minority groups largely neglected." Stereotyping statements persisted, although not to as great an extent as in the past. Toward the end of the decade, in 1977, the Council on Interracial Books for Children published a reference guide for detecting racism and sexism in various textbooks, *Stereotypes, Distortions, and Omissions in U.S. History Textbooks*. The study was an evaluation of thirteen of the most widely used textbooks in American history, all

---

10. Louis R. Harlan, *The Negro in American History* (Washington, D.C., 1965); Irving Sloan, *The Negro in Modern American History Textbooks* (Washington, D.C., 1967).

copyrighted between 1968 and 1975. The council stated that textbooks played a part in legitimizing theories of white superiority. "While it is true that newer texts do include more information about black people," the council reported, "this is usually from a white perspective, and barely touches upon black oppression."[11]

Two recent doctoral dissertations, Zachary L. Cooper's "Blacks in American History Textbooks: An Analysis of Two Middle School Textbooks" (1979) and Mark S. Hilgendorf's "Revisionist Interpretations of Slavery in Senior High School American History Textbooks" (1982), echo an enduring consensus among critical studies of the textbook treatment of minorities. American history textbooks lack balance, integration, judiciousness, and understanding in their treatment of the American black experience. Thus, as early as 1933 and as recently as 1982, evaluators of textbooks were in agreement that the accounts of Afro-American life and culture were superficial, misleading, and inadequate. Although some revisions and innovations have been made by textbook authors and publishers, the basic historical problems in the treatment and interpretation of the black experience persist.[12]

Textbook Treatment, 1973–1983

To determine the extent to which the textbook treatment of Afro-American history has changed over the past decade, an examination was made of several secondary school history books. The following books were evaluated: *Rise of the American Nation* by Lewis Todd and Merle Curti (1977), *The American Pageant* by Thomas Bailey (1975), *An American History* by Rebecca Brooks Gruver (1981), *The American Dream* by Lew Smith (1978), *A People and a Nation* by Richard Hofstadter and Clarence Ver Steeg (1979), and *History of a Free People* by Henry Bragdon and Samuel McCutchen (1981). In his examination of recent textbook accounts of

11. Kane quoted in Hilgendorf, "Revisionist Interpretations of Slavery in Senior High School American History Textbooks," 20; Michael Kane, *Minorities in Textbooks: A Study of Their Treatment in Social Studies Textbooks* (Chicago, 1970); Council on Interracial Books for Children, *Stereotypes, Distortions, and Omissions in U.S. History Textbooks* (New York, 1977).

12. Cooper, "Blacks in American History Textbooks"; Hilgendorf, "Revisionist Interpretations of Slavery in Senior High School American History Textbooks."

slavery in light of revisionist interpretations, Mark Hilgendorf learned from eight leading publishers that these textbooks were among the nine most widely purchased history books for use in public secondary schools. Further, there was complete agreement among the publishers that Todd and Curti's *Rise of the American Nation* is the most popular secondary school history textbook in the United States, controlling at least 15 percent of market sales.[13]

The textbooks are all equally evasive in their treatment of Africans' presence in the New World prior to their arrival as slaves. In February, 1975, a Smithsonian Institution team reported finding two "Negro male skeletons" in a grave in the United States Virgin Islands. This grave had been used and abandoned by native Indians long before the coming of Columbus. Soil from the earth layers in which the skeletons were found was dated to A.D. 1250. A study of the teeth showed a type of "dental mutilation characteristic of early African cultures," and clamped around the wrist of one of the skeletons was a clay vessel of pre-Columbian Indian design.[14]

Ivan Van Sertima's *They Came Before Columbus* argues that this was no isolated find. Skulls that, according to the physical anthropologist Ernest Hooton, "closely resemble crania of Negro groups coming from parts of Africa" have been found in pre-Columbian layers in the valley of the Pecos River, in northern Mexico and Texas. The historian Frederick Petersen in his study of ancient Mexico emphasized the strong Negroid substratum that intermingled with the Olmec magicians. In 1957, three professors released radio carbon datings for an Olmec ceremonial center at La Venta, Mexico. Within this center, near the Atlantic, stood four colossal stone heads, with military-type helmets, weighing thirty to forty tons each. They were described by their discoverer, the archaeologist Matthew Stirling, as "amazingly negroid." Eleven colossal Negroid stone heads have been uncovered in Mexico along the Gulf Coast. Students of pre-Columbian America are convinced that by design and by accident, in several historical periods long before the coming of Columbus, Africans traveled to America.[15]

The authors of history textbooks, in such beginning chapters as "New

13. Hilgendorf, "Revisionist Interpretations of Slavery in Senior High School American History Textbooks," 55–56.
14. Ivan Van Sertima, *They Came Before Columbus* (New York, 1976).
15. *Ibid.*

World Beginnings," "The First New World Settlers," or "The New World," write at length about the European discovery and exploration of the New World with no mention of the probable pre-Columbian links between Africans and Americans. The best textbooks tend to introduce the black presence in the New World with the introduction of slavery in 1619. Not even Estevanico, the sixteenth-century conquistador believed to be the first black person to have lived and flourished on this country's soil, is discussed even in passing. After noting the first cargo of Africans brought to Jamestown in 1619 by Dutch traders, the better textbooks then proceed to discuss the "African background," focusing always on the great kingdoms of Songhai, Ghana, Mali, and Ashanti from 700 to 1600. Here the obvious idea is to demonstrate the fact that highly developed civilizations flourished in Africa before the slave trade, and that black slaves did not descend from inferior cultures or civilizations. These sections are aimed more at combating earlier racist stereotypes than at accounting for the origin and development of the black presence in the Americas. Hence, the history of African culture and civilization terminate with discussion of African-Arabic and African-European relations. Omitted is the opportunity to record, as did Arab historian Ibn Fadi Allah al-Omari, the two Atlantic expeditions by Mali in the early fourteenth century, thereby properly linking Africans to the New World as free explorers and discoverers long before they came in chains.[16]

Even after history textbooks introduce the black presence at Jamestown in 1619, there is almost unanimous failure to develop the scope and nature of black life and culture in the New World during the seventeenth and eighteenth centuries. New World slavery is not treated in any kind of hemispheric perspective. Students will not grasp the reality of the African and Afro-American presence in the American colonies, the Caribbean, and Central and South America. Moreover, most secondary school history textbooks do not provide a basic picture of the scope and extent of the black presence in the United States from 1619 to 1776. A People and a Nation by Ver Steeg and Hofstadter is one of the few textbooks to give even an abbreviated account of black free persons and slaves during this period. This book documents the black percentage of the total colonial population

16. Ibid.; Roland Sanders, Lost Tribes and Promised Lands: The Origins of American Racism (Boston, 1978), 166, 169, 170–77, 246, 313.

(about 4 percent) in 1680 and points out that by the beginning of the Revolution, blacks made up one-fifth of the total population, more than 400,000 blacks out of a population of 2,000,000, with the greatest concentration in the southern colonies. This gives the teacher and students at least some notion of the vast increase in the black population from 1619 to 1776. It also informs them that by the beginning of the Revolution slaves constituted more than 43 percent of Virginia's total population and over 60 percent of the population of South Carolina. This treatment may not appear much to be grateful for, but relative to the typical textbook treatment of Afro-Americans during the seventeenth and eighteenth centuries this has to be rated as a superior performance. *The American Pageant* by Bailey and Kennedy does not even document the vast increase in Africans and Afro-Americans from 1619 to 1776 and, of course, makes no attempt to explain this development or its impact on American life and culture. Todd and Curti's *Rise of the American Nation* is only slightly better. Bragdon and McCutchen's *History of a Free People* also treats the enslaved people as virtually invisible during the 1619 to 1776 period. The history textbooks, after introducing slavery in the early seventeenth century, usually provide the next major discussion of the black presence during discussions of the Missouri Compromise (1820) and related forces of union and disunion. The few facts about blacks from 1619 to 1776 that we usually encounter are not only misleading but abstract, confusing, and, above all, lifeless. Secondary school history textbooks hardly discuss blacks during this period. When they do discuss them it is seldom as human beings trying to develop in families and communities while dealing with the tremendous oppression of slave society. Hence, high school students read that between 1619 and 1776 America contained a few enslaved Africans scattered along the eastern seaboard. This is most unfortunate because students read virtually nothing about the black experience during that moment in history when Africans were transformed into Afro-Americans.

A major problem with most textbook analyses of early American history is the failure to document and explain the institutionalization of bondage in America and the increasing importance of black human beings to the economic and political power and overall way of life of about half the colonies and states in the Union. The textbooks should document the institutionalization of slavery in a form similar to Edmund Morgan's *American Slavery/American Freedom: The Ordeal of Colonial Virginia.*

Instead of treating slavery and the black presence as fundamental dimensions of the growth of the American republic, authors of textbooks treat
them as adjuncts to the American experience, aberrations of Jeffersonian
democracy, and thus not a central part of the real American pageant.
Gruver's *An American History*, for instance, discusses the introduction of
slavery in the colonies in chapter 3 under the section on "The Southern
Colonies." This is interesting in its own right, since slavery was not confined to the southern colonies. Gruver, like other authors, seems to cate-
gorize slavery as merely a peculiar way of life in the South. The fact that
the institutionalization of slavery required and received the legal and political support of the whole nation is not made evident. Hence, the reader
comes away without an understanding of the nature and extent to which
slavery was interwoven into the very fabric of American law, politics, and
economic system.

Thus, when Gruver tells us that "it was relatively easy for the colonists
to make slaves of the Africans, since by the sixteenth century the English
had come to believe that black people were inferior," we are led to believe
that the institutionalization of bondage was a relatively easy and even
quiet process (p. 59). The next mention of the black presence in America
comes in chapter 5. "Eventually some five thousand blacks served in the
Continental army in both integrated and all-black units" (p. 121). Then
there is a very short discussion of free blacks in the early nineteenth century. The next real discussion of the black presence in America comes in a
feature essay on Harriet Tubman at the close of chapter 15, following a
discussion of the beginning of the Civil War. This is typical of the frag-
mented manner in which secondary school history textbooks treat the
evolution of blacks in America from 1619 to 1860. By 1776 one in every
five Americans was black and enslaved. The textbooks give us virtually no
understanding of what life was like for this one-fifth of the American population between 1776 and 1860, and virtually no understanding of its role
in the rise of the American nation.

The failure to present and integrate Africans and Afro-Americans into
American history during the seventeenth and eighteenth centuries is accompanied by the related failure to discuss or explain the formation and
development of racism in America during the colonial and revolutionary
periods. This is very unfortunate, since the racism of the present seems
depressingly continuous with the past. One cannot help being struck by

the fact that such textbooks as *The Rise of the American Nation, History of a Free People, A People and a Nation,* and *The American Pageant* do not include the word *racism* in their indexes. The absence of *racism* in the index is more than symbolic. The textbooks generally obscure the fundamental realities of racial thought, racial oppression, and race relations in American history. Nor do we receive any notion that racism was an important component of America's domestic and foreign policy, as demonstrated in works by Reginald Horsman (*Race and Manifest Destiny*), George Fredrickson (*Black Image in the White Mind*), Winthrop Jordan (*White over Black*), Leon Litwack (*North of Slavery*), Eugene Berwanger (*The Frontier Against Slavery*), and V. Jacque Voegeli (*Free But Not Equal*). These and many other works demonstrate the antiquity, persistence, and intensity of white racism in American institutional and intellectual life. Moreover, slavery was destroyed, yet racism persisted in intense and militant forms. How this was achieved, not to mention its impact on nonwhite minorities, is not addressed by history textbooks. Apparently, the authors and publishers of secondary school history textbooks believe that students do not need to understand how racism has permeated the whole country since colonial times, or they believe that high school students are not able to digest the nation's racist history. Even more distressing is the textbooks' denial of American racism. Bailey and Kennedy in *The American Pageant* inform us that "Colonial America was a melting pot and had been from the outset" (p. 62).

Frequently, interpretations that might be and ought to be critical are stated with a mellowness that make past realities seem far less drastic than they really were. Bailey and Kennedy tell us that free blacks were "unpopular" in the North (p. 332). Todd and Curti (*Rise of the American Nation*) record that twenty Africans "arrived" in the Virginia colony. These "newcomers" were the first of countless thousands of Africans "brought" to the New World. "In the years that followed, Africans worked with people from many other lands in building the English colonies." True, but the whole tone of this passage transforms the Middle Passage and slavery into a kind of group-participation project for the building of America. Similarly, *The American Pageant* informs its readers that "the Africans made a significant contribution to America's early development through their labor, chiefly the sweaty toil of clearing swamps, grubbing out trees, and other menial tasks." The exploitation of slave labor should not be framed in the context of "contributors" since this approach treats slavery as though it were typical of the many contributions made by diverse ethnic groups to America's early development. More importantly, such passages tend to serve in lieu of any real understanding of the black experience in the United States. The history textbooks (or rather their authors) are already guilty of giving only the obligatory page or two to particular periods of the black presence in American history. Hence, it is criminal to waste valuable space with such indirect and misleading passages.

Secondary school history textbooks put great emphasis on consensus in American history, and this approach often precludes any meaningful treatment of the black experience. The textbook view, that American history records a continuous unfolding of the democratic ideal, sacrifices slavery to the "dawning democratic age." In their discussion of the triumph of Jeffersonian democracy, Bailey and Kennedy (*The American Pageant*) inform their readers that Jefferson "cherished uncommon sympathy for the common man, especially the downtrodden, the oppressed, and the persecuted" (p. 148). But what of his slaves? Were they not common men, downtrodden, and oppressed? Clearly, such passages afford appropriate opportunities to examine Jefferson's relationship to slavery (including his own slaves) and to consider his understanding of the Declaration's concept "all men are created equal." Moreover, a discussion of the ideology of racism and its contradiction of democratic idealism would expand the student's understanding of Jeffersonian and Jacksonian democracy. The authors, however, avoid any discussion of racism and treat slavery as though it is merely an aberration of Jeffersonian democracy. We are told that Jefferson was "consistently inconsistent," and that he did not free his slaves because "he had fallen upon distressful times" (p. 328). Hence, it is not surprising that *The American Pageant* discusses "Jeffersonian Idealism and Idealists" in chapter 8 (p. 147) and the "Black Bondsmen" in chapter 19 (p. 332). The authors seem to imply that slavery and racism were not important components of Jeffersonian democracy.

Similarly, Gruver's *An American History* deals with the contradiction between Jefferson the slaveholder and Jefferson the democratic statesman by telling us that Jefferson "reflected the contradictions of his time" (p. 182). This approach is analogous to an analysis of the English king's repression of the colonists that would seek to explain the whole conflict by asserting that the king simply reflected the contradiction of his times. In the beginning of *An American History* Gruver instructs her readers that they should study history to discover something useful about human experience. "We want to know why people did certain things and what the results of their actions were. We want to probe the motives of individuals and groups in earlier times in an effort to comprehend their connection with subsequent history" (p. vii). Yet, there is no attempt to explain why the Founding Fathers, who allegedly demonstrated their commitment to freedom and democracy by overthrowing corrupt British rulers, were themselves slaveholders and thereby reigned over one of the most oppressive and antidemocratic societies of their times. Consequently, readers may conclude that, unlike the tyranny of the king against the colonies, there was something more legitimate, more compassionate, and therefore more justifiable about the tyranny of Washington and Jefferson over their subjects. Indeed, Todd and Curti, in *Rise of the American Nation*, tell us that some southern slaveholders, "even though they believed that slavery was wrong or unprofitable," hesitated to free their slaves because they "worried that their slaves would be unable to take care of themselves in a different and even hostile society" (p. 301). Clearly, these are double standards. England's rulers are portrayed as repressive and corrupt rulers who sought to establish an intolerable tyranny over the colonies. Washington and Jefferson are portrayed as compassionate slaveholders who sought to protect their subjects from a hostile environment. In the end the textbooks seem to conclude that black slavery was a very small price to pay for the building of the American nation.

Without question, the textbook treatment of black slavery has advanced somewhat during the past decade. But the inclusion of slaves and their culture into American history textbooks has been piecemeal and exceedingly slow. Two fundamental changes have taken place since the mid-1960s: (1) slavery has been universally condemned by most textbook authors, and (2) textbooks generally describe some features of the brutality of the slave system. However, there are virtually no attempts (except Litwack and Jordan's *The United States*) to develop an understanding of the formation and development of Afro-American life and culture. Students, having learned everything offered in secondary history textbooks, will not be able to speak intelligently about any aspect of Afro-American life and culture during slavery. The textbooks do not give an account of slavery and the black experience that is coherent, balanced, and integrated. Any hopes that (through history textbooks) high school students might learn something of the historical development of black language, family, religion, folklore, music, and political thought are without foundation. Students are much more likely to be confused than enlightened.[17]

Secondary school history textbooks provide the most extensive coverage of the black presence in United States history during the Civil War and Reconstruction eras. Yet, the treatment of the black experience during the Reconstruction era continues to lag behind W. E. B. Du Bois' *Black Reconstruction*, which was published in 1935. Usually the textbooks provide brief information about "Negro contributions to the war effort," postwar racial discrimination, and black elected officials in southern governments. The textbooks present Afro-Americans as more abstract, passive, and lifeless during this period than during the era of American slavery.

The Dunning school's version of Reconstruction has all but disappeared. However, some textbooks remind us of Dunning's crushing indictment of the Republican reconstruction program. For instance, *The American Pageant*'s presentation of the "Unfettered Freedmen" proclaims that "Blacks had suffered many cruelties during slavery, but one of the cruelest strokes of all was to jerk them overnight from chains to freedom without any preparation or safeguards" (p. 430). This statement implies that some means of gradual emancipation would have been more appropriate. The book also gives us the Dunning version of white carpetbaggers and freedmen attempting to make the process of reconstruction as humiliating, as difficult, and as prolonged as possible for southern whites. Some slaves tested their freedom by "'sassing' former masters, refusing to work, and jostling whites from sidewalks into gutters" (p. 431). Beginning in 1867, according to *The American Pageant*, southern state governments "promptly fell under the control of the much-maligned 'scalawags' and 'carpetbaggers' who in turn used the blacks as political henchmen." This interpretation is quite representative of the Dunning version of Reconstruction.

The former slaves were now free persons, but the authors of *The American Pageant* are clearly doubtful that they should have been granted the full rights of citizenship, including the right to vote: "The ex-slaves themselves were often bewildered by such unaccustomed responsibilities. When

17. Hilgendorf, "Revisionist Interpretations of Slavery in Senior High School American Textbooks," 8–20.

they registered to vote many of them did not know their ages; even boys of sixteen signed the rolls. Some of these future voters could not even give their last names, if indeed they had any, and many took any surname that popped into their heads, often that of old 'Massa'" (p. 442). The masses of former slaves, the story continues, were "without even the knowledge of how to survive in free society." To cope with this problem, Congress created in 1865 the Freedmen's Bureau, "a kind of primitive welfare agency." Hence, the masses of blacks came out of slavery and onto "primitive welfare" (p. 432). At least, that is the impression that students are most likely to receive.

Fortunately, some textbooks give a more balanced account of the Republican reconstruction program. In *An American History*, for example, Gruver includes a feature essay on "Reconstruction and Education." She points to the fact that "it was Southern blacks who took the lead in creating pressure for a new approach to education in the South, leaving most whites to oppose or ignore their efforts" (p. 437). Thus there is some evidence that Du Bois' historical scholarship is finally winding its way into the textbook treatment of blacks during the Reconstruction era. Still, most textbooks say very little, if anything at all, about the inner life and culture of the millions of black people who formed one-fifth of the American population and more than two-fifths of the American South in 1860. The attention given black history during the Civil War and Reconstruction period is focused almost completely on white American treatment of the former slaves.

Except for a paragraph or two on Booker T. Washington and W. E. B. Du Bois, the textbook treatment of the black experience during the nineteenth century generally ends with the Reconstruction period. The reader then realizes that he has passed through 280 years of the black experience in America. What did it mean for blacks to endure 250 years of slavery and racial oppression? The question is not even raised by textbook writers, and students could not begin to address this question based on what the typical history textbook tells them about black America. What were the languages, religion, music, dance, food, family structure, and general culture of the imported slaves? How did their cultural forms and values change during the seventeenth and eighteenth centuries? In what ways did the Africans of 1676 differ from the Afro-Americans of 1776? What were the hopes, aspirations, burdens, and common experiences of black Americans on the eve of the Civil War? Clearly, students cannot answer these questions from the current textbook treatment of the black experience in America.

The problems are even more critical with respect to postslavery developments. Why did black Americans not develop in much the same way as Irish, Polish, Italians, Germans, and other late-nineteenth-century immigrant groups? Why did a group that was 20 percent of the national population at the time of the American Revolution need special congressional legislation in the 1960s for equal protection under the law, due process, and above all else, the right to vote? These are all natural questions, especially regarding the development of northern urban blacks who were not living and working under the Jim Crow laws of the South. Elizabeth H. Pleck in *Black Migration and Poverty: Boston, 1865 to 1900*, Vincent P. Franklin in *The Education of Black Philadelphia: A Social and Educational History of a Minority Community, 1900–1950*, Kenneth Kusmer in *A Ghetto Takes Shape: Black Cleveland from 1870 to 1930*, and David M. Katzman in *Before the Ghetto: Black Detroit in the Nineteenth Century* provide some answers to these questions. However, the development of northern urban blacks has not become a significant component of secondary school history books.

In fact, it is difficult to see how high school students could gain from their history textbooks any coherent perspective on the social, economic, and political evolution of blacks in northern urban society. Consequently, they do not understand the historical development of institutional racism and its severe impact on the development of northern black communities. In considering the period from 1863 to 1965, for instance, one does not have to look very far to find a convincing explanation as to why there were no black students in southern white universities, no black workers in southern police and fire departments, or no racially integrated public schools in the South. Racial discrimination in the South was overt, manifest in the frequent hostile interactions between the races, and generally prescribed by law. This was not so in the North. Hence, in the absence of historical explanations such as those provided by Pleck, Franklin, Kusmer, and Katzman, students have no way of understanding why "deserving" blacks in the early-twentieth-century North could not attain the same jobs, education, and housing as the immigrants from Poland, Ireland, Italy, and Germany. This is especially critical in today's environment where about 40 percent of Americans are descendants of Ellis Island immigrants. When those students ask the question "We made it, why didn't the blacks?" the textbooks provide no clues to the answer. Therefore, it is easy for such students to embrace conventional theories of social pathology or "blaming the victim" as the most rational way to account for differences between the development of blacks and white immigrants in northern urban America.

High school history textbooks generally offer a condensed version of American history in the twentieth century, and the black experience is disproportionately abbreviated. Black Americans are usually packaged with words and pictures about the two world wars. The treatment of the Civil Rights Movement highlights the textbook treatment of the black experience in the twentieth century. Some textbooks such as Bailey and Kennedy's *The American Pageant* and Ver Steeg and Hofstadter's *A People and a Nation* provide more information and a more balanced and comprehensive treatment of the recent civil rights movements than others. However, they do not come to grips conceptually, factually, and realistically with blacks' on-going struggle for equal rights since the post–Civil War era. Hence, the recent Civil Rights Movement is disconnected from the past and its causes are unduly located in the 1950s. Ver Steeg and Hofstadter, for example, argue in *A People and a Nation* that the black protest of the 1950s and 1960s "was a response to improving conditions and a greater aggressiveness and self-confidence among black people" (p. 773). This may be true in part, but Aldon Morris' *The Origins of the Civil Rights Movement* is a large-scale version of what is needed to make the fundamental point that the black rebellion of the 1950s and 1960s stemmed from a continuous struggle and long-standing awareness that Jim Crow society by its very nature was an oppressive and inhumane system. Whether material conditions worsened or improved during the 1950s within the context of Jim Crow society was not as important as blacks' realization and resentment of the very nature of that society and their long-standing efforts to topple one of the most racist and oppressive social systems in the Western world. Secondary school history textbooks should document the beginning struggle for equal civil rights during the Reconstruction era and trace its ebb and flow to the recent Civil Rights Movement. The Civil Rights Movement has been under way since blacks were disfranchised during the post-Reconstruction period and continues into our own present as manifested in the struggle of the 98th Congress to pass major civil rights legislation.

Another major problem with textbook treatment of the Civil Rights Movement is the tendency to focus excessively on prominent personalities and sensational events rather than the beliefs and behavior of the masses who made and sustained the movement. In order to understand the Civil Rights Movement one needs to understand the culture and consciousness of the black masses. They were the essence of the movement. They made it with their discipline, their spirit, their songs and church rallies, as well as with their bus boycotts, sit-ins, economic boycotts, peaceful mass demonstrations, and voter registration drives. More importantly, they made the Civil Rights Movement with their courage. A focus on the activities of the masses, and on their beliefs and aspirations would yield a more concrete and realistic understanding of this historic movement and a better understanding of the consciousness and culture of contemporary black America.

Until the 1960s blacks hardly entered the pages of high school history textbooks. There has been some progress over the past two decades. However, it is still the case that high school students cannot learn much about the historical development of black Americans from what they read in their leading textbooks. The overall portrayal of the black experience is misleading, superficial, and even racist, not so much in an overt manner as during the pre-1960s, but certainly in an institutionalized sense. To unfairly and disproportionately screen the black experience out of the nation's historical record is a form of institutional racism. It covertly reinforces notions among all students that blacks were not a significant part of the American past. This is racism not merely because such actions underscore the continuing effects of past discrimination, but because such actions misrepresent the Afro-American presence in American history and constitute in their own right a form of unfair discrimination against black people. To be sure, the historical analyses in high school history textbooks are generally poor and frequently reflect race, class, and sex biases. But the continuing discrimination against blacks and other minorities represents something much more problematic than the usual problems of omissions and distortions. The studies examined in the first part of this chapter reveal that the historical discrimination against blacks is a special problem of racism that needs to be addressed on its own terms. It seems doubtful that such problems can be corrected as part and parcel of larger reforms in the writing of history textbooks. Moreover, it appears that in the absence of concerted actions by concerned groups and individuals there is little chance for major changes in the immediate future.

XI   THE BLACK SCHOLAR

Responsibilities of the Black Scholar to the Community

VINCENT HARDING

There is a great tradition on the theme of the black scholar's responsibility, a tradition that I feel very much a part of. No one can think about, be concerned about, the role of the black scholar in the black community without realizing that black historians were led in this tradition by Carter G. Woodson in *The Mis-Education of the Negro* (1933). The issue is addressed also by W. E. B. Du Bois in his very powerful collection of essays called *The Education of Black People: Ten Critiques from 1906 to 1960* (1973). I recommend it very strongly for revisiting the power of Du Bois and the audacity of his spirit and his mind and his deep concern for the future of our people and our society. But then, too, there is a tradition that I was able to be a part of, and this is the study produced by the Institute of the Black World called *Education and Black Struggle: Notes from the Colonized World*, which was published back in 1974.

In that volume I tried to write about something that was called the vocation of the black scholar and the struggles of the black community. My theme took off from our Indianapolis friend Mari Evans and her great poem "Speak the Truth to the People," which seemed to me to be the primary responsibility of those who are called scholars in the black community: to speak the truth, to write the truth, and, most important of all, to seek to live one's understanding of the truth. I tried to offer four or five examples of persons who seemed to me to exemplify this living of the truth, and writing of the truth, and envisioning of the truth, among them

Du Bois, C. L. R. James, Walter Rodney, and Franz Fanon. In the work I quoted extensively from Fanon, including a statement that I would like to call upon now. In *The Wretched of the Earth* (1963), his last work, written while he was dying, Fanon said this (I paraphrase for a nonsexist time): The colonized persons who write for their people ought to use the past with the intention of opening the future, as an invitation to action and a basis for hope.

On a certain level it was this concern that took me and my family to Denver more than two years ago. We moved there in part because of the conviction that black people must assume major responsibility for the re-visioning and reshaping of this society. I felt intuitively that there were certain powers extant in the Southwest that I needed to be in touch with, among them the power of the natives of this land and the power of the Chicanos. And so part of my reason for going was to find a way to understand more fully and to participate more deeply in the life of native American and Chicago communities, and to see the ways in which children of Africa could come into a deeper relationship with children of Mexico and children of the earth. My deep conviction is that there will be no future for American society if it does not take to heart the wisdom, the insight, the history, and the vision of these peoples among others. It was because I am convinced that the historian has a responsibility for the opening toward the future that I went to try to understand more fully these people, who I believe are not only openings to the past but also openings to the future and who can join in a conversation with the children of Africa and all other children of God who seek a new beginning for a society that badly needs one.

In that setting I came again upon the magnificent poetry of Pablo Neruda, and one of his poems, called "So Is My Life," I want to offer here.

> My duty moves along with my song:
> I am I am not: that is my destiny.
> I exist not if I do not attend to the pain
> of those who suffer: they are my pains.
> For I cannot be without existing for all,
> for all who are silent and oppressed,
> I come from the people and I sing for them:
> my poetry is song and punishment.

> I am told: you belong to darkness.
> Perhaps, perhaps, but I walk toward the light.
> I am the man of bread and fish
> and you will not find me among books,
> but with women and men:
> they have taught me the infinite.

I hope that, with the help of Neruda's words, it is understood what I mean by responsibility. What are the responsibilities of the black scholar to the community? Perhaps the first responsibility is to recognize that there is a responsibility. Indeed, debt may be a better word; scholars have a debt to that community, and they must always be thinking about how it will be repaid. It can never be repaid sufficiently, for individuals are never complete in themselves, and the community, when it is allowed to, is constantly making its members and remaking them as they enter the dance with it, as they seek to make and remake it. Black scholars must remember their sources, and by this I mean no technically historical sources. I mean human sources. I mean that they were not created as persons, as historians, as teachers, by Purdue University or by UCLA or by the AHA or the OAH or any other set of letters. They are the products of their source—the great pained community of the Afro-Americans of this land. And they can forget the source only at great peril to their spirit, their work, and their souls.

Second, I think that it is terribly important to remember that this community is one with all of the rich variety that Carole Merritt has revealed in discussing material culture. For those trained in a certain way of being and acting and thinking and writing, it is good to remember that the community is a source of passion as well as properness, a source that includes the warmness of human life as well as the coolness of scholarly objectivity. It is a source whose people can speak in measured terms but are not ashamed to shout and cry when they need to. It is a source of stick dolls and Atlanta mansions.

As creative people black scholars must recognize that this source is not a block of wood simply laid out for examination. One of their major responsibilities is to revision this community as fully and as continuously as possible, to keep seeing it again and again from a variety of perspectives and understandings, and most importantly to join with it in a constant revisioning of itself so that no name it has is ever satisfactory because such a name may not be adequate for the next moment. The responsibility of the black scholar is constantly to be alive to the movement of history and to recognize that we ourselves are constantly being remade and revisioned.

I think that the black scholar's responsibility to the community is to see it in the way Lerone Bennett does. I know how much I learned from Lerone Bennett, outside of the academy, in *Ebony Magazine*. Whoever heard of scholarship coming from *Ebony Magazine*? Thank God for Lerone Bennett, and even sometimes for John Johnson. As Bennett constantly reminds us, the community is not static but is constantly dancing between the past, the present, and the future. It is those who have died, those who are living, and those who have yet to be born. This is the community, the total community to which the scholars are responsible.

I think, too, that part of their responsibility is to learn from it and teach it that it is part of a larger community, that it must never be parochial in its understanding of itself, and that it is especially a part of the larger community of those who have experienced the pain of oppression, of those who have known the driving force of domination, of those who have known the rape of exploitation. Wherever these are found, they are a part of the Afro-American community, and black scholars ought never to let their community fall into a parochialism of any kind, whether it be the parochialism of a narrow black nationalism or the parochialism of a narrow Euro-American nationalism. So they must help their community to see that the Vietnamese are part of their community; to see that the Central Americans and all of their suffering now at the hands of our government are a part of it; to see that the native Americans in their long oppression are a part of it; to see indeed that deluded poor whites, who do not know that they are deluded, are a part of it; to see Africans, yes, and to know with all these peoples that those who are black in America are uniquely a part of the larger community of the pained humanity.

I think that the black scholar's responsibility, as Neruda put it, is to remember, "I exist not if I do not attend to the pain / of those who suffer: they are my pains." Black scholars should attend to the pain, meaning pay attention to, not to avoid, the pain or to live lives complaining about it. Their calling is always to seek for the meaning of the pain, to minister to the pain by pointing to its possible significance.

I think that part of the responsibility of black scholars is to help remind themselves and the community that they have constantly moved through darkness to light, constantly moved through pain to healing. Scholars have the responsibility to speak to the community and to live in the community in such a way that their lives bespeak the truth that a people cannot exist if it does not attend to the pain. In this age of the fourth, fifth, or sixth generation of historians, scholars must certainly say as loudly and clearly through their work and their lives that this people has not come through this pain in order to attain equal opportunity with the pain inflictors of this nation and this world. It has not been healed in order to join the inflictors of wounds. There must be some other reason for pain than equal opportunity employment with the pain deliverers. No, I think that our community's pain is meant to open it toward the light. "I am told: you belong to the darkness. Perhaps, perhaps, but I walk toward the light," Neruda said; toward action based on hope, Fanon said. This is the responsibility: to keep remembering that to be human, to say nothing of being scholarly, is to be constantly moving toward the light.

I think that a part of this responsibility is to sing, constantly to sing, to and with the people; in other words, to affirm the people, to celebrate the people, to clarify all those elements of their life that have been built through the pain of the land, all those elements of their life that have been built on the way to a new life. I think that part of the responsibility is to help the people to see themselves in a new light, to see themselves not primarily as victims of America but as cocreators of the past, as cocreators of the present, and as cocreators of a new vision for creating the American future. Historians must sing to them of their humanity and their hope based on the singing of the ninety-year-old woman, based on the singing of the families lined up for pictures, based on the singing of those who somehow endured slavery and prevailed.

And of course to sing to them, scholars must sing to themselves. Wherever and however possible, they must direct as much of their writing, their speaking, their teaching, and their singing to—directly to—the life and heart and growth of the community of pain and hope. I know what people have to do to get promoted. I know what people have to do in order to get spoken well of in academic circles. But I also know that these are not the sources that created the people who are these scholars. In the midst of all of the seeking and gaining of the traditional professional credentials, the scholar's responsibility is not to forget his sources, not to get so enmeshed in something called professionalism that he forgets his sources. The responsibility of black scholars is to return to the people a higher, deeper, cleaner version of the light that the people have given them, for they would have nothing to write their thousand monographs about were it not for the people. And the question is, What can the scholar return to them other than gold-bordered certificates of their Ph.D.'s? What can they return to the community that has given them so much at such great cost? There is a responsibility never to let ourselves veer from the answering of that question, which may be answered in different ways at different moments but must always be asked and must always be answered if one is to have any integrity and any humanity.

I think it is especially important at this point to remember that there are many people now in the world of academe and business and government who are creators of what I might call a new darkness, a darkness that used to call the African continent the dark continent. As late as 1963 H. Trevor Roper said that of course African Americans had no history. But I think now that there are creators of a new darkness in our own bright and shining country, people who are creating the darkness of cynicism, people who are creating the darkness of militarism, people who are creating the darkness of imperialism, people who are creating the darkness of personal opportunism and careerism and what they call realism. And all of these people are now very happy to call others away from any attention they might want to give to their sources, to call them and say, "Oh, we are now interested in you," to call them away from their hope and to offer them the appearance and even some of the substance of equality in darkness. They say, "Ah, you are well trained," "Ah, you are well published," "Ah, you are *really* approvable now; you belong to the darkness—with us."

Our great responsibility is to consider very seriously that the Hopi people of this land saw much further than we can see even now when they predicted long before slavery the coming of a people from the East, the coming to this land of a dark people from the land of the morning, as they called it. They call Africans "the people of the light." And they said that the land could not be healed without the coming of the people of the light. When black scholars hear the call to equal opportunity in darkness, they must remember that they do not belong in the darkness of an American culture that refuses to move toward the light. They are not meant to be pliant captives and agents of institutions that deny light all over the world. No, they must speak the truth to themselves and to the community and to all who invite them into the new darkness. They must affirm the light, the light movement of their past, the light movement of their people. They must affirm their capacities to move forward toward new alternatives for light in America.

I think that the black scholar's responsibility is to do whatever he has to do to catch a light-filled vision, to catch a new vision of an America where there is work for all people who need it, to catch a new vision of an America where there is housing for all of its people, to catch a new vision of an America where there are health facilities that help to create and maintain wellness without regard to ability to pay. I think that part of the responsibility to a life-affirming people is to try to catch a vision of an America where the old people no longer must live in anxiety about their future. Black scholars need to catch a vision of an America where we refuse anymore to poison the unborn children with all of our radioactive and chemical garbage. They need to envision an America where women no longer need to walk the streets in fear. They need to envision an America where there are no more missiles of world annihilation pointing anywhere.

If African Americans are remembered as a people, if they are concerned about getting into the history books, then what I ask is What shall they be there for? If they are to be remembered as a people, as a human people, by future generations or by future worlds, then let it be because they worked for such a new vision of community. Moving with Neruda and with their ancestors and with their children toward the light may mean moving toward a radical new vision of community. It may mean being called to a redefining of the community itself. For now this calling is based on the life and the history and the struggle of an ancestral community. But from this base black people may soon be called, audaciously called, to leap and to fly toward the creation of a new American community based no longer on ancestry or on color or on race but on vision and on commitment and on hope. Transformed black people must be at every level of the leadership in the struggle for this kind of a new America. In the new age yet to be envisioned, they must be part of the governing structures of this kind of a new society.

So it seems to me that the responsibility is to struggle for such a vision within oneself; to recognize how much darkness and cynicism and careerism and foolishness there is within ourselves; to recognize that one cannot carry out his responsibilities to the black community if he is not carrying out at the same time his responsibility to himself; to recognize, to see again, to reenvision those places where glimmerings of this light have shown among the black people and among all the people of pain; to recognize those visions of a new world that flashed for just such quick seconds in the 1960s, visions that then were put away because it would just take too much toil and trouble to bring them into being. Black scholars must return to some of those best visions and create new visions and then go on to share that insight, that vision, that conviction, as fully as they can in their writing, in their teaching, in their lives.

And I return to Fanon. I think that we are called upon to hear him when he says to us: Black scholars! Black, green, white, yellow human beings! Come then comrades! It would be well to decide at once to change our ways. We must shake off the heavy darkness in which we were plunged and leave it behind. The new day, the light day which is already at hand, must find us firm, prudent, and resolute. If we want humanity to advance a step further, if we want to bring it up to a different level from that which Europe or America has shown it, then we must invent, and we must make new discoveries. We must turn over a new page; we must work out new concepts and try to set afoot a new woman and a new man. In other words, I come from the people, and I sing for them.

NOTES ON CONTRIBUTORS

JAMES D. ANDERSON, Associate Professor of History of Education, Department of Educational Policy Studies, University of Illinois, Urbana, is the co-editor, with Vincent P. Franklin, of *New Perspectives in Black Educational History* (1978) and is the co-director of the Research Training Program on Institutional Racism funded by the National Institute of Mental Health. He is presently working on a book entitled "Northern Philanthropy and Black Education in the American South, 1870–1930."

JOHN E. FLEMING, Museum Director of the National Afro-American Museum in Wilberforce, Ohio, pioneered the development of the first national black museum in America. He is the author of *The Lengthening Shadow of Slavery* (1976) and, with Gerald Gill and David Swinton, of *The Case for Affirmative Action for Blacks in Higher Education* (1978). He has been a senior fellow at the Institute for the Study of Educational Policy at Howard University in Washington, D.C., and is currently at work on a major museum exhibit, "Black Life in America Since 1945."

ERIC FONER, Professor of History at Columbia University in New York City, is the author of *Nothing But Freedom: Emancipation and Its Legacy* (1983); *Tom Paine and Revolutionary America* (1976); *Free Soil, Free Labor, Free Men: The Ideology of the Republican Party Before the Civil War* (1970). He is editor of *Nat Turner* (1971) and *America's Black Past: A*

Reader in Afro-American History (1970). He has received a Guggenheim Fellowship and a National Endowment for the Humanities Fellowship. At present he is completing a history of the Reconstruction period, based on both the extensive literature that has appeared in the past ten years and new research of his own.

JOHN HOPE FRANKLIN, formerly the John M. Manly Distinguished Service Professor at the University of Chicago, is the James P. Duke Professor of History at Duke University. In 1980 he was appointed a Senior Mellon Fellow at the National Humanities Center in Research Triangle Park, North Carolina. A recipient of over seventy-five honorary degrees, he received in 1984 the Jefferson Medal Award of the Council for Advancement and Support of Education. He has been the president of the American Historical Association, the Organization of American Historians, and of the Southern Historical Association. He is the author of *From Slavery to Freedom: A History of Negro Americans* (first published in 1947, fifth edition, 1980); *The Free Negro in North Carolina, 1790–1860* (1943); *The Militant South* (1956); *Reconstruction After the Civil War* (1961); *The Emancipation Proclamation* (1963); *A Southern Odyssey: Travelers in the Antebellum North* (1976); *Racial Equality in America* (1976); and most recently, *George Washington Williams: A Biography* (1985). He co-edited, with August Meier, *Black Leaders of the Twentieth Century* (1982). He is currently researching a new study, "Plantation Dissidents: Runaway Slaves."

BETTYE J. GARDNER is Professor of History and Dean of the Division of Arts and Sciences at Coppin State College in Baltimore, Maryland. Under her leadership the Division of Arts and Sciences received support from the National Endowment for the Humanities to conduct a four-week seminar for high school juniors on the theme "The American Dream in the Twentieth Century: The Interrelationship of History and the Literature of the Black American." She is currently working on a study of black housing patterns in Baltimore, 1850–1890.

EUGENE D. GENOVESE is Distinguished Professor of Arts and Sciences, University of Rochester, New York. He is the author of *Roll, Jordan, Roll: The*

World the Slaves Made (1974); *From Rebellion to Revolution: Afro-American Slave Revolts in the Making of the Modern World* (1979); *The Political Economy of Slavery: Studies in the Economy and Society of the Slave South* (1965). He co-authored, with Elizabeth Fox-Genovese, *Fruits of Merchant Capital* (1983). Currently he is working with Fox-Genovese on a book entitled "The Mind of the Master Class: The Southern Slaveholders."

VINCENT HARDING, now a professor at the Iliff School of Theology, the University of Denver, was chairman of the Department of History and Sociology at Spelman College in Atlanta, Georgia, before becoming in 1968 the director of the Martin Luther King, Jr., Memorial Center and coordinator of the nationally televised CBS "Black Heritage" series. He was an organizer of the Institute of the Black World in Atlanta. Among his books are *Must Walls Divide?* and *The Other American Revolution.* He co-edited, with John Henrik Clarke, *Slave Trade and Slavery* (1970). His most recent book is *There Is a River: The Black Struggle for Freedom in America* (1981).

WILLIAM H. HARRIS is president of Paine College in Augusta, Georgia. He was formerly professor of history and associate dean of the graduate school at Indiana University, Bloomington, Indiana. He is the author of *The Harder We Run: Black Workers Since the Civil War* (1982) and *Keeping the Faith: A. Philip Randolph, Milton P. Webster, and the Brotherhood of Sleeping Car Porters, 1925–1937* (1977). He has been a United States Foreign Affairs Scholar, a Ford Foundation Fellow, a Fulbright Fellow at the University of Hamburg, and an American Council of Learned Societies Fellow.

ROBERT C. HAYDEN is the executive assistant to the superintendent of the Boston public schools. He is a lecturer in the Department of Afro-American Studies at Northeastern University in Boston and is the author of *Faith, Culture, and Leadership: A History of the Black Church in Boston* (1983); *Nine Black American Doctors* (1976); *Eight Black American Inventors* (1972); and *Seven Black American Scientists* (1970). He is a recipient of the Human Relations Award of the Massachusetts Teachers

Association, and the Educational Contributors Award of the Black Educators Alliance of Massachusetts. He is currently working on a history of the Metropolitan Council for Educational Opportunity in Boston.

DARLENE CLARK HINE is Professor of History and Vice-Provost of Purdue University. She is the author of *Black Victory: The Rise and Fall of the White Primary in Texas* (1979) and *When the Truth Is Told: A History of Black Women's Culture and Community in Indiana, 1875–1950* (1981). She was the director of the Black Women in the Middle West project, funded by the National Endowment for the Humanities (1982–1985). She has been the recipient of a Rockefeller Foundation Fellowship for Minority Group Scholars. She has recently completed a history of black women in the nursing profession and is currently working on a study of blacks in the medical profession.

THOMAS CLEVELAND HOLT is Professor of History and Director of Afroamerican and African Studies at the University of Michigan in Ann Arbor. He is the author of *Black Over White: Negro Political Leadership in South Carolina During Reconstruction* (1977), for which he received the Charles S. Sydnor Award of the Southern Historical Association in 1978. He has been a fellow at the Center for Advanced Study in the Behavioral Sciences and a recipient of fellowships and grants from the National Endowment for the Humanities and the Social Science Research Council. He is currently working on two books: "The Problem of Freedom: The Political Economy of Jamaica, 1832–1938"; and a biography of W. E. B. Du Bois.

JAMES O. HORTON is Associate Professor of History and American Civilization at George Washington University in Washington, D.C. He also serves as director of the Afro-American Communities Project, sponsored by the National Museum of American History, Smithsonian Institution. He has received research grants from the National Endowment for the Humanities, the D.C. Community Humanities Council, and the Smithsonian Institution. He is the author of *City of Magnificent Intentions: A History of the District of Columbia* (1983) and, with Lois E. Horton, *Black Bostonians: Family Life and Community Struggle in the Antebellum North* (1979).

NATHAN IRVIN HUGGINS is director of the W. E. B. Du Bois Institute for Afro-American Research and W. E. B. Du Bois Professor of History and Afro-American Studies at Harvard University. He is the author of *Black Odyssey* (1979); *Harlem Renaissance* (1971); *Protestants Against Poverty* (1970). He has edited *Voices from the Harlem Renaissance* (1976) and is co-editor, with Martin Kilson and Daniel Fox, of *Key Issues in the Afro-American Experience*, 2 vols. (1971). He has been a Fulbright Senior Lecturer in France, a Guggenheim Fellow, and a Rockefeller Humanities Fellow. He is presently working on a biography of Ralph Bunche.

JACQUELINE JONES is Associate Professor of History and Chair of the Department of History at Wellesley College. She is the author of *Labor of Love, Labor of Sorrow: Black Women, Work, and Family from Slavery to the Present* (1985) and *Soldiers of Light and Love: Northern Teachers and Georgia Blacks, 1865–1873* (1980). She has been the recipient of a National Endowment for the Humanities Fellowship and is currently researching the roles of black and white women in the households of sharecroppers and seasonal migratory laborers on the East Coast, 1865 to the present.

KENNETH L. KUSMER, Associate Professor of History at Temple University, is the author of *A Ghetto Takes Shape: Black Cleveland, 1870–1930* (1976). He won the Lewis Pelzer Award of the Organization of American Historians in 1973. He is currently working on a history of the underclass in the United States prior to 1940 and a series of review articles on ethnic, black, and labor history.

LAWRENCE W. LEVINE, Margaret Byrne Professor of History, University of California, Berkeley, is the author of *Black Culture and Black Consciousness: Afro-American Folk Thought from Slavery to Freedom* (1977) and *Defender of the Faith: William Jennings Bryan, the Last Decade, 1915–1925* (1965). He has been a Social Science Research Council Fellow, a Regents Fellow of the National Museum of American History, Smithsonian Institution, a Wilson Fellow, and a MacArthur Foundation Prize Fellow. He is currently researching and writing two books: "The Fragmentation of American Culture," a study of the transformation of

American culture in the late nineteenth century, and a study of American culture during the Great Depression.

CAROLE MERRITT is the director of the Herndon Home, an historic house museum and archives of the family of Alonzo Herndon, founder of the Atlanta Life Insurance Company. She is the author of *Historic Black Resources: A Handbook for the Identification, Documentation, and Evaluation of Historic African-American Properties in Georgia* (1984) and *Homecoming: African-American Family History in Georgia* (1982). She is a former president of the African-American Family History Association, Atlanta, Georgia. She is currently completing her Ph.D. dissertation in African-American family history at Emory University.

LESLIE HOWARD OWENS is Professor of History and director of the Africana Studies Program at the State University of New York at Stony Brook. He is the author of *This Species of Property: Slave Life and Culture in the Old South* (1976).

NELL IRVIN PAINTER, Professor of History, University of North Carolina at Chapel Hill, is the author of *Standing at Armageddon: The United States, 1877–1919* (1986); *The Narrative of Hosea Hudson: His Life as a Negro Communist in the South* (1979); *Exodusters: Black Migration After Reconstruction* (1977). She has been a Russel Sage Fellow, Guggenheim Fellow, National Humanities Center Fellow, and a Fellow of the American Council of Learned Societies. She is presently writing a book entitled "American Views of the South from Emancipation to Richard Wright, William Alexander Percy, and Wilbur Cash."

ARMSTEAD L. ROBINSON is Associate Professor of History and director of the Carter G. Woodson Institute for Afro-American and African Studies at the University of Virginia. He is the author of *Bitter Fruits of Bondage: The Demise of Slavery and the Collapse of the Confederacy, 1861–1865* (1986) and the editor of *Black Studies in the University* (1969). He has received a National Research Council Post Doctoral Fellowship and a National Humanities Center Fellowship. Currently at work on a book entitled "Day of Jubilo, Years of Sorrow: The Civil War Emancipation Experience, 1860–1865," he is also editing the trial record of a hitherto undiscovered file concerning the Gabriel Prosser conspiracy. Moreover, he is completing work on an instructional manual intended to enable teachers of eleventh-grade American history to incorporate the black experience into their courses.

ROBERT BRENT TOPLIN, Professor of History, University of North Carolina at Wilmington, is the author of *Freedom and Prejudice: The Legacy of Slavery in the United States and Brazil* (1982); *Unchallenged Violence: An American Ordeal* (1975); *The Abolition of Slavery in Brazil* (1972). He is the editor of *Slavery and Race Relations in Latin America* (1974). He has received a National Endowment for the Humanities Younger Humanist Fellowship, a Ford Foundation Fellowship, and an American Philosophical Society Fellowship. He has received several grants for television productions from the National Endowment for the Humanities and won the Eric Barnouw Prize from the Organization of American Historians for *Solomon Northup's Odyssey* (Best Dramatic Film on American History, 1984). He is presently producing a documentary film on World War I and completing a book entitled "Slavery in Crisis: The Specter of Violence in the Antebellum South."

INDEX

Abbott, Robert S., 116
Aframerican Woman's Journal, The, 244
Africa and Africans, 4, 26, 27, 35–36,
37, 265, 275, 280–83; family ties,
27; impact of slavery on, 28; role in
the plantation economy, 29; able to
harness Paradise, 30, 37; place of
women in African cultures, 30–31,
32; resistance to bondage, 30, 31, 36;
treatment of in textbooks, 262
African Methodist Episcopal Church,
229
Afro-American historians: four generations of, 1–6, 14–22; "contributionists," 2; Carter G. Woodson's
generation, 2; need for an Afrocentric
perspective, 4; fifth generation, 6; as
products of history, 7, 18; fourth
generation, 18–19; role of in black
community, 277–83. *See also* Afro-
American history
Afro-American history, 1–6; funding of
research, 139, 140; need for institutional histories, 150; new perspectives
on, 151; teaching of in schools and colleges, 171–93; course syllabi, 173; use
of primary sources in teaching, 174;
use of slave narratives, 174–75; in
public schools, 184–93; slavery as central fact of, 2; mobilization of black
labor, 3; new periodization of, 3–4; as

"centerpiece" of American history, 5;
involvement of white historians in, 17;
and publishers, 19–20. *See also* Black
Women's History; Emancipation Stud-
ies; Slavery Studies; Urban History;
Textbooks
Alabama State College, 246
Albridge, Ira, 203
Allen, Richard, 189, 229
*All the Women Are White, All the Blacks
Are Men, But Some of Us Are Brave*,
44
Alpha Home for Colored Aged, 239
American Council on Education, 255
American Historical Association, xiii,
139, 150, 174, 279; Committee of
Seven, 171
American History, An, 261, 265, 266,
267, 269, 270
American Pageant, The, 261, 264, 266,
269, 272
American Revolution, 185, 264, 271
Anderson, James D., 253, 275
Anderson, Karen Tucker, 242
Angelou, Maya, 249
Anti-Defamation League, 258, 260
Aptheker, Herbert, 159
Arkansas, University of, 182
Ashanti, 263
Association for the Study of Negro Life
and History, 9, 15, 16–17, 172, 255;